Goal Setting

"Turning Your Mountains Into Molehills"

by Gene Greeson

Published by: Potential Unlimited, P.O. Box 1073, St. Charles, MO 63302

Published in St. Louis, Missouri, by Potential Unlimited.

ISBN 0-9638658-0-3

Published in the United States of America

Dedication

I dedicate this book to my two children whom I'll always love.

KIMBERLY KAY GREESON

and

JOEL NATHAN GREESON

I've written this book for many reasons, but the primary reason has been that you will have access to my mind long after I'm gone into eternity.

Acknowledgments

Space does not permit me to properly acknowledge all those who have a part in this book, as that would include everyone who has influenced me positively over the past 45 years. I easily recognize that I am not a self-made man, but one whose life has been molded by the positives and negatives which I have encountered along the journey of life.

Early in life, and throughout my life, my mother has been a great encouragement. She was always there to inform me that I could do whatever I wanted to do in life. Three of my high school teachers: Mrs. Martin, Mrs. Kettering, and Mr. Drake all contributed greatly. Mrs. Martin and Mrs. Kettering both were continually on my case for being an underachiever, and Mr. Drake showed genuine interest in helping my brother and me, even though we didn't deserve it. As I reflect, I'm amazed at the love and patience these three demonstrated in light of my mischievous antics. (I once won a contest for being the student who received the most "whacks" in one semester.)

My teenage years would have been a total disaster had it not been for the interest shown in me by two sets of my aunts and uncles. George, Ethel, Carl, and Nancy all assisted mightily in giving me a sense of self-worth. Words cannot adequately express my gratitude. Each of them, in a different way, contributed to my making it through my teenage years without committing suicide. (Nobody ever knew how close I really was.)

I did most of my growing up in Vietnam, having experienced my 19th, 20th, and 21st birthdays there. While nobody provided a positive influence for me over there, I believe it was the tremendous negativism and disgusting actions of the multitude of my fellow soldiers that helped me to improve my own self-esteem. I had one goal — to die for my country and to give my best while doing so. While I didn't think very highly of myself in the beginning, I soon realized that I was not outclassed by the majority. Thus, they too, contributed in a strange way to the things you are about to read and learn.

God used one man, Roger Post, in 1970 to provide me with the information that most turned my life around — the gospel of the Lord Jesus Christ. Once

I understood that God loved even me and wanted to give me purpose, I knew life would never be the same again. His influence, and that of my instructors and friends later at Florida Bible College, instilled in me an intense desire to become the person I'm capable of becoming. The puzzle was finally fitting together.

During college, and since, I built a library of approximately 5,000 books. Many of them have contributed to helping me become the person I am today, but none more than Zig Ziglar's book, *See You At The Top*. His was the first book I read of that type in 1977. Perhaps it was his book, and a few others, that have motivated and persuaded me to write this book. I've recognized that no one book has all the answers, nor can reach all the people, so I must do my part. No author appeals to everyone. Nor will I.

I've been challenged to write this book by the thousands I've witnessed rising up and overcoming their negative circumstances. They have challenged me by their courage and determination. They have helped me develop the "if they can do it, so can I" attitude. I have been equally challenged by the millions I've witnessed who have allowed circumstances to imprison them with lives of mediocrity. Perhaps they have influenced me the most. My fear of being like them drives me daily.

My friends have also contributed. Fredric (Ric) L. Kinne, Marion Stephens, Tom Abbott, David Stephens, Terry Bright, Max McLean, Marvin McMillian, Joe Buttici, David Meintrup, Kevin Olsen, and James Coakley are just a few who have had a tremendous impact on my life. My employees inspire and challenge me daily, holding me accountable while we all have fun together.

Those who have assisted me the most in getting this book to press are Rick Madsen (editing), Scott Lisech and Cynthia Prosser (typesetting), Dee DeLoy (drawing and painting the cover), and Debbie Woodall (drawing the illustrations inside). Countless others have read the drafts, helping me look for those little mistakes that frustrate or embarrass me. Western Press of St. Louis, Missouri, has done the printing of this book.

Thank you all. This book is not just my work — you have all had a part in it too.

Introduction

The fact that you have this book in your hands is one of the biggest blessings of my life. The writing and publishing of this book has been a passion of mine for many years. I'm almost embarrassed to tell you how many years. These past several years, I've often said that the only thing I've needed to do before I'm totally prepared to die is complete this book.

I am extremely thankful I've lived long enough to finish it. I'm also thankful I did wait until now to complete it. If I had put it to rest eight years ago, when I first intended to, it would only be about one-third the size it is now and would be missing several key ingredients which I've needed to learn along the way.

I actually began this book during the summer of 1985, the summer I purchased my first computer. I wrote with the passion of a possessed person for two months, typing almost every night between the hours of 10:00 P.M. and 4:00 A.M. while my family slept. After completing the bulk of what is now the first six chapters of this book that summer, I thought that the only thing I needed to do was to have someone review it for me and I would get it printed.

Fortunately, I still felt something was missing so, I put the book on the shelf for the next two years. I purchased my first laser printer in 1987. Because I was extremely excited over the quality of print I was then able to produce, I picked up the book and began working on it again. With two additional years of experience in owning my own business, I felt I knew what I needed to add. Once again I began typing with the fervor of a possessed man. I couldn't stop typing until, a few weeks later, I felt I had given my all. I sent the manuscript off for some editing assistance. It was months before I saw it again. The scratch marks and suggestions it contained seemed overwhelming.

I was very busy operating my own computer store, so I continued to allow the book to sit on a shelf until the year 1990 arrived. That year I actually determined to make it a goal to finish the book and to get it printed. This time I was between businesses, having sold my previous store and moved to Florida for (what turned out to be) a year. I made the changes that the person I'd hired to edit the manuscript had suggested. Once again, to my amazement, there seemed to be so much more inside of me that I felt it was necessary to add to the book. It was in this year that I added chapters 10 through 14. In addition, a friend (Rick Madsen) offered to provide some editing for me. During that time, we decided to move back to Missouri and begin another business. Once again, I decided to shelve the book. I did, however, set a goal to finish it in July of 1993. Thank God I did. Otherwise, I might not ever have taken the time to do it.

While waiting for 1993 to arrive, I hired Dee DeLoy of Orlando, Florida to draw and paint the front cover. He read the book and came up with the subtitle and picture which now grace the cover. It took him a full 18 months to complete the work in his spare time. During that time, I almost lost the edited manuscript when my computer business burned to the ground with it inside. It was only saved by the grace of God and over 300,000 gallons of water. Burnt around the edges, and water soaked so badly that the pages literally had to be peeled apart and laid out in five rooms of my house to dry, the manuscript somehow survived. That was in February of 1992, just two days after the painting was completed. Fortunately, I had not yet received the painting or it would have been destroyed in the fire.

I've heard it said that an artist never finishes a painting; he simply gives up on it. I think that is what I have decided to do with the writing of this book. It has not been easy to quit while knowing there may be a few mistakes we have not yet found. I pray that God will give you the grace to read it as He has given me to write it. More importantly, I pray that it will be worthy of your investment in time. I'm confident it will be.

I believe the truths contained herein can be used to transform your life into one that is exciting, vibrant and purposeful. I've not written this book just to make me feel good (although it does). Nor have I written it to earn money (I won't mind if it does). I've written it to assist me in fulfilling my life's purpose — helping others get visions for the persons they can become. If you leave this book with such a vision planted firmly in your mind, I'll rejoice with you.

I can say without hesitation that not one idea or principle is presented herein that I haven't personally tested and found true. Can I say that I absolutely apply everything to my life every day? No way! I've written this book to challenge myself as much as I've written it to challenge you. My mind, like yours, has a tendency to forget what it has learned unless it is given the opportunity for review. Thus, I expect to use my own book as a refresher course each of the remaining years of my life.

I don't claim to know it all, nor will I ever. I am confident that you can use goal setting as a tool to gain control of your life. With goal setting, and its accompanying principles, you can tackle those mountains. You can cut them down to size — literally make them appear as molehills. Instead of having to say to others, "I'm fine, under the circumstances," you can show them that you have everything under control. You'll actually become excited over the opportunities that the mountains present.

I'll close this introduction by challenging you to set a goal to complete this book within three weeks. It contains slightly more than 120,000 words. If you read it at only 125 words per minute (half the speed of an average reader), you'll complete the book in 17 hours. Thus, spend one hour per day reading this book and you'll have learned how to take charge and change your life into whatever you want it to be. Go to it! God bless you.

Contents

·One·
Anything You Really Want

Did you ever wonder why some people seem to get whatever they want, while you don't — why some people seem to get all the breaks, while life for you seems just one big problem after another — why some people have more friends than they can count, while you don't have even two?

Why is it that some people get to go wherever they want, do whatever they want, whenever they want? Have you ever thought, "No wonder they're happy; I'd be happy too if I had it made like they do?" "Sure," you reply, "hasn't everyone thought that way at times?" And I guess you'd be right; everyone probably has. We've all found ourselves, at times, being envious of what another owns, is, or has accomplished. The real question, however, is what do we do about it when we begin to think this way?

Are we envious to the degree that we go off and sulk? Do we allow other people's success to make us think less of ourselves? Do we become ungrateful and thankless for the many blessings we do have? Do we even become bitter toward others whom we decide to blame? Those others may be God, our parents, our spouses, our children, our employers, past teachers — anyone, in fact, who we think might be responsible for having limited our potential. I'm sure you've heard the phrase, "I once complained because I had no shoes, until I met a man who had no feet."

How we respond when we see others who have things we desire is extremely important. Envy can, and should, serve as a motivating factor in our lives. Often we can't visualize ourselves as attaining a particular thing until we accept the responsibility for getting it. The real failures are those who do not accept the responsibility for their lives, those who blame others for their failures. Many will testify, "I am a self-made success!" Few of us, however, have ever heard someone say, "I am a self-made bum!" Yes, we want the credit for our successes, but not for our failures.

Once we accept responsibility for our own lives, we are on our way to better lives. We cannot control everything that happens to us, good or bad. We can control how we respond to whatever happens. Our responses ultimately determine what our lots in life will be. I know many people who have had the most tragic events take place in their lives; yet they appear to be among the happiest people I know. On the other hand, I also know those who have had everything handed to them on a silver platter. They are among the most miserable people on the earth. Can we learn something from this?

List Your Trials And Disappointments

Before beginning your study, reflect for a moment on your own life. On a sheet of paper (or several sheets), list the things that had or have the greatest negative impact in your life. These "negatives" may include everything from your physical characteristics to your family life, to your job responsibilities, to events that have occurred. You might want to include the people you feel have harmed you, have held you back, or spoken against you. Include, if you wish, the fact that you have not been as lucky as others: perhaps you feel bad that it was someone else who won the last Publishers Clearing House Sweepstakes.

To make you feel more comfortable in making your list, I'll share some of my personal disappointments and negatives. Only by admitting them (at least to myself) and facing them have I been able to deal with them.

Included in my list are:

- Too short (5' 8")
- Divorced parents (when I was age 3)
- Family was poor (very poor)
- Not too athletic (certainly no star)
- Bad eyesight (20/400)
- I speak with a lisp
- Very lonely childhood (often considered suicide)
- Too shy
- Experienced major personal financial disaster

- Sexually abused as a child
- Sterile (result of childhood mumps)
- Giant inferiority complex as a child
- Business burned to the ground — result of arson

List the things in your life which have displeased you most. List all the negatives so we can deal with them.

Stop Reading and Make Your List Now

_____

_____

_____

_____

_____

_____

_____

_____

_____

_____

_____

_____

_____

_____

_____

_____

_____

_____

_____

_____

_____

_____

_____

_____

_____

_____

_____

_____

_____

_____

_____

_____

_____

_____

_____

_____

_____

_____

_____

_____

_____

_____

_____

_____

_____

_____

_____

_____

_____

_____

_____

_____

Add additional pages as needed.

You may or may not realize it, but your feelings regarding these items are affecting your ability to accomplish your current goals. It may have been very painful to write some things down. You may have even refused to write some down, but I encourage you at least to make a mark or code to jog your memory. This is *your* list — you don't need to show it to anyone else.

Count Your Blessings

I'll instruct you what to do with that list soon. We are now ready for the fun part. List all the blessings you've received in your life. These "positives" may include those people, events, possessions, and accomplishments, of which you have been most pleased. Take your time and enjoy making this list. You also might want to include compliments that you have received from others.

Again, to give you an example, my list includes the following:

- Saundra, my wife
- Kimberly, my daughter
- Joel, my son
- Rose, my encouraging mother
- My dedicated, hard-working employees
- Ric Kinne, my best friend
- My Uncle George and Aunt Ethel
- My Uncle Carl and Aunt Nancy
- Eternal life through Jesus Christ, my Saviour
- A wonderful house
- My church
- My library (books, cassettes, videos)
- My 4-H and F.F.A. experiences
- High School wrestling experiences
- Safe return from 27 months in Vietnam
- Four years of education at Florida Bible College
- Great health for my whole family all my life to this day
- Nice dependable car
- Excellent computer system & office equipment
- Great neighbors and neighborhood
- Thousands of learning experiences

This is only a sampling. My personal list includes additional family members, past teachers, friends, employers, and neighbors, as well as many other blessings I've had. I hope your list will be lengthy too.

Stop Reading and Make Your List Now

_____
_____
_____
_____
_____
_____
_____
_____
_____
_____
_____
_____
_____
_____
_____
_____
_____
_____
_____
_____
_____
_____
_____
_____
_____
_____
_____
_____
_____
_____
_____
_____
_____
_____
_____
_____

_____
_____
_____
_____
_____
_____
_____
_____
_____
_____
_____
_____
_____
_____
_____
_____
_____
_____
_____
_____
_____
_____
_____

Add additional pages as needed.

Did you do it? Did you count your many blessings, taking the time to name them "one by one," as the song goes? How do you feel after making this list? I've found this to be a really encouraging experience, one I give to myself at least once each year — usually on Thanksgiving Day.

It might be interesting to see how many items in this second list are related to the negatives in the first list. If you stop and think about it, you'll see that many of your greatest blessings have come as a direct result of some of your greatest trials.

In my case, my parents' divorce served to strengthen my resolve to build healthy relationships in my family. Since my father wasn't available, and I had an unhealthy relationship with my stepfather, my two uncles took up the slack. In different ways, they were tremendous blessings to me and have helped me become the person I am. I've learned from my personal financial disaster, and have become much wiser and more financially stable because of it. All the personal characteristics I didn't, or don't, like about myself have helped me too; I'm not likely to become proud and think more highly of myself than I ought. Instead of focusing on myself, I focus on helping meet the needs of others. While growing up poor, I learned to appreciate hard work and the value of a dollar; I'm confident I wouldn't be where I am in life now if it hadn't been for this fact.

My shyness prevented me from trying to win a girl I was crazy about. She eventually married another. This disappointment forced me to resolve never to allow that to happen again. Had it not been for this resolve, I would have never married my wife, Saundra. Actually the lesson I learned from that situation has helped me countless times by encouraging me to pursue diligently whatever I earnestly desire.

Probably no trial in my life was more difficult to deal with than finding out I was sterile. We had been married five years when we learned of this. We determined to adopt children and our adopted daughter was born less than two months later and our son came eleven months after that. You who have adopted children know that our joy couldn't have been greater. Even my having been sexually abused as an adolescent has served to impress upon me the ugliness involved in immorality, and helped me to avoid it at all cost.

Compare your two lists to see if you agree that your blessings, too, have come as a result of your trials. Think about each item on them, and attempt to match the blessings with the trials. The one positive thing that has occurred as a result of a trial may be an event or experience, accomplishment, character quality, or lesson you've learned.

This may surprise you, but those who accomplish the most in life, and become the most successful, are usually those who have had the greatest obstacles to overcome. They've learned that every negative has a positive with it. Thus, in essence, it is really the negatives in our lives that can become our greatest positives.

While you may not be able to ignore the pain that has resulted from those negative things on your list, you can accept it and go on. The mind has a way of minimizing pain after an unpleasant event has occurred. Let's be thankful it does. We've all experienced trials that seemed tremendous at the time. We might have considered death as preferential over going through the trial, but somehow we made it. We can now see that we are better persons for having had the experiences, and more prepared to live life.

As we grow and mature, we can even look back on some of those trials and laugh, as they seem so small. One way we can recognize growth in our lives is by realizing that our past mountains are now molehills. Projects that used to seem impossible become projects taken in stride.

Dream List

Now, let's begin another list. We'll call this a "dream list," as it will include all those things you've dreamed of accomplishing, acquiring, or experiencing in your life.

I've heard it said that children begin to lose the ability to dream by ten years of age. So, what I'm now asking you to do may not be easy. Some of you have been put down so often, and for so long, that you don't even allow yourselves the luxury of dreaming. You might even scold yourselves when desires, or aspirations, enter your minds. If you have that attitude, shake it off, and force yourself to dream awhile. Perhaps you'll feel guilty when you attempt this exercise, thinking you don't deserve the things you're writing. We will deal with that later.

Don't attempt to qualify or classify things that come to mind — simply list them. Don't refuse to list "travel around the world" just because you are currently working for minimum wage. Don't fail to list "win a beauty contest" if that is one of your dreams — even if your class voted you the Ugliest Girl in school. If it's something you'd truly like to have, something you'd like to do, or be — list it! From this list you will learn a lot about yourself. Make this list as if you have no restrictions concerning time, money, skill, etc.

As you begin this list, try to isolate yourself from interruptions. If need be, drive to a park, or go to a quiet restaurant. It's important that you be alone, without interruptions, and have time to think. Get away from the telephone, and give yourself at least 30 minutes.

Your list may become several pages long and should continue to grow throughout your lifetime. Whenever you see or think of something that you'd like, add it to your list.

This list becomes the menu from which you will choose your selections for the rest of your life.

Here are some of the things on my dream list:

- Go to the moon
- Ride a Jet Ski
- Complete a 26-mile marathon
- Earn over $100,000 in a single sale
- Write a book on selling
- Memorize the Biblical book of Proverbs
- Take a fishing trip to the Congo
- Own a helicopter
- Visit at least 50 countries of the world
- Learn to snow ski
- Learn to swim well (at least 100 yards)
- Earn at least one million dollars in one year
- Take a six-week U.S. tour, including Alaska
- Drive a race car and win two races
- Get a pilot's license
- Learn to speak Spanish
- Develop a relationship with 10 neighborhood families

Things I've had on my list which have become realities are:

- Take a Canada fishing trip (I've gone 10 times)
- Develop a Seminar to teach Goal Setting
- Develop a Twelve-Week Sales Course
- Write this book
- Install new carpet in house
- Remodel house
- Cruise to the Caribbean
- Take a Venezuelan fishing trip
- Over $25,000 profit or commission on one sale
- Purchase a house in Florida with a swimming pool and spa

- Increase my income overnight from $2,000 per mo. to $6,500+
- Get out of debt
- Submarine ride
- Earn over $100,000 in a year
- Purchase desktop publishing equipment
- Purchase a custom Dodge Maxi-van
- Lose 52 pounds in 89 days
- Catch a 10 lb. bass
- Catch a Tiger fish in Africa
- White-water raft trip down the Zambezi River in Africa
- Drive a race car
- Trips to Mexico and Honduras
- Parachute out of an airplane
- Develop the habit of Daily Exercise
- Sell my Computer Store for $135,000
- Step 1,000 floors (8,000 steps) on a LifeStep in 49:53 at age 43
             (my goal was to do this in less than 50 minutes)

I've had many additional things come true from my list, many of which I would never have done had I not made such a list. Some required much work, like clean out my garage, and others required simple discipline, like developing the habit of brushing my teeth regularly. When some of you read this book, I already will have accomplished more of the items you've just read on my dream list.

What I'm really asking you to do is to make a shopping list for the rest of your life. You'll be able to continue adding to it throughout your life. You'll also reserve the right to decide if and when you'll make the purchases of these items with your time and money.

Stop Reading and Make Your List Now

_____

_____

_____

_____

_____

_____

Add additional pages as needed.

Now, how do you feel? This list was only a beginning, but a very important one. One of my goals in writing this book is that you will accomplish some of your dreams as a result of reading and applying what I've written. I'm especially referring to those dreams that you long ago abandoned. For all practical purposes, your dream list is the beginning of your experience in goal setting. From this list you will decide which desires will become your goals. In essence, when you write or add to a dream list, you are listing everything you would ever like to do, to become, or to have.

You will think of many more things to add to this list as you continue reading this book. I suggest you begin a notebook, possibly using a three-ring binder, titled *This Is My Life.* In it include the three lists you've already made, plus any additional writing activity you have as you plan your life.

Your Life Will Be What You Make It

Your life doesn't have to be filled with boredom or chaos. You can live life to its fullest and truly enjoy it, including the trials. You'll know you're growing when you encounter trials that used to sidetrack you and you react calmly to them.

Life is said to have its peaks and valleys. You can't totally eliminate the valleys, and the peaks are so enjoyable you wouldn't want to eliminate them. Most people spend their time focusing on getting to, or creating, the peaks. Some call these "mountain top" experiences. Actually, you'd be wise to focus on raising the level of your valleys. You see, if the valleys aren't so low, you won't mind coming down from the peaks. Instead of having good and bad days, you can experience good and great days.

The problem with living for the "peaks" or "mountain tops" is that they seldom occur, and when they do, they seldom meet your expectations. Many people realize this regularly when they endure their jobs all week in hopes that the weekend will prove to have been worth it. It seldom is.

I learned this lesson the hard way while in the Army. I was stationed with the Army's 46th Construction Engineer Unit in Vietnam. We each worked an average of 12 to 15 hours per day, seven days a week. We would each get one day off per month, and an extra day per year on our birthday. I so looked forward to getting my day off that it was often the driving force that would get me through the day. I'd think, "Just five more days, then I'll have my day off." Can you imagine what my most disappointing day of the month would be? You're right — my off day! In fact, as I'd lie around relaxing on that day, my predominant thought would be, "Now, I must wait another whole month before my next day off!" I couldn't even allow myself the enjoyment of a day off because of my attitude toward those other days (the valleys).

Maybe that is a reason the suicide rate is so high in January, after the Christmas season. Most people don't really enjoy living life on the normal days; so they look forward to that special Holiday Season to provide the joy they've been missing. Their expectations are seldom met, and they dread going back to their valleys.

I approach the Holiday Season without extraordinary expectations. Oh, I expect to enjoy it, but not necessarily any more than any other day. I expect to enjoy every day, and I'm seldom disappointed. I'm often encouraged by a Bible verse I've memorized. Psalm 118:24 says,

> *This is the day which the LORD hath made; we will rejoice and be glad in it.* (KJV)

We're supposed to rejoice and be glad every day. Someone once challenged me to drive to a cemetery anytime I felt like complaining about the day. Buried there are the bodies of many who probably wished they could have had "another day."

That Bible verse also seems to show that our joy and happiness are the results of our choices. Happiness comes from within; we can choose to be happy! We should choose to be happy every day.

You might be thinking, "I do choose to be happy every day, but someone else chooses to make me unhappy. I can't control my circumstances." I agree you can't totally control your circumstances, but you can control your reactions to them. Since I developed the attitude many years ago of fully enjoying every day, I find I no longer need to look forward to, or even desire, the mountain-top experiences. Oh, I have plenty of them, more than I can count, but the real thrill is that the valleys are also enjoyable. I have often said that I could die today and not feel cheated one bit. I have probably found more enjoyment in the past 25 years than most people will find if they live to be 100.

The steps to enjoying life are really quite simple. Many of the profound truths I've learned are that way. Most are so simple that I ignore them for years before they finally get my attention. I believe you'll find, as I have, that the three steps we are going to examine are things you *can* do.

Be Thankful For Who You Are And What You Have

Be thankful for who you are. God created you in His own Image. God makes no mistakes. You may neither like, nor appreciate, everything about your design. This fact affects your ability to enjoy life. God designed you with, and for, a purpose.

Who among us has not regretted something about his physical appearance? We think we're too short, too tall, too skinny, too fat, too dark, or too light. We dislike our hair, eyes, noses, ears, or some other features. We are disappointed that we have poor eyesight or poor hearing, distinguishing birthmarks, or other features that cause people to make fun of us. We ask ourselves, "Why can't I be as handsome or as pretty as so-and-so?" Playing the comparison game makes most others seem to have the edge over us in appearance.

While we're riding the Pity Wagon, we might as well also ask these questions:

- Why was I born into a poor family?
- Why can't I have parents and siblings like so-and-so?
- Why do I have to live in this place?
- Why can't we buy the kinds of things everyone else does?
- Why do I have a beat-up junker while everyone else has a new car?

The list goes on. Have you ever asked yourself questions like these? Of course you have! The more you dwell on them, the more worthless you feel. You can't play the "comparison game" and come out a winner. Someone will always be prettier, smarter, more talented, or more blessed in another area. The "grass will always be greener on the other side of the fence" as long as you play these games.

Be thankful for what you have. We'd be amazed to find out just how blessed we are that we don't possess many of the things, situations, or qualities we most covet. We are acutely aware of the trials we already have, but we can't even begin to imagine the trials of those we are envying. Talk to them sometime; they think they have the worst problems on the face of the earth. Often, people who already possess that which we desire, don't enjoy it. Does this surprise you? It shouldn't. If you don't enjoy what you have, why should they be any different?

Again, the answer is simple. Happiness is not found in the getting of possessions, situations, events, physical qualities, talents, or any of the other things we desire. Real happiness can only come from within ourselves. This is why it is very important that we thank God for what He has given us. One of my favorite Bible verses is **1 Thessalonians 5:18** which says,

> *In everything give thanks: for this is the will of God in Christ Jesus concerning you.* (KJV)

I hope this book will help you see that it is the trials that can provide the greatest blessings in your life. I've taken the time to thank God for everything that is on my "Trials And Disappointments" list, and it proved to be a liberating experience. Try it; you'll see what I mean.

Expect To Enjoy Life

We tend to get what we expect to get. If we expect to have fun and excitement in life, we will. If we expect to be mistreated, to fail always at everything we attempt, we will. If we expect the trials to turn out fine, to be an opportunity to grow and learn, then that will be the case.

Our expectations prove to be self-fulfilling prophecies. It is a universal law that our bodies cannot move us in directions contrary to where our minds tell us to move. Denis Waitley says it this way:

It is impossible to move toward the reverse of an idea!

Attempt to focus on whatever you don't want, and you will receive that which you've focused on.

Earl Nightingale sold more than a million records from a recording he made in 1956 entitled *The Strangest Secret.* In brief, the strangest secret was, and still is, that we become what we think about most of the time. Thus, this is my challenge to you and its hope of reward: Expect to enjoy life, and you will.

Plan To Enjoy Life

Very few things that are worthwhile happen by accident. I can name a few but they are exceptions, not the rule. You will enjoy life more, and have fewer regrets in your later years, if you will take the time to plan your life now. I've written this book to help you fulfill this third rule. I want you to enjoy life.

Your life cannot go according to plan if you have no plan. A goal without a plan to make it happen is only wishful thinking — a dream. A quotation I recall hearing many years ago is:

Luck occurs when preparation meets opportunity.

If you are upset because others seem luckier than you are, it might just be that they planned it that way. I've told you to expect to enjoy life. It is far easier to expect something you've planned than something you just hope might happen. Make plans!

Just as you would never attempt to build your "dream house" without a good set of blueprints, you should not attempt to live the rest of your life expecting your dreams to come true, without an equally good set of blueprints.

·Two·
Success And Failure

Success: What Is It?

Success is something we all want to obtain. I often ask groups of people, "How many of you want to be successful?" Not surprisingly, everyone raises his hand. The world is full of people who want to be successful. Yet, the amazing thing is that only a few people have actually taken the time to define success, let alone figure out how to achieve it.

Take a moment to write down your definition of success. You probably will find it an interesting and revealing experience.

Write it here. Success is:

_____

_____

_____

_____

_____

Did you do it? How did such an experience make you feel? By your own definition, are you already successful? Or, did you define success as something you "hope" to someday achieve — in the distant future?

Did your definition include a measuring stick? In other words, can you use your definition to determine your own current level of success? What measuring stick did you use?

In a book I highly recommend, *FAILURE: The Back Door to Success*, Erwin W. Lutzer gave the following example of the importance of choosing the proper yardstick.

A coed wrote the following letter to her parents:

> *Dear Mom and Dad,*
>
> *Just thought I'd drop you a note to clue you in on my plans. I've fallen in love with a guy called Jim. He quit high school after grade eleven to get married. About a year ago he got a divorce.*
>
> *We've been going steady for two months and plan to get married in the fall. Until then, we've decided to move into his apartment (I think I might be pregnant).*
>
> *At any rate, I dropped out of school last week, although I'd like to finish college sometime in the future.*
>
> *(ON THE NEXT PAGE THE LETTER CONTINUED)*
>
> *Mom and Dad, I just want you to know that everything I've written so far in this letter is false. NONE of it is true.*
>
> *But, Mom and Dad, it IS true that I got a C- in French and flunked my Math . . . It is true that I'm going to need some more money for my tuition payments.*

Erwin W. Lutzer then added: "This girl made her point! Even bad news can sound like good news if it is seen from a different perspective! Success and failure are relative; their meaning depends on the standard of comparison we use."

Let's consider definitions of success and failure in an attempt to clarify the standard of comparison we want to use to measure our own lives.

Definitions of Success

I have read and heard many good definitions of success. Each of these shed light on the subject, and could possibly help you improve your definition.

Paul J. Meyer of Waco, Texas, defined success:

> *Success is the progressive realization of predetermined, worthwhile personal goals.*

Let's examine that in detail.

"Progressive" is defined in the *Webster's Collegiate Dictionary* as, "a moving forward or onward; a succession, as of acts, happenings, etc." "Realize" is defined as, "to make real, or to bring into being."

"Predetermined" implies that the bull's-eye was drawn before the arrow was shot — not afterward.

What is "worthwhile" to one person may not be worthwhile to another. Saving money for a vacation home on a lake in the country may not be worthwhile to you if the sacrifice you have to make to achieve it is worth even more!

"Personal" implies that you are doing what you want to do — not what someone else has said you must do. (That doesn't mean that you cannot adopt someone else's goal as your own.)

"Goal" implies that you do have an objective, something you are attempting to achieve.

Thus, this definition of success teaches that we are successful when we are moving toward the fulfillment of an objective that we personally are excited about and believe the price we are paying to be reasonable and worthwhile.

Bill Gothard, founder of the Institute in Basic Life Principles, gives us another definition.

> *Success is not determined by what we are but rather by what we are compared to what we could be. It is not measured by what we have done but rather by what we have done compared to what we could have done.*

Gothard is telling us that the measuring stick we should be using is one that evaluates our potentials. He adds, "Each person has a total set of aptitudes, interests, and capacities in his spirit, his soul, and his body. If we can only integrate part of these aptitudes and capacities into our life's work, the remaining part will constitute our boredom factor." He breaks down the aptitudes and capacities that are possible in each category (body, soul, and spirit), and says, "In determining the total potential of our lives, we must add up all the above aptitudes and abilities."

To apply this definition, making it practical, we must know ourselves. To know ourselves, we must take the time to evaluate who we really are. What are our strengths and weaknesses? What are our likes and dislikes? Do we attempt to do whatever we do the best we can? Are we continually challenging ourselves physically, mentally, and spiritually to assure ourselves of growth in each area?

Here is another definition for success:

> *Success is not what you have done compared to what others have done, but what you are doing compared with what you have done!*

This definition brings out a very interesting point. Your measuring stick should not be the level of someone else's achievement. Someone may consistently have a golf game in the 70s, and you have just completed your best day with a 95. Can you consider your game successful, though your partner beat you by 20 strokes? You bet you can! If you usually score over 100, you have made a major improvement.

It is foolish to play the comparison game. Are you to consider yourself successful simply because you accomplish more in a particular area than the average person? Or, are you less than successful because you are in the bottom ten percent in some category? No, the real consideration shouldn't be based on how you compare to others, but how you compare to your own potential. Your potential is determined, of course, by several factors. Some of them include your aptitude, intelligence, desire, resources, additional responsibilities, and the time you are willing to devote to a particular activity or project.

Success not only involves achievements, but also character, as borne out in the next definition:

> *Success is much more than a matter of achieving the right things.*
> *It is also a matter of being the right person.*

This definition strikes at the very heart of the issue. A man once encouraged me after a discouraging situation by saying, "What lies before us and what lies behind us are tiny matters compared to what lies within us." It is impossible to be successful without having the goal of becoming a better person. If you truly want to improve what you do, then you ought to focus upon improving who you are. It comes back to cause and effect. Who you are affects what you do and how well you do it.

In his excellent book, *Success, Motivation, and the Scriptures*, William H. Cook stated:

> *Success involves the continued achievement of being the person*
> *God wants me to be, and the continued achievement of established*
> *goals which God helps me set.*

This definition adds the idea that being successful depends upon measuring up to God's standard. It is both interesting and sad, to note that most books on success neglect this teaching. The reason might be simple. Those writers may not know Him, and cannot include an element into the formula of which they have no knowledge.

God, the Creator of mankind, knows more about success and how to obtain it than all men combined. He created man and woman, then gave them a set of clear instructions concerning how to live successfully. The Bible records those instructions.

I used to think the Bible was a book with rules to keep me from having fun. I was 22 years old before I learned that it was really a book with guidelines, authored by God, to show me how to enjoy life. One would be foolish indeed, to have a very expensive piece of equipment and hope to receive the maximum

use from it without carefully reading the owner's manual prepared by the manufacturer. Don't you agree?

If so, think about this. Which is more valuable, an expensive piece of equipment or your life? Even if you only make the comparison from a strictly monetary viewpoint, how much are you worth, in income, over the period of a lifetime? How much could you be worth if you realized your potential?

God is not against our success. In fact, He gives many guidelines for achieving success. I'll explain more about this in a later chapter.

The last definition of success that I will present is excerpted from *They Call Me Coach* — a book written by former U.C.L.A. basketball coach John Wooden. You will not read very far in his book before you begin to realize that his unparalleled success as a coach was no accident or fluke. His definition is:

> *Success is peace of mind that is a direct result of self-satisfaction, in knowing you did your best to become the best you are capable of becoming.*

Wooden pointed out that the only person who can judge whether you are successful is you. He said, "You can fool everyone else, but in the final analysis only you know whether you goofed off or not. You know if you took the shortcut, the easy way out, or cheated. No one else does."

John Wooden's U.C.L.A. college basketball teams won ten national titles for him in his last twelve years of coaching, including seven in a row. His players testify that "winning" was never their stated goal; the goal was to "play their best." This principle has served him well all his life. As a high school basketball player, his team won the Indiana state title his senior year. From over 600 teams in the state tourney, Wooden was named "Mr. Basketball," the title given to the best player in the state. In his senior year at Purdue University, Wooden's team won the national title and he was named the top college player in the country! Was his success a fluke? I think not. What do you think?

Now, I'd like to give you another opportunity to rewrite your definition of success, using the principles taught in the definitions we have considered. Make it a definition you'll use to measure yourself the rest of your life.

_____

_____

_____

_____

_____

Failure... Must It Be?

Having a proper attitude toward failure is a key ingredient in one's quest for success. Success does not exist without failure — it is a necessary element! Failure has been a misunderstood subject in the minds of men too long. I'll attempt to shed some light on it as I discuss the positive and negative aspects of it.

First, let's admit it, we've all failed! The only person who has never failed is the person who has never attempted anything. Often, people will allow their fear of failure to hinder them from even trying! The person who does this will receive what he fears most — failure! This is one of those lessons I've learned the hard way. I failed repeatedly because I was too timid even to try. Finally, one day I said, "Enough!" I began to take risks, and reap many benefits — both from my failures and my successes!

There is no shame in failure, not when we have given our best. The Bible teaches, "A just man falls seven times, and gets up again" (Proverbs 24:16). Or paraphrased, "Seven times down, eight times up." Real failure occurs in staying down when you have fallen. No one is ever really defeated until he is defeated on the inside.

I've learned it doesn't matter how often I fail, if my successes offset the failures. I could fail nine out of every ten attempts if the successes are grandiose enough. Even a baseball player would be ecstatic if he only failed six out of every ten times at bat. He'd be batting .400 and be a shoo-in for the Hall of Fame.

Learn From Failure

Failure can have many positive benefits, not the least of which is education. While one can gain a great education by studying ones own failures, I don't necessarily recommend you always do it that way. Only a fool learns from his mistakes when he could have learned from someone else's mistakes. Thus, it makes sense first to find out all you can about your project by attempting to learn from the success and failure of others.

I'm always open to learn from the failures of the other person — when I can. If I'll take the time to ask questions, often I can figure out two or three key issues that will spell "failure" should I ignore them. I'm confident I've avoided many mistakes and failures by doing this. We should take the time to learn from others' mistakes because there isn't enough time left for us to make all of them ourselves!

Someone asked Thomas Edison how he felt about having "failed 10,000 times to invent the electric light bulb." I love his reply. He said, "I didn't fail 10,000 times; I simply found 10,000 ways that wouldn't work." History's most prolific inventor understood the value of learning from mistakes and failures.

Sometimes we don't have the luxury of learning from someone else's failure. We have to "fail" some ourselves. Always remember, however, that the only true failure is the one in which you fail to learn anything!

As a sales trainer, I often teach the following principle to those in my class.

I tell them I don't want to make *all* the sales, only the next one. Whenever I fail to make a sale, I feel like the commission I've just lost is the tuition I've paid for an education. I don't know about you, but whenever I pay for something, I like to keep it. I wouldn't want to walk into a store to purchase an expensive item, only to walk out without it and never receive it. I hate losing a sale and then compounding the failure by failing to learn from it. If the commission I failed to earn is the tuition I've paid for an education, then I should be diligent to see that I receive the education.

I sometimes might call the person to whom I failed to sell and ask for his assistance. I explain what I have just explained to you — that I teach this principle in my sales course and desire to practice what I preach. Therefore I wonder if he would take the time to help me. I would like to know what I did, or didn't do, that lost the sale for me, or what my competitor did that gained the sale for him.

I have done this many times and have been extremely impressed at the helpfulness of those I have asked. It is true that I lost one sale, but I have no desire to lose more sales for the same reason. In fact, I consider education an investment. I want to get a good return on my investment. Therefore, I calculate the commission I lost and determine to use the lesson I gained to earn me at least twice as many dollars as I lost. Then I feel I am doubling my investment. I have turned some lessons into literally thousands of dollars, after they had only cost me a few hundred dollars. I once earned a speaking engagement for a major company, after having learned a lesson in this manner from that same company in another city. In other words, I used what I learned to make a sale to the same company who had taught me the lesson.

One of the best examples of learning from failure was one I read in *Think And Grow Rich* by Napoleon Hill.

> *One of the most common causes of failure is the habit of quitting when one is overtaken by temporary defeat. Every person is guilty of this mistake at one time or another.*

> *An uncle of R. U. Darby was caught by the "gold fever" in the gold-rush days, and went west to dig and grow rich. He had never heard that more gold has been mined from the thoughts of men than has ever been taken from the earth. He staked a claim and went to work with pick and shovel.*

> *After weeks of labor, he was rewarded by the discovery of the shining ore. He needed machinery to bring the ore to the surface. Quietly, he covered up the mine, retraced his footsteps to his home in Williamsburg, Maryland, told his relatives and a few neighbors*

of the "strike." They got together money for the needed machinery, and had it shipped. The uncle and Darby went back to work the mine.

The first car of ore was mined and shipped to a smelter. The returns proved they had one of the richest mines in Colorado! A few more cars of that ore would clear the debts. Then would come the big killing in profits.

Down went the drills! Up went the hopes of Darby and Uncle! Then something happened. The vein of gold ore disappeared! They drilled on, desperately trying to pick up the vein again —all to no avail.

Finally, they decided to quit.

They sold the machinery to a junk man for a few hundred dollars, and took the train back home. The junk man called in a mining engineer to look at the mine and do a little calculating. The engineer advised that the project had failed because the owners were not familiar with "fault lines." His calculations showed that the vein would be found just three feet from where the Darbys had stopped drilling! That is exactly where it was found!

The junk man took millions of dollars in ore from the mine because he knew enough to seek expert counsel before giving up.

Long afterward, Mr. Darby recouped his loss many times over, when he made the discovery that desire can be transmitted into gold. The discovery came after he went into the business of selling life insurance.

Remembering that he lost a huge fortune because he stopped three feet from gold, Darby profited by the experience in his chosen work, by the simple method of saying to himself, "I stopped three feet from gold, but I will never stop because men say `no' when I ask them to buy insurance."

We should learn many lessons from failure. When you finish reading this chapter, you may not consider failure your "best friend," but you should consider it a friend. Someone once said,

> *Failure is a better teacher than success, but she seldom finds an apple on her desk.*

If it were not for failures, how would we even know when we were experiencing true success — in light of the definitions for success? The pole-vaulter knows what is an excellent vault for him only after he has failed. Remember, we measure success by what we do compared to what we've done.

Only In Sports

It is only in sports, and some contests, that failure takes on a little different dimension. Certain limits are placed upon both individuals and teams that help to define success and failure.

In baseball, the batter is allowed only three strikes, the pitcher is allowed four balls per batter, and a team allowed only twenty-seven outs. Except for the possibility of the game being called because of rain or darkness, there is no time limit. In college basketball, each player is allowed only five fouls. The game is played with a time limit: two twenty-minute halves. In football, each team must move the ball at least ten yards within the allotted four downs; and, of course, there are time limits. Most sporting events are governed by series of rules and regulations regarding time and method.

While these limits exist in sports, they don't always exist in life. We usually don't have to be too concerned with such limitations. We live until we die, and the game of life continues until then. Many have faced immense failure until, through persistence, they stumble upon the right formula or opportunity and accomplish a great deal. Remember, it was Colonel Sanders who hit the road after age sixty with only his recipe to his name.

Perhaps you have heard about this man. He:

- Lost his job in 1832
- Was defeated for the legislature in 1832
- Failed in business in 1833
- Lost his sweetheart to death in 1835
- Had a nervous breakdown in 1836
- Was defeated for Speaker in 1838
- Was defeated in bid for Congress in 1843
- Was elected to Congress in 1846
- Lost nomination bid for Congress in 1848
- Was rejected for Land Officer in 1849
- Was defeated for Senate in 1854
- Lost nomination for Vice Presidency in 1856
- Was defeated for Senate in 1858
- Was elected President of the United States in 1860

His name, of course, is Abraham Lincoln. He had a deep conviction that God had a purpose for him to fulfill. In other words, Lincoln had a purpose and refused to allow short range frustrations to hinder him from accomplishing his long range objectives.

Thoughts About Success And Failure

You've probably heard the following quotes:

(1) It isn't whether you win or lose, but how you play the game that counts.
(2) Winning is all that really matters.
(3) Show me a good loser, and I will show you a loser.
(4) In life, you have the winners and the "also-rans."

Often, we hear the above quotes and accept them without taking the time to properly analyze them. It makes sense to focus on their ramifications if we are to accept them as fact.

Let me discuss these briefly:

(1) It isn't whether you win or lose, but how you play the game that counts.

Although this quotation is sometimes a hard pill to swallow, right after a close loss, it's so true. Let's face it; Sometimes you don't stand a chance to win, and you shouldn't get caught up in measuring our success by whether you win. The proper measurement might be found by comparing how you did to what you have done in the past — or how you did compared to what you know you are capable of doing.

I will never forget the first night I played racquetball against Mike. I'd just beaten another friend eight straight games, some by the score of 21-0. But then Mike beat me seven straight games by a total score of 147-10. Then I found out that Mike had been playing for at least twelve years. (I had played for two years.) He was also ten years younger than I. I soon realized it wasn't realistic for me to expect to beat Mike, at least without great improvement. I did, however, set a goal to score at least ten points against him in one game, and a few weeks later I realized that goal. I actually scored eleven! And I felt successful — because I was.

(2) Winning is all that really matters (or) Winning isn't one thing, it's the only thing.

It's sad to say, too many people have this attitude toward winning and losing. They don't realize that there are some things at which one can never win.

Yes, in sports, one measurement of success and failure has to do with the final score. Of course, just as an army might lose a battle and still win the war, almost every champion has lost several events on the way to becoming champion. Of course, even champions eventually lose — or retire.

I really get excited when one of my favorite teams plays for a national championship or world title. I've learned the hard way how dangerous it is to allow my joy to be determined by the outcome of the game. This is especially true because I have absolutely no control over the final score — the circumstances! Even the team playing doesn't have total control over the final score.

Remember John Wooden? He knew his teams did not have total control over the final score. He also knew that there would be times when winning might not be a realistic objective. Thus, his teams set their goals on something they could control — playing their best. If they played their best, they were true winners! Interestingly enough, they won more games than any other team.

If that surprises you, it shouldn't. You see, when a team has as their goal to win the game, they approach the game with a particular attitude. If they get ahead by ten or twenty points, they feel they can let up somewhat. After all, they got the lead once, so they can do it again if need be — or so they think. All too often, the team with the big lead early in the game loses. No, winning or losing is not the proper way to measure success.

(3) Show me a good loser, and I will show you a loser.

Depending upon what is meant by "good loser," I either agree or strongly disagree with this statement. If "good loser" means that the person didn't care whether he won or lost, and therefore, felt no emotion over losing — then I agree he will probably make it a habit of losing more often than he wins.

If "good loser," however, describes him as a good sport who demonstrates his sportsmanlike conduct in the aftermath of defeat, then I disagree with the statement. He who does his best, and loses, shouldn't be ashamed. There is no reason not to be sportsmanlike and congratulate the opponent for his victory. Even if you don't do your best, and lose, you can still maintain enough self-control to congratulate the winner. Be upset, but be upset at yourself, and turn that anger into your ally.

(4) In life, you have the winners and the "also rans."

Again, this statement shows an improper understanding about what really constitutes a winner. A winner is not necessarily only to the individual or team who comes in first. In actuality, it may even be true that the "also ran" won in more ways than did the one declared "winner." Success and failure are not so easily defined. Thus, the one who scores the most and wins the game may, or may not, be a winner in the true sense.

Practical Exercise

I've discussed success and failure, and hopefully have provoked your thinking on the subject. Now, I'd like for you to make two more lists for your *This Is My Life* notebook.

Accomplishments

On this first list, record all of your accomplishments that you can recall since the day you learned to walk. The following list is provided only to stimulate your thinking in this area. Surprisingly, most people have a difficult time remembering their accomplishments.

Physical Accomplishments
- Athletic events
- Awards received
- Exercise program
- Weight loss
- Skills Endurance

Mental Accomplishments
- Grade School
- High school
- College Awards
- Seminars
- Books read
- Cassette albums listened to
- Memorization
- Vocabulary

Spiritual Accomplishments
- Received gift of eternal life
- Bible study
- Prayer life
- Ministry to others
- Habits developed
- Church attendance

Family Accomplishments
- Marriage
- Raising children
- Other family relationships
- Family vacations
- Special times

Social Accomplishments
- Friendships
- Neighborhood relationships
- Organizational activities
- Volunteer activities

Financial Accomplishments
- Earnings
- Savings
- Investments
- Giving
- Debt reduction or elimination
- Items purchased

Career Accomplishments
- Jobs obtained
- Companies worked for
- Positions attained
- Job responsibilities fulfilled
- Skills developed
- Knowledge obtained

Stop Reading and Make Your List Now

_____

_____

_____

_____

_____

_____

_____

_____

_____

_____

_____

_____

_____

_____

_____

_____

_____

_____

_____

_____

_____

_____

_____

_____

_____

_____

_____

_____

What I'm hoping to accomplish by having you make this list is to help you see that you already have many successes. Often you are tempted to compare your success to someone else who is held in high esteem, and you begin to lose self-esteem. This may help to restore some of it.

Failures

Now for the flip side. List your failures. Include everything you can think of that you have purposed to do, but failed. Include, also, those things that you should have done but didn't even try. Don't be easy on yourself. Even if you don't bear the total responsibility, list it — with your share of the blame. While this may seem a negative experience, it can have great benefits. Those failures are fixed in your mind and your subconscious cannot ignore them, even when you attempt consciously to do so. By getting them out and on the table, so to speak, you can deal with them.

Stop Reading and Make Your List Now

_____
_____
_____
_____
_____
_____
_____

Now for the positive part. Beside each failure you've written down, list the positive benefits. Perhaps the benefits are among the following:

Provides education (What did you learn from the failure?)
- About the project
- About yourself

Develops character
- Persistence (seven times down, eight times up)
- Humility ("Pride goeth before destruction" — Proverbs 16:18)
- Gratefulness
- Compassion for others
- Alertness
- Discretion
- Sensitivity
- Objectivity
- Frugality
- Generosity
- Honesty
- Discipline
- Aspiration

Builds a sense of humor

Increases your ministry in the lives of others

Helps you to recognize your need for God's wisdom and strength

While you're at it, you also might attempt to evaluate the reason for your failure.

Some common reasons for failure are:

- Lack of preparation (knowledge and/or planning)
- Lack of ability and/or talent
- Lack of resources (time, money, personnel)
- Lack of focus
- Unavoidable circumstances
- Poor health
  (see chapter on "Obstacles and Roadblocks")

Failing does not make one a failure. Every successful person I've ever known, or read about, failed often, and sometimes big. Read the biographies of men like Walt Disney, Harry Truman, Ulysses S. Grant, Abraham Lincoln, Babe Ruth, and Thomas Edison to understand this principle more. You'll be challenged.

The only true failure is the person who has given up. Many think they can avoid failure by simply refusing to "play the game." Others may think they are not failures; they just started at the bottom and liked it there. It is obvious you are not in that category or you wouldn't be reading this book.

All failures have one thing in common. They either blame somebody or something for their failure, rather than accept responsibility for it. On the other hand, all successful people acknowledge that they are ultimately responsible — they continually move toward their worthwhile personal goals, attempting to realize their God-given potential.

I've written this chapter to challenge you to consider the true meaning of "success." I hope that the light shed on this subject proves beneficial to you. It does not matter where you are today on your scale of success, as you've chosen to define it. What really matters is that today is the first day of the rest of your life. Not only can you have a new beginning, but today you can begin determining a "new ending" to the story of your life! The past does not have to equal the future. The rest of the book is dedicated to helping you achieve the success you desire.

· *Three* ·
Bring About A Change In Your Life

In 1975 I graduated from college and went to work for a life insurance company. I'd been working only a few months when one day I found myself discussing the subject of change with my sales manager, Ken Crowe. It seemed he wanted me to make a couple of changes for the better. I informed him that I was already planning to make these changes.

Ken then made a statement I have never forgotten: "Gene, people change, but they don't change very much, and they don't change very often." I believe that statement bears repeating even now. Let's study it together for a moment.

> *People change, but they don't change very much and they don't change very often! (Kenneth Crowe)*

What do you think of that statement? Do you agree or disagree? How would you respond to it if your supervisor just had made it to you? Without taking any time for analysis, I quickly replied, "Ken, I don't care about what people do or don't do, I am Gene Greeson and I **am** going to make a change." I know that might sound arrogant to you, and it may have to him. Over the years, I've had the time to evaluate his statement and I've found it to be very true. It is so true, in fact, that sometimes it's downright painful. In observing myself and others over the years, I determined that recognizable changes don't occur often. Incidentally, I did make the necessary changes. I must admit, however, that my implementing those changes was probably made infinitely easier and more certain because of my desire to prove that statement wrong.

James Cash Penney, founder of the department store chain, said . . .

> *No man need live a minute longer as he is, because the Creator endowed him with the ability to change himself.*

I hope that statement does for you what it did for me. It takes the negative aspect of Ken's statement and replaces it with a positive. It may be very true that change doesn't come easily, and, therefore, people don't change very often or very much. That doesn't mean that we cannot change if we determine to change. It may take determination and work, but is it worth it? That depends on the change that we're considering.

J. C. Penney also said,

The hardest part of any job is getting started.

It has also been said,

Getting started is at least half the job.

I think most of us would agree with these statements. The question is: Are we going to be encouraged, or discouraged by them? We can decide whether we will be challenged and encouraged by a statement, or defeated and discouraged by it. As for me, I'd rather be challenged and encouraged. I say to myself, "If getting started is half the job, then all I need to do is start and I'll be half way there." Isn't that exciting?

Change Comes In One Of Two Ways

Change is all around us, and it cannot be avoided. Change is certain. The weather is always changing. Circumstances in our lives are always changing. The streets we drive on, the places we shop, and the people we associate with all change. Is this good or bad? Change is forced upon us — we cannot easily avoid it, and it behooves us to learn to live with it.

Personal change, or changes you make to improve yourself, to cope with a situation, or simply to survive, comes in one of two ways: through a **tragic event** or through **discipline**.

Here's an example of what I mean. Many people have developed the habit of smoking. Among those, I've known three kinds of smokers: those who have quit through self-discipline, those who have tried to quit but couldn't, and those who thought they couldn't and didn't even try. I suspect, however, that there is a fairly high success ratio of people who are able to quit when told by their doctor that they will be dead in six months if they don't. This tragic event, the deterioration of their health to the edge of death, is usually enough to force them to change. Yet others, sad to say, are so hooked that even imminent death doesn't give them the strength and determination to quit. They die without ever achieving a victory over this habit.

We're forced to examine our own lives when faced with certain circumstances. We all have changes we know we should make, but we don't seem to have the time, discipline, or inclination to do so. It takes something to move us off dead center — maybe loss of job, family, health, possessions, or being confronted with other situations that "shake" our very foundations. Actually, it is fortunate that we may not have to lose anything — except our sense of security in any of these areas to get our attention. These are all tragic events that can be used to bring about changes. It is sad, but true, that most of us sit and wait for tragic events before we decide to make changes.

The second way to bring about change is through discipline. This is the most sensible, and certainly the least painful way. This occurs when we examine our lives, figure out what we like and dislike about ourselves, and design plans to change. We then commit ourselves to do whatever is necessary to change those things we believe must be improved to give us the qualities of life we desire. To say the least, this is the more enjoyable way! The benefits are tremendous. The person who decides to TAKE CHARGE of and CONTROL his life never lacks something to do. He always has a big project he can be working on — himself. This person, the one who constantly sees room for growth and is working to bring it about, is the one who truly enjoys life.

Elements Necessary To Bring About Change

Some changes are much easier to bring about than others. What might be very easy for one person to change in his life may prove quite difficult for another. While it is true that some habits are easier to make or break than others, the following truths are for everyone. Let's examine in some detail the three elements necessary to bring about a change.

A Clear Definition Of Exactly What Is To Change

Changing anything without a plan is difficult; making a plan without knowing what to change is harder still. Being dissatisfied with the present set of circumstances is not enough. We must take the time to understand exactly what the circumstances are, and then clearly define what we would like them to be. The difference between those two situations outlines the distance that must be covered to bring about the desired change. If you are earning $30,000 per year and you want to earn $50,000, then you must outline a change that will be worth an additional $20,000 per year to you. That is one way to look at it. Another way is to "scrap" the job which only pays you $30,000, and come up with a plan that is worth $50,000. You see, it may be that attempting to add $20,000 to your income without quitting the $30,000 job would hinder the accomplishment of some of your other goals.

In attempting to figure out just what it is that needs to be changed, ask yourself the following questions:

● Do I need to change something about me (my attitude, work habits, character qualities, skills, appearance, personality, knowledge, or position)?

● Is there something about my circumstances, over which I have control, that I can change?

● Do I need a change in environment?

I've heard it said, "If you cannot clearly state the change you wish to bring about, you probably don't understand it yourself." Think about that. The biggest obstacle to bringing about a change is clearly defining what you want to change.

For example, if you are unhappy with your family life and would like improvement, simply stating that you want to have a happier family life is not enough. Nor is it enough to say that you want to increase your appreciation for your spouse, or to see your children become more respectful. What do these things mean? How will you measure them? You must clearly define what it is you want and how you will recognize it when you have it.

A clear definition of exactly what is to change is as follows:

"I am not pleased with my present family life. My love and appreciation for my wife has deteriorated. I used to dread being separated, even if only for a few hours. While away, I anxiously looked forward to our reunion. When together, we would spend hours planning and discussing our future. I was so enamored with her that I wouldn't even think of what it might be like to be involved with another girl. We could go to the beach and I wouldn't even see another girl."

"I want that kind of experience again. I want to appreciate her and find myself looking for creative ways to show her I still love her. I want to be excited because we are married to each other and not find myself envying anyone else."

An Action Plan To Make It Happen

A goal without an action plan to make it happen is only wishful thinking. We can spend our lives daydreaming, or we can do something about the things we want to accomplish. It's foolish to build a house without a blueprint. The same is true when it comes to bringing about a change.

We cannot properly set goals without an action plan. An action plan allows ones dreams to become believable, realistic, and worthwhile. A goal can be written, specific, personal, measurable, desirable, challenging, and scheduled for regular review without a detailed plan. The plan, however, is necessary to maximize ones chances of realizing the goal.

Action plans must be detailed. Ask questions when you are developing your plan.

- Why hasn't this change occurred already?
- Has it been attempted one or more times already?

- Why do you believe you haven't previously changed?
- What obstacles must you overcome?
- Who might attempt to stand in your way?
- What additional resources will you need?
- How will the change be measured?
- When will the measurements take place?
- What will be the additional demands placed on your schedule?
- Who else can assist you?
- How long will it take to make this change?
- Is there a deadline?
- What are the risks?

Realize that action planning takes time. You may need to work 10 to 20 hours, or more, in this planning process. You may need to research material. You may get discouraged, but consider that many corporate executives feel they save four hours in execution for every hour they spend in planning. The quality of your plan can mean the difference between success and failure. Your plan need not take a great amount of time. If you can simplify your plan and put it together in just a few minutes, that's great — if it is a quality plan. "The proof will be in the pudding." You'll probably find out in a few days just how good your plan really is.

A good plan to improve one's love, admiration, and appreciation for his wife might be as follows:

I will develop a daily check list and do the following each day:

- I will praise her sincerely for something.

- I will go out of my way to show her I appreciate her.

- I will give her the opportunity to share her burdens of the day with me.

- I will make sure we always part company properly, with a kiss.

- I will show her the courtesies I once did (open her car door, ask her preferences, etc.).

- I will not allow myself to get into any situation where I find myself desiring another female's company more than I do my wife's company.

- At least once weekly, I will date my wife, take her someplace special where she will be treated like a queen.

- I will show appreciation for the many things she does for me.

- I will be determined never again to take her for granted.

- I will focus my thoughts on the many things I admire and appreciate about her and not waste time focusing on her shortcomings.

- I will evaluate weekly how I am doing and how I feel about our marriage.

- I will become accountable to a friend to fulfill this plan.

A Firm Commitment To Carry It Out

Let's face it. Everyone can have a goal, a desired change, and even an action plan to bring it to pass. But unless one is really committed to carrying out his plan, it probably will never happen.

What does the word "commitment" mean to you? The *Webster's New World Dictionary* defines "commit" as "to pledge or bind." To make a commitment, therefore, means that you promise to do a particular thing. A commitment can only be as good as your word. If you find it easy to break your promise when the going gets tough, then your commitment will not mean very much!

Let's look at commitment considering the change we talked about in the first two steps. I chose improving your marriage because it is one of the more difficult goals to define and develop. It would have been far easier to walk you through these steps while showing you how to change your eating habits.

Let's first think about it. What you really want to do is renew the original commitment you made when you said your marriage vows. You promised to love and cherish, honor and protect, prefer over all others, "until death do us part." One doesn't have to look at the divorce rate very long to see just how weak most of those commitments are. An excellent definition of character is "that which allows you to keep a commitment long after the emotion in which it was made has passed."

So, you need to renew your commitment. You must do it in a way that will help you more than did the making of the original commitment. A technique that often proves helpful to me in making and keeping commitments is what I call the Penalty Principle. Psychologists tell us that we tend to act quicker to avoid a loss than we will to gain a benefit. This is why only a few people in this country really work hard to get ahead, while most will do just about anything to keep from going backward. Few people will work two jobs for a nicer house, but they will work two jobs to keep the one they have.

How, then, can you use this principle to your advantage? There is often a cost to pay to keep a commitment. The cost may include time, money, energy, and pain (especially in the elimination of a habit). Recognizing this, you simply assign a similar, but greater, cost as a penalty if you fail to keep your commitment. Thus, the unattractiveness of what you must do to keep the commitment pales in comparison to the unattractiveness of what you must do if you fail to keep it. As an example, if it will take you approximately 10 hours of hard work to fulfill a commitment, you might assign a penalty of 100 hours of similar work for failure to fulfill it.

If you doubt the validity of this principle, consider the reason tens of millions of people all over this country work like crazy to file their taxes on the final day, April 15th. Might it have anything to do with the penalty for failure to file on time?

Now, back to our example. You want to improve your marriage, and believe you can do so by adhering to the plan outlined. You're now wanting to commit yourself to that plan. In this case, you'll use the Penalty Principle and make the penalty something that will move you closer to the objective.

Any day that you do not fulfill your daily objectives, you will place "x" number of dollars into a fund to use for a special weekend (or longer) together. (Note: make the "x" an amount that you cannot easily afford.) By assigning this penalty, you are putting yourself in a WIN-WIN situation. Even the failure of your objective will still help to move you closer to your stated objectives.

You are already losing a great deal (more than you realize) by not keeping your marriage commitments to the degree that you should. Therefore, you can also benefit by focusing upon the loss that you've experienced already and the benefits you stand to gain.

Are there different levels of commitment? I believe there are. The greater the level of the commitment, the greater your chances are that you will succeed in bringing about the desired change.

I'll share with you a story that explains how I learned the value of the **Penalty Principle**, almost accidentally. Since then I've used it often and it has never failed me.

While in Vietnam, I developed the habit of drinking beer to quench my thirst. When I first arrived in February of 1967, the only thing I could get cold to drink was beer. Once I started drinking, I developed the practice of drinking 18 beers, if I drank one. (I seldom do anything halfheartedly.) When I returned to the United States, I brought my habit back with me.

Usually I'd drink only when I'd go to a party or bar. At times, however, I'd be lonely and feeling sorry for myself, so I would purchase four quarts of beer and drive around until I had finished them. I'm not proud of this fact and thank God that I didn't cause bodily harm to someone during those times.

Then one day an event happened to change all that. I was drinking my 18th beer with a friend when I mentioned, "You know, one of these days I'm going to quit." He told me, "You can't quit and you know it." I detest being told I can't do something, so I immediately accepted the challenge. I replied, "If I ever take another drink, I'll give you my car." Realizing I was serious, and he might be about to lose a drinking buddy, he replied, "I was only kidding; I don't want you to quit and I wouldn't take your car."

"I don't care if you would take it or not; I will park it in your front yard and it will sit there and rust the rest of its days — if I ever take another drink!", I insisted.

Now, I need to tell you what my car meant to me. I grew up in a very poor family. We never had a car newer than ten years old. I had saved over $7,000 while in the Army and was determined to purchase a new car when released.

After returning home, I spent thirty days test driving new cars until I found the one I was "in love" with: a 1969 Dodge Charger SE, and what a beauty! I washed it every day and waxed it once a week. I would almost prefer that you cut my arm off than dent my car. This was the car I was willing to give away if I ever took another drink!

You can bet it was not difficult to quit, after I made this commitment. No beer, or alcoholic beverage was worth more than my car to me.

I was tempted only once, two years later. I was working on a construction crew, preparing a field to pour concrete streets for a new housing addition. The temperature was over 100 degrees, and I had been swinging a sledge hammer for three hours without a drink of water. Finally, a truck arrived with a cooler, but instead of bringing us water, it was full of ice cold beer. In fact, the boss had purchased enough for each of us to have three. I guess he felt bad for having left us out there so long without anything to drink. Now I was faced with a decision. When I looked at that bottle of beer, with the frost running down the side, I recalled my Vietnam days and how great an ice cold beer could taste in such heat. I also remembered my commitment. I rationalized that these circumstances were certainly unique. Two years had passed since I'd made that commitment, and over a thousand miles now separated us. No one on the construction crew knew of my commitment, or even knew anyone else who knew me. If I drank a beer or two, nobody would ever know. Nobody but me, that is. I remembered something I had memorized some time before about honesty. It was:

Character is that which allows you to keep a commitment long after the emotion in which it was made has passed.

I had to live with myself. I knew if I drank a beer and didn't give my car away, I'd continue to lie the rest of my life. I'd already learned to hate lying. If I couldn't tolerate lying in others, I would not tolerate it in myself. So what did I do? Well, I did what I wanted to do in Vietnam five years earlier — I quenched my thirst by sucking on an ice cube. I made it through that day and knew I probably wouldn't be confronted with a greater test of my integrity or commitment again in my whole life. Since that day, I've had no trouble at all keeping my commitment. Today, if I were to take a drink, I would still give away whatever car I am driving.

That story shows what a strong commitment can do for you. This example taught me a lot about myself and about the tremendous assistance a strong commitment can give me. I've used this example to provoke myself to make many similar commitments since then. Now, when I make a commitment, I usually write a note promising to do a certain thing (always something I'd never want to do) if I fail to keep my commitment. I give the note to a friend and ask him to hold me accountable. The matter is then sealed. I've accomplished many things using this method that otherwise would not have been accomplished.

Now, I admit, I do not enter those situations very quickly; I am not masochistic. First, I study the situation very carefully to figure out what the issues really are. Often we think we have the answers, and we don't even have the questions! You'd be surprised what such an approach to making a commitment can do for you. If you're going to assign yourself a penalty for failure, make sure you'd prefer what you might lose over the habit you're attempting to change. As I mentioned previously, people act quicker to avoid a loss than they do to gain a benefit.

Consider this statement again. People act quicker to avoid a loss than they do to gain a benefit. They will act quicker to avoid the pain of a loss than they will to gain the pleasure of an additional benefit. If you really want to change and can't seem to make yourself do it, make the loss for not changing greater than the loss for changing. Losing my new car was a greater loss than not enjoying a cold beer or even 18 beers.

Of course, I'm assuming that you will realize many benefits from the change you want to make. Otherwise, you would not desire to change. Then, as you focus on those benefits, realize they, also, will be a part of your loss if you do not change. Your desire to avoid the loss you will have by not changing must be even greater than your desire to avoid the loss you will experience with the change.

The idea is this — when the pain of not changing becomes greater than the pain of changing, your ability to make yourself change becomes easy. The smoker finds it difficult to quit smoking because of the nicotine craving, or withdrawal pains, he experiences whenever he attempts to quit. Once the pain of not quitting becomes great enough, the nicotine craving will pale in significance.

While you can already feel and experience the benefits you're receiving by not changing, it is more difficult to feel and experience the benefits you will receive if you make the change — until after the change has been made. It's tough to give up what you already have for what you hope to receive. You can, however, attempt to visualize and imagine what it will be like.

One thing this commitment will do is help you decide if you really want to change. Talk is cheap. If after studying the situation carefully, you decide you don't really want to change, then don't. Don't talk about it any more, either. That is, until you begin considering the change again. Then, look over the real questions involved and make an intelligent decision. Talk to people who have been successful in making the same change you are contemplating. Find out how they did it, what their biggest obstacles were, and how they overcame them. What they did may, or may not, work for you. If you, however, interview enough people and read enough books on the subject, you should eventually have all the information you need. Then, it's up to you to act on what you perceive to be the best advice you've received.

In closing this discussion on commitment, let me give you another example I heard recently while giving a seminar on this subject. I was told of a Jewish woman who, many years ago, committed herself to giving so many hours per week to fight the Nazi Party. She wrote out a contract with herself stating that she'd write a check for $50 to the Nazi Party and send it every week she didn't keep her commitment. I don't know the whole story, but I suspect that she didn't have to send very many checks, if any. What do you think?

Why Do We Resist Change?

It is very helpful in developing a good attitude toward change to first understand why we resist it. Let's discuss the most common reasons for resisting change. They are:

- Complacency
- Insecurity
- Fear of the unknown

Complacency

Complacency is one major reason we resist change. We become satisfied and don't want anybody to rock the boat. We are especially against change if it might involve great effort on our part.

How to Murder A Minister was written, anonymously, to young men considering the ministry. It was written to explain the "facts of life" in the pastorate, so they would know the price they'd have to pay to be and to remain pastors. One quotation has stuck in my mind these many years:

> *Make a man think he is thinking, and he will love you; make a man think, and he will hate you.*

Think about that for a moment. If a pastor simply presents nice messages that pacify the congregation, he may be loved. His congregation can walk out of church every week thinking they are thinkers. But if, on the other hand, he challenges them and, thereby, forces them to think (maybe even study), he may soon have them hating him. They may even ask for his resignation — on some other grounds, of course. They would not admit that they detest being forced to be thinking people.

Everyone wants to learn, but few are willing to study, because they find themselves in ruts. *Webster's New World Dictionary* defines a "rut" as "a fixed, routine procedure, course of action, etc." I define it as "a grave with the ends knocked out." Many people settle into these ruts, and there they stay until their dying days. They remind me of a sign I've heard about, beside an old road in Alabama:

> *Choose your ruts carefully because you will be in them for the next several miles*

We can, and will, do something about an attitude of complacency only when we recognize it and realize it is stifling our growth. We must recognize and accept the fact that:

> *It is impossible to grow, or improve, without change!*

Insecurity

We can't get excited about change when we feel insecure. Insecurity in setting goals manifests itself as fear over the costs or possible risks of change, doubts about ones own ability to change, or in ones reluctance to commit to making a change at all.

We especially won't desire a change if we're insecure and believe change involves too great a risk. While it's true that some of us are, by nature, more disposed toward taking risks than others, even we will shy away when we feel insecure.

Feelings of insecurity appear when we are not confident in our own abilities and skills. A person with a healthy self-image feels secure, and a person without one does not. The key, then, is knowing how to have a healthy self-image. I'll discuss this later in the book.

I feel sorry for individuals who work all their lives in jobs they hate because they feel they need the security the jobs offer. Every month I meet or hear of someone who has been with his company for 20 plus years, only to lose what he thought was a secure job.

I work with sales people who believe their incomes are more secure because they work on salary instead of commission. They need to realize that, unless they produce, they will be out on their ears. Security is not to be found in a job, a company, or in another human. The person who hired you may like you, and may have promised you the moon, but what would happen if he gets transferred, fired, or retires, or leaves for some other reason today?

Real security can only be found in one person. Who is that person? I'm tempted, at times, to answer, "Myself!" But even that isn't the real answer. Even though I have more security in myself, with the skills and knowledge I possess, than in any company, my real sufficiency is from God — my Creator and Heavenly Father. The Apostle Paul wrote in his second epistle to the Corinthians.

> *Not that we are sufficient of ourselves to think any thing of ourselves; but our sufficiency is of God.* **2 Corinthians 3:5 (KJV)**

God is the Giver of life, and the Giver of health. Sure, we can ruin our health disregarding His principles and guidelines; we can even take our own lives, but we do not hold the power to keep them. When we forget this truth and think ourselves to be secure apart from God and His grace, we're opening ourselves up to fall. We're guilty of PRIDE. Notice what God says about this pride.

A man's pride will bring him low, But the humble in spirit will retain honor. **Proverbs 29:23 (NKJV)**

God resists the proud, but gives grace to the humble. (James 4:6). Humble yourselves in the sight of the Lord, and He will lift you up. **James 4:10 (NKJV)**

When pride comes, then comes shame; But with the humble is wisdom. **Proverbs 11:2 (NKJV)**

Read the parable of the rich fool which Jesus told to his disciples, recorded in **Luke 12:13-21:**

Then one from the crowd said to Him, "Teacher, tell my brother to divide the inheritance with me." But He said to him, "Man who made Me a judge or an arbitrator over you?" And He said to them, "Take heed and beware of covetousness, for one's life does not consist in the abundance of the things he possesses." And He spoke a parable to them, saying: "The ground of a certain rich man yielded plentifully. And he thought within himself, saying, 'What shall I do, since I have no room to store my crops?' So he said, 'I will do this: I will pull down my barns and build greater, and there I will store all my crops and my goods. And I will say to my soul, "Soul, you have many goods laid up for many years; take your ease; eat, drink, and be merry."' But God said to him, 'You fool! This night your soul will be required of you; then whose will those things be which you have provided?' So is he who lays up treasure for himself, and is not rich toward God." **(NKJV)**

Consider the security of the man of whom God said, "You fool!" (We would all be wise to remember this warning when we begin to feel sufficient in and of ourselves.)

> *Wherefore let him that thinketh he standeth take heed lest he fall.*
> **I Corinthians 10:12 (KJV)**

Thus, we see the real reason for feelings of insecurity. We, at first, place too much confidence in ourselves, then we fall. After we fall, we place little or no confidence in ourselves. All the while, we leave the Almighty God completely out of the picture. The All-Powerful, All-Knowing God says:

> *My grace is sufficient for thee: for my strength is made perfect in*
> *weakness.* **2 Corinthians 12:9 (KJV)**

God desires for us to look to Him for our sufficiency. He is All-Powerful and is both willing and anxious to exercise His power through us. If we will only yield ourselves to Him, insecurity will not hinder us from changing.

Fear Of The Unknown

The most popular answer to, "Why do we resist change?" is related to insecurity. The most common answer is "Fear of the unknown." In other words, we fear that the changes may be worse than what we already have! In actuality, however, the benefits may far outweigh any negative aspects of change, but we don't seem to focus on that fact. Again, this is because people act more quickly to avoid a loss than to gain a benefit. We all want something better than we have, but we don't wish to lose what we already have to obtain it.

As I think back to the changes I have resisted, I remember two in particular, both from my youth. Now, I'm very thankful they were forced on me, but at the time I fought them, at least emotionally.

The first change occurred when I was only ten years old. My family was very poor and was living in the slums of Indianapolis. I despised the life-style, the neighborhood, the school system, and just about everything else connected with my life. My childhood in Indianapolis was very unhappy; today I cannot reflect on even one happy day there.

Then one day, my parents announced that we were moving out to the country to live in an old farmhouse, which was owned by my aunt. The house was more than 100 years old, lacked running water, and seemed to be located in the middle of nowhere. The idea of moving to an unknown area did not appeal to me, although, looking back, there was probably nothing I thought I'd miss about the city life I'd hated so much.

We moved in 1958, and it wasn't long before I fell in love with the country. We didn't own a thing; we were just as poor as we were in the city, but it didn't seem to matter as much. We could grow a garden and be assured of always having food. I was away from a school I hated, and in a school I could at least tolerate. All twelve grades were under one roof, with less than 300 in the whole school. My brother and I enjoyed the hundreds of acres we considered our playground. (In the city, our yard was smaller than most cars.) That Christmas, we each received a bicycle and felt like we'd died and gone to heaven! Life was really beginning to move in the right direction.

In the years that followed, I could look back and give thanks, with tears in my eyes, that my mother had worked so hard to get us out of the city. She and my stepfather worked full-time in a factory making wheels. I don't believe either one of them ever earned over $2.25 per hour in their lives. She knew what I didn't, that the change to the country would be good for her two boys. It provided me with some of the greatest learning experiences of my life. I learned to work, to appreciate the small things in life. Neither time nor space will permit me to state all the benefits that came from that change. It was one of the best things that ever happened to me.

The second change I resisted occurred when, at age 17, our little country school was forced to consolidate with a large one, a city school. Perhaps it was my memory of my earlier experiences with the Indianapolis school, or simply my desire to remain at the school I felt so much a part of. Don't get me wrong. It wasn't the school I liked but the social life, the sports, and the interaction with friends. My junior class had only 12 students. Knowing it would be our last year together, we took a class trip to Washington, D. C. and the New York World's Fair. I'd never before been on a vacation, and that was some trip!

I was really torn up emotionally over the forced change in schools. I'd even sworn that I'd quit school before I'd go to the city school. Whiteland, the city, was only three miles away and had a population of about 5,000. The senior class, of which I would be a part, had about 125 students in it. Since one of my major goals in life had been to graduate from high school, I finally decided to swallow my pride and attend the "large" school anyway. The decision wasn't easy, but I didn't have any choice if I wanted to graduate.

I entered school with a chip on my shoulder. I didn't expect to like it at all. Knowing how our expectations influence what we receive, I'm now amazed that I ever opened up to the opportunities awaiting me. I found that being a farm boy in this city school made me somewhat special. Many city kids were intrigued by farm life.

Blessings abounded that year! At our small school, all I had to do was go out for basketball to make the team. That was not the case at Whiteland. Though I didn't make the basketball team (we had one of the best teams in the state that year), I tried out for the wrestling team. I'd never even seen a wrestling match before the night of my first meet. My self-esteem grew more through participating in wrestling than in all the other school activities I'd ever experienced. I received a varsity letter in wrestling and cross-country. I also received a State Farmer award in F.F.A. (Future Farmers of America) and the Chapter Star Farmer Award. Again, the benefits of making that change, against which I'd fought so hard, are too numerous to mention.

I had finally learned a lesson that has helped me to this day: CHANGE CAN BE VERY, VERY GOOD! In fact, instead of fearing the unknown, I now expect change to be good, and I'm seldom, if ever, disappointed! I've learned that the change needs time to produce its benefits.

It is extremely important that you develop a positive attitude toward change, as you must deal with changes for the rest of your life. I'll close this chapter with three ideas that can help you develop that attitude.

How Can We Develop A Positive Attitude Toward Change

I've just related to you two events that helped me to develop a positive attitude toward change. Perhaps you, also, can remember similar events in your life. What changes were forced upon you that you initially resisted, but later appreciated?

Now, I want you to take the time to add to your *This Is My Life* notebook. Make a list of major changes that have taken place in your life. Record your thoughts regarding the changes. Did you resist them? Are you now glad they have occurred? What insight have you gained to assist you in the future?

You might find it helpful to do what I do. Purchase a book with blank pages to begin writing daily lessons you're learning. It's easy to forget to apply a lesson you learned if you don't write it down and review it.

These three ideas can help you to develop a better attitude toward change:

1) Keep an open mind.
2) Accept change as an opportunity to grow.
3) Realize that God brings change into your life to improve it.

Let's look at those in detail.

Keep An Open Mind

What is an open mind, and why is it important? An open mind is one that asks questions. A closed mind is one that does not ask questions. When you are confronted with change and quickly form a negative opinion about it, then we may be guilty of having a closed mind. Emotionally, a closed mind causes us to be scared, prompting you to fight or flight (run). An open mind doesn't always produce the positive emotion of gladness, but at its worst, it will be neutral. With a neutral mind, at least you can think clearly; you cannot do so with a mind that is mad, sad, or scared!

Therefore, I suggest that we respond to change by asking questions. This will keep our emotions in check, assist us in gaining valuable data, and demonstrate that we are maturing. We choose how we respond to forced changes. Even in the face of an impending disaster, it's wise to keep an open mind in order to think quickly and act accordingly. An unwise decision can make the consequences even worse than they needed to be.

Some questions to ask are:

● What are the odds this change will occur?

● What areas of my life might this affect?

● Who else will it affect?

● What are the possible benefits of such a change?
(Attempt to list at least ten.)

● What are the possible negatives? (Don't look too hard; if there are some, you will see them easily.)

● How can I minimize the negatives and go along with the change?

● What are the possible consequences of refusing to go along with the change?

● What, do I perceive, are the risk factors involved?

● What are my options if I refuse to accept this change?

● Which option is the most attractive?

● Is this a change that I would desire to make, even if it were not being forced upon me?

● Where are the greatest opportunities for my growth?

The answers to these and other questions will assist you in making wise decisions as to how you should respond to change. Sometimes we should accept the changes, and sometimes we should not. Sometimes we should fight change, and sometimes we should run from change. The primary point, however, is that there always will be some benefits in every change, and we should approach the decision-making process with an open mind to determine how we should respond.

Accept Change As An Opportunity To Grow

Even if the change is one that you would reject, if it is forced upon you, and if its negatives appear to outweigh its benefits, you can still grow because of it! Ask yourself, "How can I grow as a result of having been presented with this change?" If you cannot think of any possibilities for growth, ask someone who knows you, someone who you consider to be wise.

Personal growth is something for which we should all strive. We cannot be successful without growth! I have never seen a good definition of success that didn't demand personal growth. Think about each major area of your life and ask, "How can I be successful in each area?" Then recognize the need for growth in each area.

- **Physical**
- **Mental**
- **Spiritual**
- **Family**
- **Social**
- **Financial**
- **Career**

To approach it from the other side, ask yourself how the change might limit, or reduce, your rate of growth. You will always grow in some areas if you accept the change. These areas, however, might not be as important to you, and you may decide the opportunities for growth are greater elsewhere. Should you, therefore, decide not to accept the change but to select a different option, then you will still have grown because of the proposed change. You see, you cannot stay the same. You must change! Just make sure those changes are taking you in the direction you wish to go.

Realize God Brings Change So You Can Grow

God loves each of us. That fact is clear to anyone who reads the Bible. Those who look only at circumstances have greater difficulty in understanding and accepting His love. He is very concerned about us . . . even more concerned than we are ourselves, and He desires the best for us. The problem is that we don't always understand what's best for us.

We tend to look at our lives like the underside of a tapestry rug. Everything seems to be going in a different direction and lacks reason. God sees it from the top. He can see the beauty of what is happening and knows the beautiful design He plans to accomplish.

Many verses in the Bible are very comforting to me and provide me with much assurance when things seem to be going haywire. The first is found in **Proverbs 16:20**:

> *He that handleth a matter wisely shall find good: and whoso trusteth in the LORD, happy is he.* (**KJV**)

Happiness is not something to be based on our circumstance of life but on our response to those circumstances. If we find ourselves unhappy, then it is evidence that we are not trusting Him. If we are trusting Him, we will be happy. It is as simple as that!

John Wanamaker used to say,

> *We should work like it all depends upon us and trust God like it all depends upon Him.*

Man has a responsibility to think and act maturely. Once man has done all he can, God will provide. God does not teach that "He helps those who help themselves." God helps those who are unable to help themselves and instead trust Him for that help. Man has limitations. When man has done what he is responsible to do, God takes over from there.

Changes come into your life for many reasons. Sometimes you, yourself, are responsible for them. You have done something, good or bad, to attract them. At other times, you have done nothing to affect the change. Take time to figure out the cause of the change. You can learn from it. The important thing is to make sure you respond the correct way. If it is a change over which you have no control, you can have a real peace of mind by trusting God to fulfill His Word. A verse I have found comforting and consoling is Romans 8:28:

And we know that all things work together for good to them that love God, to them who are the called according to His purpose. (KJV)

I became a Christian in 1970. Soon, after that, I was introduced to this verse. I can recall how enthusiastically I received this truth. It was not long before I found myself immediately asking after an accident or mistake, "God, how is this one going to work for good?" Or I would look up to heaven and say, "God, I'm really looking to see how You work this one out for good!" I'd keep track and honestly can say I was amazed at just how faithful He is.

You might be asking these questions about that verse:

- Who are the "we" ?
- Can it include me?
- How do we "know"?
- What does it mean to "be the called according to His purpose"?
- Does this verse only apply to Christians?

I will give only brief answers to these questions. I do suggest, however, that you spend some time studying the remainder of the chapter, and you will see God's motivation for giving this promise. For example, verses 31 and 32 say:

What shall we then say to these things? If God be for us, who can be against us? He that spared not his own Son, but delivered Him up for us all, how shall he not with him also freely give us all things? **Romans 8:31-32 (KJV)**

The "we" includes any Christian who loves God and is fitting into His plans. We can "know" because God is always true to His Word; He is faithful! He loves us and wants the best for us. He is more concerned about our character development than He is that we all become rich. In fact, He knows how we would respond in every given situation that could occur and protects us from situations we are not yet mature enough to handle.

Does this mean that God is not concerned, nor working to help the non-Christian? No, it doesn't! He is not required to answer the prayers of the person who is separated from Him, but He does work to bring that person into a relationship with Himself. I have heard many people testify that they lacked use for God until they found themselves flat on their back in a hospital bed. Then they found it easier to look to God. You are probably familiar with the saying:

You can lead a horse to water, but you cannot make him drink.

I believe God is in the business of working in individuals' lives to make them want to drink. I guess you could say, **He puts salt in the horse's feed and makes him want to drink**. We should all be very thankful that He does this out of His love for us. Yes, changes — even bad ones — can be GOOD!

• *Four* •
The Importance Of Goal Setting

Consider These Questions:

If you do as much in the next ten years as you did in the last ten years, will that satisfy you? If not, how do you plan to assure yourself of an improvement?

Research shows that most people rarely use over 10% of their actual potential. If you had an automobile functioning at 10% of its capacity, what would you do with it?

Why does one man get paid $4.00 per hour and another man receive $100.00 per hour?

Would you like to get paid what you are worth, instead of just what your job is worth?

Would you like an opportunity to have anything you want to have, or to be anything you want to be? If so, what would it be and how would you make it happen?

The purpose of these questions is to stimulate your thinking regarding the necessity of goal setting, and the possibility of becoming the best that you can be. It has been said that goal setting is "the strongest human force for self-motivation." It has also been said that "a person without a goal is really a person without purpose."

No wonder most people live in a "rut." Remember, a rut is simply a grave with the ends knocked out. I've read that 97% of all people are living their lives without specific goals for direction — without clearly defined purposes. In essence, they died long ago and are just waiting for their hearts to stop beating.

This may sound like a harsh judgment on mankind. You might argue that everyone has goals. "They might not have them written down," you argue, "but they know what they want to do with their life." Is this really true? Stop and think about it. What do you want your life to *count for*? After your demise, how do you want others to remember you? When you are 65 or 70 and looking back on your life, what will you have to look back on? What will you have done? What kind of person will you be?

Motivational speaker, Cavett Robert, once challenged me when he asked:

> *If you could look into the mirror and see the person you will be at age 65 or 70, what would that person look like? Let's even say you could reach into the mirror and shake that person's hand. Now, while you are holding onto him, you pull him into your room, place your arm around him, and walk together over to a corner to sit and*

chat. What would he say to you? Would he pat you on the back and sincerely thank you *for helping him to become the person he has become? Or would he look you in the eye and say, "Look at me; look at what you have made me!" Would he be upset?*

You might think this is ridiculous. Is it really? If you should live long enough, isn't it just possible that one day you'll be looking back on your "younger" self with either fond memories, or with disappointment?

You will usually do more on purpose than you will by accident. Only a fool would spend his life savings in building a house without a blueprint. If you have ever attempted to build something as simple as a doghouse or a picnic table without first developing a plan, you probably found yourself making many mistakes. Or perhaps you've experienced the frustration of trying to locate an unfamiliar destination without a map. How often have we had to learn the hard way that it makes sense to stop and ask for directions when lost?

Only a fool learns from his mistakes when he could have learned from someone else's. Any fool can learn from his mistake, but it takes a wise person to learn from a book. Does it then make sense to study a particular situation before jumping into it? We know it's important to use a blueprint to build a house and to use a map to arrive at an unfamiliar destination on time. Then isn't it even more important to have a plan to get the most out of life? Your life cannot go according to plan if you have no plan. Most people don't plan to fail — they simply fail to plan!

Why Don't People Set Goals?

Why do an overwhelming majority of all people fail to establish goals for themselves? Let's examine some reasons that are commonly given.

No Realization Of The Importance Or Value

We aren't apt to do something requiring work that we don't think is important or valuable. Goal setting *does* require work. This work, however, reaps tremendous benefits.

Life is too valuable to waste! Yet, many well-meaning, intelligent people live day after day, month after month, and year after year without a plan. Often, these people are so busy, and yet so frustrated, because they aren't getting anywhere. Their dreams remain just that — dreams. How about you? Are you one of them?

If so, get excited, because goal setting is the answer. It is the tool you've been searching for to fix your problem. I must confess, I lived without a plan until 1978, when I discovered goal setting. Oh, I had dreams like everyone else. Yet, I couldn't begin to tell you how they were going to become reality. All I could do was hope they might — someday.

The importance of our dreams will cause us to live life with purpose. Instead of simply hoping that they will somehow miraculously happen, our dreams become living realities through goal setting.

I never cease to be amazed at the number of people who excitedly tell me what a life-changing experience this material has been to them. Their testimony usually goes something like this:

"I can't believe I never saw this. It's so simple! If you want to get something done, develop a plan of action and stick to it, and it's yours! I've been in this job for many years, trying to do some things that now have taken just a month or so with a plan."

The reason for this is simple. It is awfully difficult to do anything worthwhile without clear direction. In order for a dream to become a goal, an action plan giving clear direction is necessary. Once we obtain clear direction, we can focus our efforts and eliminate confusion.

Lack Of Knowledge

Goal setting is not a skill with which we are born. It must be learned. We've often attempted to set goals, only to fall flat on our faces, and we decide never to try again. We improperly set goals and they work against us instead of for us.

Most of us will not attempt to work on expensive equipment if we think it too difficult or complicated. Also, we will not spend much time setting goals if we don't know how. Not knowing something is not shameful. The only shame is in not being willing to learn something vitally important to our futures. If you recognize that you don't know how to set goals, you should make it your first goal to learn how!

If you've done that, continue reading this book. My goal is to give you the knowledge you need to properly set and accomplish your goals!

Fear Of Failure

Fear of failure keeps us from setting goals. We see failure as something to be avoided at all costs. Perhaps, people have laughed at us in the past after a failure, and we don't want to experience that again.

As I discussed in Chapter Two, failure is not necessarily negative. We can gain many benefits from failure. You see, falling down doesn't make you a failure, but staying down might. Babe Ruth, known as the "Home-run King," also held the record for the most strike-outs. A very large percentage of millionaires in this country have been bankrupt at least once — some several times.

Lloyd Jones said, "The men who try to do something and fail are infinitely better than those who try to do nothing and succeed." I've heard Jim Cathcart say, "Most men aim at nothing in life and hit it with amazing accuracy."

My point is: Don't allow fear of failure to keep your dreams in the dark.

Interestingly, the fear of failure usually brings about the failure that you fear the most. Think about it — if you really want to do something and you fail to try because you might fail, the result will be the same. There are many ways to become a true failure, but never taking a chance is the most sure.

The only thing we have to fear is not doing something about the fears we have. Courage is not the absence of fear, but the conquest of it. I'll discuss more about fear and how to deal with it in a later chapter.

Lack Of Confidence

If we have little or no confidence, we will attempt to accomplish very little; so, since we tend to get what we expect to get out of life, we'll get very little. If we expect very little from ourselves, we won't be disappointed. An adage that bears repeating is,

If you think you can, you're right. If you think you can't, you're right again.

How do we obtain a greater confidence in ourselves? Simple — success breeds success, and confidence grows as success becomes more common in our lives. We begin by setting goals that are just out of reach, but not out of sight (we must see the reaching). Once we accomplish these goals, we set larger goals. We know we're growing, and our confidence level is improving when the tasks we're attempting are becoming larger.

A little success never hurt anybody. Much success has hurt many — those who were not properly prepared to handle it. If you have been failing to set goals because you lack the confidence that you can accomplish them, now is the time to discard that misconception. You can obtain the confidence as you build your blueprint for success!

Poor Self-Image

A poor self-image might be the primary reason you don't set goals. You don't feel you deserve the fulfillment of our desires. Self-image refers to the way you see yourself. You cannot consistently act in a manner inconsistent with the way you see yourself. If the mental picture you have of yourself is one of failing, then you most assuredly will fail.

Can you picture yourself successfully navigating your way down the length of a board 20 feet long and one foot wide that is lying on the ground? Sure you can! Now, visualize yourself attempting to walk the length of the same board as it spans two skyscrapers. What do you see? I suspect the proper answer is "disaster!"

You probably would fall if that is the picture you really see when you think about such an event. Your self-image works through your subconscious mind either to help you, or prevent us from doing anything that is inconsistent with itself.

It also attempts to convince you that you don't deserve some things that are inconsistent with the way you see yourself. If you've always been poor, for example, your self image might hinder you from setting a goal to travel around the world. It may even stop you from planning to attend college to become a doctor.

Many things can be done to improve our self-images. The greatest boost to my self-image occurred in 1970 when I met the Creator, God who created me in His own image. I received His forgiveness, and the free gift of eternal life. It was such a boost to finally know that He, indeed, loves me.

When I understood that God loves even me, it did more toward improving my self-image than had the President of the United States, or my favorite sports hero, announced to the world that I was his best friend. My self-image has continued to grow as I've studied the Bible and applied its teaching to my life. It is impossible to develop a close relationship with God without receiving also the by-product of a healthy self-image.

There are other things you can do to improve your self-image:

- Listen to and appreciate your creative ideas
- Forgive yourself for your failures and mistakes
- Accept what cannot be changed, and improve what can be
- Commit yourself to a great cause
- Dress and look your best always
- Accept compliments with a "Thank you"
- Don't compare yourself to others
- Finish what you start
- Improve your physical appearance when possible
- Increase your education
- Use encouraging language when talking about yourself

- Quit harmful habits: overeating, smoking, drinking, cursing, etc.
- Avoid: pornography, hard rock, soap operas, horoscopes
- Improve your management of time
- Make your enemies your friends
- Develop your personality
- Look for the good in others
- Do your best when attempting anything
- Be punctual
- Associate with those you admire
- Go out of your way to help others
- Let others know you appreciate them
- Never allow another person to make you feel inferior
- Learn Biblical principles and apply them to your life

Work at improving you, and you'll improve the image you have of yourself. There are many manifestations of a poor self-image besides the failure to set goals. A person with a poor self-image will minimize something really magnificent, or someone else's accomplishments. He might spend much time attempting to impress others with how great his accomplishments or possessions are. If a poor self-image has been hindering you from setting goals, why not begin today building a healthy one? If you've never trusted Jesus Christ as your Saviour, do yourself a favor and do it today.

Too Great A Price

Certainly, many things we could do in life are not worthwhile to us. Yet, when we claim that we don't set goals because the price is too great, I believe we haven't really considered the price of not setting goals.

We pay a price either way. Think about it. If we do not set goals, we'll pay with anxiety, disappointment, poverty, boredom, rejection, and possibly even jobs we hate. This compares unfavorably with the price of success, which includes burning desire, persistence, enthusiasm, knowledge, creativity, flexibility, and enjoyable jobs. There is no such thing as "not paying a price" for what we choose to do in life. Everything has a price tag.

I've heard Zig Ziglar say,

We don't pay the price of success; we enjoy the price.

I doubt that many can say they enjoy the price of failure.

Disease Of Laziness

People with the disease of laziness seem to think that they are eligible for "medical discharge" from the responsibility of setting goals. Perhaps it's possible they've had this disease from birth.

Everything comes to them on a silver platter, and they feel the world owes them a living. They're content to sit back and receive all the handouts they can get. Suggesting that these people set goals simply asks too much of them. I think there is only one cure for this disease — total abstinence! They should be made to do without until goal setting becomes a part of their lives — at least the goal of getting jobs and working for a living.

Time is so precious. The Bible teaches in James 4:14 that your life is but a vapor that appears for a little while, and then vanishes. Since this is true, doesn't it make sense that we make the most of the time we have?

I was fortunate that I learned to enjoy working at an early age. Perhaps it was the benefits (paycheck, praise, etc.), or perhaps it was that I sensed a fulfillment of purpose by working. This one thing I do know: It is more fun and productive to fight laziness with good, old fashioned hard work. Someone once said,

A lazy person is not afraid of work; he can lie beside it and sleep all day long.

Lack Of Discipline

We must be disciplined to be able to do those things that have not yet become habit or are not necessarily enticing in and of themselves.

It requires discipline to begin an exercise program. It requires discipline to do today what our bodies beg us to put off until tomorrow. The act of sitting down and planning the rest of our lives is not necessarily something that must be done today; it can wait until tomorrow. Since it can wait, it probably will. As we all know, tomorrow never comes. Goal setting is something we're all going to get to "one of these days."

Overcome Those Reasons

There are ways to combat each of these reasons. Some solutions are simple and even quick. Others, are neither quick nor simple. It does make sense to take the time and steps necessary to set goals. The alternatives are not attractive. We can either be goal setters and help to control our circumstances or we can be, as most are, "under the circumstances." The choice is ours!

It matters not what our lots are in life. We can change them for the better. Often those who accomplish the most are those who have had to overcome the greatest numbers of obstacles. Simply trying to survive forced them to set goals. Once they became survivors, they learned the tremendous benefits of goal setting and continued setting goals until they surpassed those who have never experienced the limitations or obstacles.

Goal setting can help you get the most out of your life. Life is too short to waste! With only 24 hours in a day, we should feel behooved to spend time wisely. One cannot save time; one can only spend it. Killing time is another way of committing suicide. Think about it! Murder is considered one of the most hideous crimes. Yet, murder is simply taking away the time of the victim. When we decide to kill time, we should remember that we cannot resurrect time. If we have no desire to kill time, then we must do something to avoid it. Goal setting is the answer!

Most would probably admit there just isn't enough time to do all we really want to do. In fact, I have days that I leave 50 things on my *Things to do* list uncompleted. I never have to look for something to do. I do need to look at the list and decide which items are the most important, and which ones will help me in reaching my goals. Many activities I sincerely love, and many more I'd like to learn and experience. The only hope I have in getting to these is to plan to do them. Otherwise, it is unlikely they will ever find their way into my busy schedule.

Now and then I encounter a person in his "last years," telling how he wishes he had a second chance. I hear how he always wanted to do something, learn something, go somewhere, or change occupations, but never found the time. Now, it's too late. (Sometimes, it really is too late; most times it isn't.) If finding time has been your problem, change your thinking now. You don't find time. You make time by scheduling what you want to do.

I've come to believe that at least 75% of all people are unhappy with their jobs (most because of dissatisfaction with themselves). Others are guilty of thinking the grass is greener on the other side of the fence. Still others really should be working somewhere else, but they just don't have the courage to make the change. Some say they can't afford to change. Actually, they have gotten to the point where they no longer own their possessions — but their possessions own them. Sad indeed!

Goal setting can change all this. Or, at least, it's the beginning to bringing about a change. We must first decide what we want and then develop action plans to make it happen. As we walk through our plans or blueprints, we will see the changes we want. Our goals may be as short-range as cleaning out our garages (simple, hey?), or as long-range as having million-dollar savings accounts by retirement. They can, and should, include both long-range and short-range goals. I'll share more about this later.

In my first year of goal setting I accomplished more than I had in any previous year of my life. Since then, as I sit down each November to plan the next year's activities, I review my accomplishments for that past year and get even more excited. I have achieved many things that I never would have achieved had it not been for goal setting.

I've been inspired by John Goddard's life. He is now almost seventy and has done more in his life than 100 average men do. You can read about him in the October 1983 issue of Reader's Digest in an article entitled, *I Wanted To Do*

It All. When he was only 25, he made a list like the dream list I've already challenged you to make. His first list had 127 items on it. His list included exploring the Nile and Amazon Rivers, milking a rattlesnake, going to the moon, writing a book, making a movie, climbing Mt. Everest, and visiting every country in the world. As of 1983, he had accomplished 106 of his 127 items from that first list. Of course, he had added many things to that list that he had also accomplished.

You may have no desire to do anything on his list, or anything on my list. That is OK. What's important is that you do those things on your list that you deem important. We fail to do the things we really want because we lose sight or focus of those things. We think about them now and then, but then something else grabs our attention, and we're off in another direction.

There are many benefits to be derived from goal setting. Let's look at some of them.

Goals Give You...

Purpose And Direction

John F. Kennedy said, "Efforts and courage are not enough without purpose and direction." It was in his State of the Union message of May, 1961 that he pledged that the United States would land a man on the moon and return him safely to earth "before this decade is out." I'm still impressed with the accomplishment of that goal. Aren't you?

Our goals should be determined by our stated purposes in life. Since most people cannot easily state, or even find, their purposes apart from their goals, the reverse is usually the case. Their goals give them their purposes.

You cannot be anything if you want to be everything. There is just too much that you can do. You cannot please everybody, and if you try, probably you will not please anybody — including yourself! Unless you find your purpose and direction based on your goals, you will constantly be wandering around, doing little.

A Standard Against Which To Measure Your Effectiveness

Imagine keeping score in a basketball game without a goal at either end. Or picture evaluating a football game without having the field marked off every ten yards, or with no end zone. Just as we need goals in sports to measure our effectiveness, so we need them in life. Only losers don't keep score. I really believe that a winner desires to know, and needs to know how he is doing, where he is in relation to where he wants to be. To succeed in life, we must continue to grow and improve. Properly setting goals will help us to know how well we're doing.

A Sense Of Accomplishment

I ask participants in my seminars to list their accomplishments in the different areas of their lives. I'm amazed at how many people just sit there with blank expressions on their faces, trying to figure out if they ever have done anything worth writing about. A goal setter is never at a loss when fulfilling this assignment. As one's sense of accomplishment grows, so does his self-image. You cannot consistently act in a manner inconsistent with the way you see yourself. If you think you can, or if you think you can't, you're right! Your sense of accomplishment determines if you think you can. Having and reaching goals improves your sense of accomplishment.

Goals Help You To...

Concentrate Energy And Resources

We only have so much energy and so many resources. Having goals will help in using our energy and resources to the greatest potential, and amazingly, even increase them. Goals attract the resources necessary for their fulfillment. Some resources we possess are:

- Time (24 hours per day)
- Money
- Personnel
- Equipment
- Supplies

Keep Priorities In Perspective

I mentioned earlier that my daily *Things to do* list often contains as many as 50 things that will not get done. Everything on my list must be evaluated in light of my priorities. How do I decide my priorities?

First, I evaluate each item in relation to my goals. (I even need to rank my goals.) Second, I look at each item and decide if it falls into the "must be done," "should be done," or "nice to do" category. Third, once the items are in each category, I then number them according to the importance of the goals they're going to help me attain. Otherwise, I find myself allowing the "urgent" to push aside the "important." I know of no better system than this.

Improve Your Use Of Time

Time is life. Without it, we're dead. Time is no respecter of financial position. Rich or poor, we each have only 168 hours in a week, 24 hours in a day, 60 minutes in an hour, and 60 seconds in a minute. We might not consider the seconds, or even the minutes, as important — but they are! We make our future by the best use of the present. When we have just a little time left, then we realize the importance of it. A person with goals seldom finds himself "watching the clock," wishing that time would pass a little faster. A person with goals on his job seldom says, "Thank God it's Friday." On the contrary, the person with goals finds that time passes all too quickly. Time flies when he is having fun, even in the midst of trials and adversity. He has purpose. Have you noticed that you do more when you have a deadline and excitement about meeting or beating it?

Build Enthusiasm

Is enthusiasm important? You bet it is! You see, from enthusiasm you receive most of your energy. Have you ever come home after a hard day on the job, ready to "flop," and a friend calls up for a quick racquetball or softball game? Suddenly, you have the energy of a ten-year old? Maybe racquetball or softball doesn't do that to you, but something does. You get my point.

Avoid A Life Of Mediocrity

Let's face it — just "getting by" in life is no fun. "Mediocre," according to Webster is "of middle quality; neither very good nor very bad; ordinary; average; commonplace." The best definition I've heard of "average" is that it's "the best of the worst, and worst of the best." I can't get excited about being in either of those categories, and I don't believe you can either. One cannot characterize the life of a goal setter as "average." A study was conducted asking Harvard graduates about their future; it showed only 3% of them had written down their goals and objectives for their future. Twenty years later, a follow-up study found that the three percent had earned more than the other 97% combined. Does that surprise you? It shouldn't.

Avoid Procrastination

The most valuable trait that you can acquire is the ability to make yourself do the thing you have to do — when it ought to be done — whether you like it or not.

Goal setting can even help you to like doing the things you otherwise would not like. Procrastination is the doing of a lower priority activity when a higher priority activity ought to be done. We tackle something easy instead of something difficult. We do the quick before the lengthy project. We do that which we enjoy before that which is mundane. We do that which we know before that which we must learn.

Goal setting helps us to put all projects in proper prospective. You can really "enjoy" doing an activity simply because you can see how it will help you in getting where you want to go. The hardest work in the world is that which should have been done yesterday. Procrastination is the fertilizer that makes difficulties grow.

Summary

You ought to be setting goals and developing action plans. Today is the best time to begin. Tomorrow never comes! You can, and will, do more with your life if you live it on purpose instead of by accident. Today is the first day of the rest of your life. Crying over the years you've wasted won't do any good. You've already begun building a new future for yourself. Keep up the good work! Next, you're going to learn about the different categories of goals.

·*Five*·
Goal Categories

When people think of setting goals, they often think of attaining certain levels of earnings, winning sporting events, accomplishing great feats, or obtaining something they want. All these are examples of goals. Yet, goals are not limited to these.

Webster defines "goal" as "an end that one strives to attain; aim." Thus, a goal can be literally anything you want and are willing to strive to attain. It might be as grandiose as becoming the president of a major company, or as simple as developing the habit of brushing your teeth twice daily. A goal can be something as exciting as visiting some faraway place, or as mundane as cleaning out your garage. Yes, anything that you sincerely want to do, become, or have, can be a goal, if you are going to strive to attain it. Otherwise, it's only a dream or wishful thinking.

In this chapter, you will learn about the seven major categories in which you should set goals to have a balanced life. These categories are:

- *Physical*
- *Mental*
- *Spiritual*
- *Family*
- *Social*
- *Financial*
- *Career*

Each goal you set may be classified under one of these categories. Which category do most of your past goals come under? Which categories have you omitted completely? The answers to these two questions explain why you are the person you are today.

Let's take a closer look at these categories. I will begin each category by repeating some aphorisms relating to the category, and close each with some questions that I hope will prompt you to set some goals in that particular category.

Physical

Money, achievement, fame, and success are important, but they are bought too dearly when acquired at the cost of health.

A great deal of poor health in the country may be attributed to heavy meals and light work.

Those who ignore health in the pursuit of wealth usually wind up losing both.

Good health just doesn't take care of itself, and it is most often lost by assuming that it will.

The Agriculture Department says the average American eats 1,148 pounds of food a year. Of course, a lot of it goes to "waist."

The best exercise is to exercise discretion at the dining table.

Sleep is something that always seems more important the morning after than the night before.

Oversleeping is a mighty poor way to make your dreams come true.

It doesn't do any harm to dream, providing you get up and hustle when the alarm goes off.

Why not cultivate health instead of treating disease?

It becomes easy to think of some physical goals we might set after reading those comments, doesn't it? Submitting to some physical testing determines ones condition. This is almost certainly a category in which each of us could use improvement. Many of us are too fat, too skinny, too weak, or too sluggish. Most of us want to improve, but we never find the best time to begin. Remember J. C. Penney's statement? "The hardest part of any job is getting started!" We have all kinds of excuses for waiting until tomorrow. After all, there are so many conflicting reports out there about what's good or dangerous for us, that we're not even sure where to start. The last thing I'd want you to do is to die attempting to get into shape. Everyone says, "Check with your doctor." You may find, however, that he isn't in any better shape than you are.

That is the merry-go-round most of us are on, isn't it? Why are physical goals important? Most of the reasons are obvious. We want to enjoy life, which is difficult to do when confined to a bed because of poor health. How well we care for ourselves physically is the major factor determining how long each of us will live. Continuing to breathe, itself, is a physical goal. Without breath, a body cannot function. Breathing, still, isn't the only physical goal we ought to have. Many people continue breathing but are so miserable. Because of the way they've treated their bodies, they cannot enjoy life.

Another reason to set physical goals is for our own self-esteem. We spend more time with ourselves than with anyone else. We might get tired of looking at someone else and decide to walk away for awhile, but we cannot do that with ourselves. Many of us probably don't even realize how much we've damaged our self-esteem by the way we've let ourselves go. We look in the mirror every morning and have even grown to accept the way we look. We say to ourselves, "Sure I'm overweight, but I don't really look that bad. I get along. Others don't make fun of me." And we are satisfied — until, that is, we see our pictures! We think, "Is it really possible that I look that heavy?" At that instant we decide we really ought to do something to change the way we look — but we only decide.

The need for self-control is definitely evident here. I don't know what is more difficult: to begin and maintain an exercise program, or to begin and maintain a proper diet. They're both tough, aren't they?

Don't run from this need to set physical goals. Perhaps you've tried many times in the past, and failed miserably. The fact that you are reading this book proves there is still hope. Keep going. You'll be excited when you see how easy it is to put these pieces together and apply them. Remember, anything can be made easy if you break it down into small manageable parts and tackle each part one at a time. "It's hard by the yard but it's a cinch by the inch!"

Consider the following questions as you decide what some of your physical goals should be.

1) Am I in excellent, or at least good, physical condition?

2) Am I satisfied with my current weight? What should it be?

3) Do I have a regular exercise program?

4) When was the last time I had a thorough physical checkup?

5) What physical skills do I want to improve?

6) What can I do to improve my appearance?

7) Do I need to build, or improve, my hygiene habits?

8) What do I do for family recreation?

9) What physical habits do I have that I know are detrimental to my health?

10) Do I participate in any sports or recreational activity?

Mental

The mind is like the stomach. It's not how much you put into it that counts, but how much it digests.

An open mind, like an open window, should be equipped with a screen to keep the bugs out.

If you keep your mind too open, people will throw a lot of rubbish into it.

It's impossible for anyone to learn what he thinks he already knows.

Being ignorant is not as shameful as being unwilling to learn.

Only hungry minds can become educated.

Those who really thirst for knowledge always get it.

It is not necessary to know everything, but you had better know almost all of the important things.

Knowledge has to be improved, challenged, and increased constantly, or it vanishes.

You cannot escape the results of your own thoughts.

Shortchange your education now, and you may be short of change the rest of your life.

Those who don't read have no advantage over those who can't.

A person should have enough education so he doesn't have to look up to anyone. He should also have enough to be wise enough not to look down on anyone.

Among the few things more expensive than an education these days is the lack of it.

Man is like a tack; he can only go as far as his head will let him.

Think small and you will remain small.

Mental goals are important. Nothing affects the way we live and the results of our lives as much as the material we put into our minds. Many years ago I heard Zig Ziglar say, "You can change what you are and where you are by changing what goes into your mind." That statement made sense to me then and it has proven itself to me many times since.

There is a computer term "GI-GO," meaning "Garbage In - Garbage Out." If garbage is programmed into a computer, garbage will come out. The mind works the same way! We cannot fill our minds with trash, hang around negative people, and spend our time worrying without it affecting us negatively. Remember Earl Nightingale's record entitled, *The Strangest Secret*? His message was that we become what we think about most of the time.

It may surprise you that the average adult in America reads less than two books per year. About fifty percent of all adults have never even read one book since they left school. Think of it — not even one book! The person who does not read has no advantage over those who cannot read.

One of the most valuable lessons I've learned in my adult life has been the value of using my ability to read. I didn't graduate from high school with a desire to learn. In fact, I can remember taking my books home to do homework only once in my four years of high school. I had one primary motivation in high school: to get by, to graduate. I lacked any desire to continue my education. I don't think I was an exception; I believe most who leave high school today feel the same way. Even those who go to college often do so only because they believe it will improve their earning potential — not because they have a desire to learn.

When I left the Army as a 21-year old, I took advantage of the GI Bill's educational opportunity. I enrolled in Purdue University, thinking I might become an engineer. Before one semester was over, I realized I hadn't changed. I still did very little homework, and my heart just wasn't in it. I had no desire to waste my time, or the government's money, so I quit after just one semester. As far as I was concerned, I would never return to college, at least not until I could become motivated to study something. I really didn't know if that motivation would ever come.

A year passed before I found a subject that interested me. When I became a Christian, I realized that the Bible, God's Word, was worth studying. I was 22 years old and knew nothing about it, except that it contained answers to many of my questions. I decided to return to college and to apply myself to learning something exciting. I attended four years of Bible college and consider it the wisest investment I'll ever make. I learned how to study the Bible, for which I will be forever thankful.

I have a desire to improve every area of my life, and can do that only when I know how. I even use my ability to learn to help me catch more fish during my Canadian trips. I read articles in fishing magazines, written by those successful in catching the kind of fish I want; then I apply what I learn. I spend much time and money when I go fishing and I want to get the most for my investment.

What are you attempting to do in life that could be made easier through studying? How much does your attitude affect your actions? Are you constantly improving your mind? Plan now to take time to set goals in the mental category. Consider the following questions to help you in setting some of these goals.

1) What books do I want to read?

2) Do I listen to cassette tapes?

3) Do I read and study the Bible?

4) Am I satisfied with my memory skills?

5) Should I consider working on my reading skills?

6) Do I feel I'm being hindered in my progress because of a lack of education in some area?

7) Do I take time to think, to be creative?

8) What negative influences affect the way I live daily?

9) How much do I invest in my education annually?

10) Do I plan a time to feed my mind daily?

Spiritual

The man who believes in nothing but himself lives in a very small world.

People always get into trouble when they think they can handle their lives without God.

The highest knowledge is the knowledge of God.

The best way to stand up before the world is to kneel down before God.

The man who bows humbly before God is sure to walk uprightly before men.

Some people cannot find God for the same reason that a thief cannot find a policeman.

Too many men who talk of finding God in nature, rather than in church, go hunting for Him with rod or gun.

At times we may not know where God is, but we can be confident that He knows where we are.

God still speaks to those who take the time to listen.

God never gives you anything bigger to do than you have the resources to handle.

Never be afraid to trust an unknown future to a known God.

Fear not tomorrow; God is already there.

God's promises are like life preservers. They keep the soul from sinking in the sea of trouble.

When you get to the end of your rope, be thankful — God is there!

God is never more than a prayer away.

The love of God cannot be merited or earned, but it can be spurned.

There are a thousand ways of pleasing God, but not one without faith.

Faith is the hinge that holds the believer to a personal relationship with God.

Faith is something like electricity. You can't see it, but you can see the light.

Faith gives us the courage to face the present with confidence, and the future with expectancy.

All men need a faith that will not shrink when washed in the waters of affliction and adversity.

Feed your faith, and your doubts will starve to death.

When we let God guide, He will provide.

God never intended that we do as we please, but as He pleases.

There will be no real peace of mind as long as God remains unseated at the conference table.

Greatness is not found in possessions, power, position, or prestige. It is discovered in goodness, humility, service, and character.

What lies behind us and what lies before us are tiny matters compared to what lies within us.

Death is not a period but a comma in the story of life.

Everyone should fear death until he has something that will live on after his death.

The one thing certain about life is that we must leave it.

If you are born only once —you'll die twice. If you are born twice —you'll die only once.

Yes, all these and more are true! Yet, it continues to amaze me how few people take time to give them much thought. I am often asked for examples of spiritual goals. Most people not only don't set spiritual goals, but also admit being apathetic toward them.

Consider these questions:

1) Is anything more important than getting to know the God who created us?

2) Is any information more valuable to mankind than the Word of God?

3) Does any question deserve more attention than where will we spend eternity?

4) Can any fellowship be more fulfilling than that which we might spend with God Almighty?

5) Can any power be more valuable to us than the power of God?

6) Will anything be more satisfying to the soul than to live a life well pleasing to God?

7) Can we build anything that is more important than building character into our lives?

My purpose in writing this book is to share those things that I have learned — not to preach at you. I am extremely thankful that I was introduced to this spiritual realm in 1970. At a critical time in my life, I received God's forgiveness and was born into His family. Until then, I always thought God was off in the distance somewhere. I wasn't even sure He existed, let alone that He might love me. I was very lonely at times, and often considered suicide. My spirit was deeply troubled, and I had no peace of mind. I was looking for purpose and wasn't sure if I would find it. I probably wouldn't have if I had continued in the direction I was heading.

Several years ago while I was teaching a sales seminar in Pittsburgh, someone posed this question. "Gene, how do you find the courage to approach presidents and vice presidents of large corporations?" I hadn't thought about it before and was surprised when I realized the answer. Here is what I told the audience.

> *I used to be very self-conscious of my appearance, my speech, and my lack of learning. I don't know if I felt inferior, or just thought everyone else thought I was inferior. At any rate, I didn't feel comfortable around others who I believed were smarter, wealthier, better looking, or more talented than I. I didn't feel accepted by even the "middle class," and therefore didn't feel very good about myself. Had I remained that way, I could not have mustered up the courage to make those contacts. When I understood, however, that God loved me and desired that I be a part of His family, my self-esteem was boosted tremendously! I developed the attitude, "Since the God of heaven loves me and calls me His own, why should I be concerned if someone else doesn't have the good judgment to do the same?" I can walk in anywhere and hold my head high, knowing I am a child of the Living God, a sinner whose sins are forgiven. I've been given eternal life, and I'll be spending eternity in heaven —all because He loves me!*

That's precisely what I told them. I can face others who appear superior because I know God personally. You can too! If you can't say with assurance that you know God, then make that one of your spiritual goals right now. You will never have a more important goal in your life. The Bible asks the question:

> *What shall it profit a man, if he shall gain the whole world, and lose his own soul?* **Mark 8:36 (KJV)**

Consider that question carefully before you dismiss this section as just a "religious" message.

It doesn't matter how many questions you have answered correctly if you get to the end of your life and still haven't answered the most important one: "Where will I spend eternity?" Study the Gospel of St. John. Read John 20:31 and you will find John's gospel can help you answer that question, and know how to have eternal life.

Just in case you haven't heard, eternal life is a free gift, not something for which you have to work. You couldn't earn it or deserve it by your works, even if you tried. Over 150 times, the New Testament clearly teaches that the way to obtain eternal life is to believe in (place your faith, rely upon, trust, place confidence in) Jesus Christ. If you're too proud to receive eternal life as a gift, you can't have it. It's as simple as that. Notice the simplicity in the following verses.

> *For God so loved the world, that He gave His only begotten Son, that whosoever believeth in him should not perish, but have everlasting life.* **John 3:16 (KJV)**

> *For by grace are ye saved through faith; and that not of yourselves: it is the gift of God: Not of works, lest any man should boast.* **Ephesians 2:8,9 (KJV)**

> *Be it known unto you therefore, men and brethren, that through this man is preached unto you the forgiveness of sins: And by him all that believe are justified [declared righteous] from all things, from which ye could not be justified by the law of Moses.* **Acts 13:38,39 (KJV)**

> *What shall we say then to these things? If God be for us, who can be against us? He that spared not his own Son, but delivered him up for us all, how shall he not with him also freely give us all things?* **Romans 8:31,32 (KJV)**

Think about this next statement for a moment.

You're not prepared to live until you're prepared to die.

Are you prepared? If so, what are you doing to help others prepare? Jim Elliott, a missionary who gave his life in Ecuador in 1956, said, "He is no fool who gives what he cannot keep to gain what he cannot lose." Elliott had a spiritual goal of winning the natives to Christ, and he gave his life for it. You ought to read the rest of the story in *Through Gates of Splendor.*

In determining some additional spiritual goals, consider these questions.

1) Do I have a relationship with the Creator?

2) Do I pray and receive answers to my prayers?

3) Do I read and study the Bible?

4) What questions do I have that the Bible could answer?

5) Where do I go to receive spiritual growth?

6) Where can I go to become involved in spiritually stimulating activities?

7) How can I make a spiritual contribution of lasting value?

8) Am I prepared to die?

9) What is God's purpose for my life?

10) What character quality changes would I like to see made?

Family

Nowadays there are more model homes than model families.

As the gardener is responsible for the products of his garden, so the parents are responsible for the character and conduct of their young children.

One does not find happiness in marriage but puts happiness into marriage.

Success in marriage is more than finding the right person. It's also a matter of being the right person.

Fewer marriages would skid if more who said "I do" did.

Too many people are finding it easier to get married than to stay married.

It is better to be laughed at for not being married than to be unable to laugh because you are.

The person who marries for money usually earns every penny of it.

To marry a woman for her beauty is like buying a house for its paint.

Children need strength to lean on, a shoulder to cry on, and an example to learn from.

It is extremely difficult for a child to live right if he has never seen it done.

The best thing you spend on your children is your time.

Every father should remember that one day his son will follow his example instead of his advice.

To train children at home, it's necessary for both the children and parents to spend some time there.

Parents who have fine children usually have children who have fine parents.

We would probably all agree that family goals are important. When asked to name the most important thing in their lives, most people reply that it is their family. How sad that we don't normally live like it! The family unit is the backbone of the nation. History shows that when the family deteriorates, so does the country. If this is true, then America beware!

As with anything, improvement must begin with you. You cannot even care very much what happens to other families, if you don't care what happens to your own. You might say you care about your family. You might even say they are more important than anything else in the world. But, if you're not willing to devote time to them — not just for them — your actions speak louder than your words.

Consider ways to improve relationships with the following: spouse, children, parents, brothers and sisters, in-laws, grandparents, grandchildren, cousins, uncles, and aunts. Certainly, some of these relationships mean more than others. Yet, none of them can really mean very much if you don't let them know you care.

Determine how much your family really means to you by analyzing the percentage of your goals directly related to them. Has your love for them diminished? Are arguments common around the house? Does your spouse seem uninterested in you or uninteresting to you? Do you get respect at home? Well, don't expect changes until you're willing to change. Your family will eventually respond, but you must change first!

Thinking we have all the answers causes major family conflicts. Having marriage licenses makes us husbands or wives, and having children makes us parents — in one sense. Yet, it doesn't make us any more qualified than we were before those events. If the only thing we've learned about those responsibilities is what we have observed, then we have a long way to go. Don't be too proud to learn from books, especially the Bible. God knows more about families than all the family experts combined. He instituted marriage, and He intended for one marriage to last a lifetime.

His Needs, Her Needs, written by Willard F. Harley, Jr., helps couples better understand each other's needs. Harley explains how and why affairs get started and presents many practical ideas on how to "affair-proof your marriage." I strongly recommend this book, and especially encourage you to read about the "Love Bank" concept.

Consider the following questions to help you in setting some of your family goals.

1) Am I satisfied with the demonstration of love between the members of my family?

2) Am I proud of the way my children are turning out?

3) Do I spend enough time with the individuals of my family to assure them of my love and concern for them? Do I schedule "family time" and stick to it?

4) Does each member of my family talk freely and comfortably with the others?

5) Do I know what the needs of my family are, and do I work to help fulfill them?

6) What am I going to do in the immediate future to improve my ability to fulfill my role as a family member?

7) Do I have a clear picture of the person I would like to be, as it relates to my role within my family?

8) Do I practice character qualities such as honesty, empathy, encouragment, and forgiveness within my family unit?

9) What families am I most familiar with that could serve as role models to help me improve?

10) What books will I read or seminars will I attend in the future to improve myself in this area?

Social

Wise is the man who fortifies his life with friendships.

The best recipe for making friends is to be one yourself.

We are on the wrong track when we think of friendship as something to get instead of something to give.

Untried friends are like uncracked eggs —you can't be sure what they are like on the inside.

The bank of friendship cannot live long without deposits.

A true friend is one who sticks by you even when he gets to know you real well.

Friends are like a priceless treasure; he who has none is a social pauper.

Your neighbor will seem like a better man when you judge him as you judge yourself.

Of the seven categories, this is my weakest area. I keep quite busy almost every waking moment, and therefore, find very little time for social activities. In fact, I must schedule time to socialize.

People are either primarily task-oriented or people-oriented. No doubt, I am task-oriented. If push comes to shove, I'm more concerned about the accomplishment of the task, even if it means someone might get his feelings hurt. I find it difficult to go to a social function to have a good time. I have a great time almost every waking moment anyway — in the pursuit of accomplishing my goals. To quit what I'm doing to attend a function where people just stand around talking is not my idea of a good time.

I've shared this with you in case you're like me. I don't believe you have to change your attitude about this to accomplish a lot socially. If you're like me, you probably feel you have all the friends you have time for already. The key now is making sure you take the time to keep those relationships alive. Aspire to help others enjoy themselves most when they are with you. You can be an inspiration and encouragement to them.

I love life and believe the way to get the most out of life is to focus on giving — not on getting. Therefore, in attempting to accomplish my objectives, of giving myself to others to help them accomplish their objectives or solve their problems, I accomplish many of my social goals.

If you aren't blessed with a job like mine, constantly meeting new people and developing new relationships, then you must work harder in this area. If you can't say you have friends you would give your life for, and believe they also would for you, then you probably ought to be setting goals to develop friendships like that.

> *Two young men had been friends their entire lifetimes. As neighbors, they had played together, gone to school together, engaged in athletics together, and finally enlisted in the Army together. Fate determined they would eventually be in the same area of battle together during World War I. After a particularly bitter battle, one of the boys was missing somewhere out in what was known as "No Man's Land." The other boy, safe and unhurt, went to the commander and requested permission to go look for his friend. He was told it was no use for no one was alive out there after the withering fire of so many hours. After great insistence, he finally received permission.*
>
> *Some time later he returned with the limp body of his friend over his shoulder. The commander said, "Didn't I tell you it was no use to go?" to which the boy replied with radiance, "But it wasn't in vain. I got there in time to hear him whisper, 'I knew you'd come.'"*

A friend walks in when the rest of the world walks out. A real friend tells you when you have spinach stuck in your teeth. A real friend is one who, when you've made a fool of yourself, doesn't feel that you've done a permanent job. Yes, a real friend sticks by you even when he gets to know you.

Friendships don't come easy. They must be earned. Friendship is usually a plant of slow growth. Although some think they can buy friends, friends who can be bought will often shortchange you if given a chance. A rich person has great difficulty determining who his real friends are.

A man never gets so rich that he can afford to lose a friend. Friendships will last if they're put first. You can, however, run your friends off by running them down. Or, you can wipe out a friendship by sponging on it. I strongly suggest you read Dale Carnegie's, *How to Win Friends and Influence People*, which can be found in almost every bookstore — and for good reason.

I can't tell you a lot about social and civic organizations because I have never joined any of them. Many professionals tell me I've really missed the boat, and they may be right. I know many salesmen who have joined to secure leads or prospects. I've never needed that reason. I do know that many organizations perform wonderful functions for their communities. These organizations present especially good opportunities to develop relationships for those who do not normally meet many people.

Be very careful with whom you build your relationships. Birds of a feather do flock together, and you will, probably, become like those with whom you associate. Determine to be a thermostat, not a thermometer. Don't let others set your mood, character, or life-style — bring them up to your level.

Ask yourself the following questions when setting some social goals.

1) How many good friends do I really have?

2) What can I do to let my friends know I really appreciate them?

3) With whom would I like to develop a better relationship?

4) What character qualities do I have that attract others; which ones repel?

5) Do I spend time with the caliber of people I aspire to be like?

6) Do the people I most associate with encourage me or discourage me?

7) What organizations should I join to improve my social life and help me accomplish my social objectives?

8) What can I do to improve my relationships with my neighbors?

9) What can I do to make myself more socially attractive without compromising any of my principles?

10) Am I committed to the growth and well-being of my friends?

Financial

A person's character is put to a severe test when he suddenly acquires or quickly loses a considerable amount of money.

Contentment is realized when your earning power equals your yearning power.

Fools sometimes make money, but money also sometimes makes fools.

Money can build a house, but it takes love to make it a home.

The guy who invented the boomerang was probably the same one who invented the credit card.

If George Washington never told a lie, what's his picture doing on a dollar bill that's worth about twenty-three cents?

The only way to make a dollar go far these days is to mail it overseas.

The value of a dollar will never drop as low as some people will stoop to get it.

The average man has quit dreaming of having enough money to last him the rest of his life. He'd settle for enough to last him the rest of the month.

Some people have more money than brains — but not for long.

Money never did buy happiness, and credit cards aren't doing any better.

It's funny how a dollar can look so big when you take it to church and so small when you take it to the supermarket.

Anybody who thinks there is a shortage of coins hasn't been to church lately.

The most expensive way to make money is to spend your life doing nothing else.

Taking your money with you when you die isn't important. The real problem is making it last until you're ready to go.

The man who overestimates the value of money will never be happy by amassing more of it.

Some people get the idea they're worth a lot of money just because they have it.

Money is a good servant but a poor master.

Money brings happiness to those who find happiness earning it.

No one really knows whether or not a person would be happy if he had all the money he wanted. There isn't that much money.

Money may be used as a universal passport to everywhere except heaven and as a universal provider for everything except happiness.

People are funny. They spend money they don't have to buy things they don't need to impress people they don't like.

Those anxious to invest their money in a "going" concern should make sure which way it's going.

Before borrowing money from a friend, decide which you need more.

It's all right to save money, but too many are trying to save it from people they owe it to.

The dollar doesn't go very far these days, but what it lacks in distance, it makes up in speed.

The above aphorisms probably provoked a chuckle or two from you, just as they did from me. They do so because they strike home — don't they? Certainly, this financial category is important to each of us.

Money greatly affects each of our lives. We must decide how we're going to:

(1) EARN IT
(2) SAVE IT
(3) INVEST IT
(4) SPEND IT WISELY, AND
(5) GIVE IT.

This is no easy task. Most people only think of earnings when financial goals are mentioned, but earning money is only one of many concerns. In fact, if we would concentrate more on the other four areas, we might not have to concentrate so much on earnings.

Let's briefly look at these areas of financial interest, as well as how to handle debt.

Earn It

Before you can do anything with your finances, you have to have some. Unless you inherit a bundle, or win it, you must have an income. There are two primary categories of income: earned and unearned. Earned income refers to wages, salary, fees, or commissions received for performing a specified function or activity. Unearned income refers to money received from investments such as interest, rent from property, and dividends from stocks. Begin by determining your current total income from all sources. Then, calculate what you expect it to be in the years to come if you continue on the same road you are presently traveling. Allowing for considerations such as inflation, are you satisfied with those expectations? If not, how can you change them?

The choices really are simple. You can either reduce your need for income, increase your work load (add a second job, work overtime, etc.), or get a higher-paying job. The point is, these options are available to you. The choice is yours to make.

You can estimate future income in one of two ways. Some look at their current situations and calculate how much they will earn. Then they develop budgets for those amounts. I have found it useful first to figure out how much I need to accomplish my objectives. Then I set the goal to bring in that amount of income. This method often forces me to stretch — as you might expect. I do believe, however, that my income grows at a much faster rate when I demand it of myself than when I just wish for it.

Save It

Few things in life are more difficult than saving money. It's a discipline, and not an easy one to acquire! When I was in Vietnam and had all my real needs provided for, I found it easy to save. But, once I returned to civilization, my saving came to a screeching halt.

I have friends who are great at saving money. When they purchase new cars or make any other large purchases, they always pay cash. They literally save thousands of dollars that otherwise would be spent in interest. I admit I became envious some years ago and determined to make my purchases in cash as well. That has been a real blessing. Not only do I save money, but I'm also not as apt to spend thousands of dollars casually.

Each of us should discipline himself to three kinds of saving: Long Range, Short Range, and Emergency. "Long Range" saving is for retirement. I don't ever expect to retire, but I do realize that I might outlive my income-producing years. Through the natural deterioration that age brings, I could find myself unable to continue producing an adequate income. Therefore, I must save for that time, should it come, so I will not burden others.

Second, short range savings will be used in the next few months or years to purchase items that require more money than one would normally maintain in his checking account. Cars, vacations, property, home improvements, etc., fall into this category. By saving toward them, I can carefully plan and decide which items are priority items. Not only do I save interest, but I know I own it when I do buy it. Paying off something already used is not as much fun as using something already paid for.

Third, emergency savings is money available when the expected unexpected occurs. Think about it. Isn't it foolish not to expect the unexpected? Though we can't always predict the exact emergencies, we know they occur with amazing regularity. Into every life a little rain must fall. Emergency savings will help take the sting out of those situations.

Invest It

In a way, investments are related to savings. Unless the investment is truly safe, you should be careful about placing very much of your savings into it. If the investment is very risky, don't risk investing your savings, at least not the Long Range, Short Range, and Emergency savings.

Investments are financial ventures that should either increase your wealth or bring in additional income (unearned income). Realize that often it's possible to lose your investment! Two kinds of people shouldn't gamble: those who can't afford to lose their money, and those who can. Although many investments can be considered a gamble, just as many are very safe. Often, however, the safer the investment is, the smaller the gain.

Be sure you have as much information as you can before you invest; and check out the reliability of that information! Simply putting something in black and white doesn't make it true. Find out how much control you will have and if there is a penalty for getting out before a deadline.

Spend It Wisely

I love this area of financial interest! I don't get real excited about earning it, saving it, or even investing it, but I can get excited about spending it. I enjoy spending, and mostly I enjoy spending on fantastic deals.

As a teenager, I purchased my first vehicle, a pickup truck, for only $150. I drove it for two years and turned it over on a gravel road. I still sold it for the same amount (after I beat the dents out with a sledge hammer). I realized then I could buy "right," use the item for awhile, and sell it for as much or more than I paid for it.

I'm convinced you can make your income go at least fifty percent further by planning carefully in this area. The following guidelines may help you in stretching your dollars.

- Plan for purchases; avoid the use of credit for impulse buying.

- Study to sharpen your negotiating skills — at least read a book on the subject.

- Don't buy the first item you look at — unless it is really a once-in-a lifetime bargain.
- Consider buying used. You can often purchase a more expensive item at less than half the price than you would have paid — and the item may have been only slightly used!

- Read the Classified Ads in your paper. Consider auctions, garage, and yard sales.

- Decide how much you really need or want an item before you purchase it. Have a priority list for purchases.

- Sometimes you can purchase two or three for about the price of one. Sell the remainder and get yours for just your effort.

I have literally made thousands of dollars and ended up with thousands of dollars worth of items to keep — simply by going to auctions with this attitude. I determine to spend my time at the auction wisely by only buying items that can easily be resold for a profit. That profit pays for the items that I keep. Then, my real cost for the item has only been my time. When I was 14 years old, I purchased an item for five dollars, which I later sold for $165. I only go to a couple of auctions each year, but I make them profitable. Here are some examples of purchases I've made at auctions:

- Gas Dryer — $2 (we used it for ten years)

- Washer — $13 (we used this also for ten years)

- Queen Ann dining room table w/chairs — $7 (we have used it for 16 years+)

- 25 cu. ft. Chest Freezer — $47.50 (we used it for two years/sold it for $275)

- 25 cu. ft. refrigerator/freezer — $80.00 (we sold it in two days for $180)

- Video Equipment — $5,600 (we sold part of it in three weeks for $12,300)

- 4 Copiers — $785 (we sold all for a total of $8,750)

These are only a few of many examples. By occasionally reading the Classified Section of the Sunday newspaper, I will often find an item I've always wanted but couldn't afford new, at a price I can easily afford. The trick is to look at your Sunday paper on Saturday afternoon or evening. Get there first. Great bargains go fast.

Give It

It may seem strange that I'd include "giving" as a category to consider when setting financial goals. Isn't giving one of those things you do when the plate is passed at church (while everyone is looking), or while you have company and someone comes to your door collecting for the Heart Association? Isn't giving what you do when your boss says the corporation **will** reach their United Way goal this year, and you **will** give your share? Yes, I guess that is giving, but not the kind I am talking about. The giving I mean is the kind God talks about in **2 Corinthians 9**.

> *So let each one give as he purposes in his heart, not grudgingly or of necessity; for God loves a cheerful giver.* **Verse 7 (NKJV)**

We've all heard that quotation, but how often have we put that one to the test? In this day when the finances seem so tight, we might find it difficult to want to give. I can tell you, as a person who has had money and one who hasn't, that giving is never easy. Granted, giving $20 is tougher when I only have $25 than when I have $2,500, but it's never easy to give a certain percentage. If I purpose to give a tithe (ten percent), then giving $250 when I make $2,500 in a week is as difficult as giving $2.50 when I make only $25.00.

Only three attitudes can provoke me to give as I should. The first is *discipline.* If I discipline myself to give and do it often enough so that it becomes habit, giving becomes easier. The second attitude is *faith*. The Bible verse that follows the above mentioned verse says: "And God is able to make all grace abound toward you, that you, always having all sufficiency in all things, have an abundance for every good work" (2 Corinthians 9:8). God will not allow the Christian who gives for the right reasons to suffer lack. Jesus taught that it is "more blessed to give than to receive" (Acts 20:35). If you believe this, giving becomes infinitely easier. The third attitude is *compassion*. Giving when you really care for others' needs makes giving less difficult.

This story provides additional food for thought regarding giving.

> *Dr. George W. Truett, a preacher of days gone by, was being entertained on one occasion in the home of a wealthy oil man in Texas. After the dinner the man took him up to the roof of his house and pointed to some huge fields of oil derricks. He then said, "Dr. Truett, that's all mine. I came to this country 25 years ago penniless, and now I own everything as far as you can see in that direction."*
>
> *He then turned to each of the other three directions and pointed to fields of grain, huge herds of cattle, and a great virgin forest, and said, "It's all mine, everything as far as you can see in every direction. I worked hard and saved, and now I own it all in every direction."*
>
> *He paused for the expected praise, but to his astonishment it didn't come. Dr. Truett laid his hand lovingly on his shoulder, pointed upward and said, "My friend, how much do you own in that direction?" The man dropped his head in shame and said, "I never thought of that."*

How easily we forget God's desires regarding our finances. Some erroneously teach that ten percent of everything belongs to God, and we should give that part back to Him. The Bible really teaches that it **all** belongs to God. We are only stewards. In reality, one is wise to consider God's will in determining what to do with every dollar. You might find it interesting to study what the Bible teaches regarding stewardship — and giving.

The Subject of Debt

I've been in debt up to my eyeballs, and can tell you first hand, it ain't fun! I've spent an average of one hour per day talking to creditors on the phone, and I can tell you first hand, it ain't fun! I've had to sell everything we owned (that was worth selling) to pay creditors, and I can tell you first hand, it ain't fun! I have had my family go almost 18 months (including one of the coldest winters in Missouri history) without hot water or gas heat. They can tell you first hand, it ain't fun! Do you get the message?

I learned the hard way that debt can become bigger than I am. Optimism can help a person accomplish a lot, but once he has overextended himself, it can't help him satisfy a creditor. I've been so down that I've considered suicide as the best way to pay my bills. I'm not proud of where I've been financially, but I'm glad I've been there. It is like the 27 months I spent in Vietnam—I'm glad I served there, but I wouldn't want to go through that again for anything. I've learned a lot through these negative experiences, and now I can better relate to others who are hurting.

Therefore, make one of your goals to become debt free! You'll be amazed at what it will do for you. I've been in financial bondage, and again repeat, "It ain't fun!" Working each day to pay for your possessions is senseless. When that happens, do you own them — or do they own you?

Eliminating debt is not as easy as getting into debt. Not only is it not as easy, but it's not as much fun. I suspect you're realizing as I did, that short term benefits are not worth long range debt!

If you only increase your debt by $2,000 per year for 20 years, at 15% interest, compounded annually, then attempt to pay it off at the rate of $25,000 per year, do you know how many years it would take to pay off the indebtedness? You would have borrowed a total of only $40,000. The answer is that it would take forever, and then some, because the interest alone each year beginning with the 21st year would exceed $27,800! If you paid back the loan at the rate of $40,000 per year, it would still take you over eight and a half years! Imagine that — it would take more than $340,000 to repay only $40,000! I don't think we foresee this when we're increasing our indebtedness by only $2,000 per year over a long period.

Some thoughts on how to get out of debt are:

(1) **Quit going further into debt.** Get rid of your credit cards if you can't handle them responsibly. Attempting to borrow your way out of debt is risky business and can quickly cause you to lose everything (possessions, friends,

self-respect, reputation, etc.). My first step was to draw the line and say, "No more!" I refused to borrow again — even for necessities.

(2) Sell what you have that is worth selling. We sold every piece of furniture that was worth selling. We received $775 for a three-year old stove, and replaced it with a $60 stove. We sold our bedroom suite for $875 and kept only the box springs and mattress that we put on a set of rails given to us. Selling these items helped us keep our house. At times we were four to six months behind with the payments.

(3) Be creative. It was when I was in the midst of these great financial trials that I heard Robert Schuller's message, "People don't have money problems; they have idea problems." That one idea stuck with me and helped me through my crisis more than anything else. Time does not permit me to share the ways I applied it, but perhaps the rest of this book can give you some ideas. I will give you this one idea that I used often: *sell yourself.* When possible, make a deal with your creditors to work off your debt by using your skills to their benefit. If you cannot sell yourself to your creditors, sell yourself to someone else who can benefit from your skill. Pre-sell your services at a discount, and use the money to eliminate the debt. It will work!

Some questions regarding financial goals are as follows:

1) What do I want my earnings to be — both now and in the future?

2) Am I in financial bondage? If so, how will I get out?

3) Am I debt free? Do I want to be?

4) Do I have a budget?

5) What safeguards have I built into my financial plan to prevent overspending and foolish impulse purchases?

6) Do I have a savings plan and invest that money wisely?

7) Regarding giving, do I carefully plan my giving and give what I should to support my church and others?

8) If I have children, do I teach them practical principles regarding their personal finances?

9) Do I have a healthy Biblical attitude regarding finances — realizing that all belongs to God and I am simply a steward?

10) Do I purchase large items such as automobiles, vacations, furniture, etc. with cash — or borrow for it and pay interest?

Career

No dream comes true until you wake up and go to work.

The fellow who is fired with enthusiasm for his work is seldom fired by his boss.

There is no future in any job. The future is in the person who holds the job.

Stick to your job until one of you is through.

Nothing is quite as embarrassing as watching your boss do something you assured him couldn't be done.

Education is to business what fertilizer is to farming.

Some people think they have ten years of experience when all they really have is one year reproduced ten times.

If you want to go far in business, you'll have to stay close to it.

Many successful people are so lonely because they sacrificed too many friends on the way up.

Go straight. Every crooked turn delays your arrival at success.

A successful person continues to look for work after he has found a job.

You certainly want to make good somewhere, so why not make good where you are?

The secret of success and happiness lies not in doing what you like, but in liking what you do.

Even the woodpecker has discovered that the only way to succeed is to use one's head.

The road to success runs uphill; so don't expect to break any records.

Between tomorrow's dream and yesterday's regret is today's opportunity.

The gates of opportunity swing on four hinges: initiative, insight, industry, and integrity.

The basic rules for success may be defined as follows: Know what you want. Find out what it takes to get it. Act on it and persevere.

Most people think about careers when they think about goal setting. Even high school students are asked if they've determined their career goals. Yet, sadly, very few really define their goals.

Your career goals range from what you want to do in life, to where you want to do it, to how much you want to earn while doing it. They range from the education and skills you wish to attain to the type of people with whom you wish to work, to the company for which you want to work. Your career goals might be awards and achievements to have to your credit, and might be your attitude toward your job. You may wish to own your own company, or to work for someone else. Career goals can be these and much more.

Is your job worth giving your life for? Because that's exactly what you are doing! You have only 168 hours in a week. If you sleep 56 of them away and spend only 50 hours of the remaining 112 hours per week on your job (including driving, lunches, etc.), then you're spending about 45% of your waking moments (your life) on the job. Doesn't it make sense that you enjoy it?

How sad that many people really don't like their jobs. Approximately 75% of the people I question don't enjoy their jobs. Yet life doesn't have to be that way. Now, I'm not suggesting those 75% should quit their jobs. I am suggesting that they take time to make the necessary changes so they can enjoy their jobs. They could either change some aspect of the jobs, or change their attitude toward their jobs.

I advise job seekers to ask: "If I could do whatever I want for whomever I want, what would it be?" Often they can't even answer that question. Then I ask them to list their likes and dislikes, their assets and liabilities, their skills and shortcomings. This project might look like this: Rate the following on a 1-10 Scale. (10 = great!)

1) I enjoy working indoors.
2) I enjoy working outdoors most of the time.
3) I enjoy working alone most of the time.
4) I enjoy working with others most of the time.
5) I enjoy working with the public.
6) I enjoy variety — a different project each day.
7) I prefer becoming an expert at one thing.
8) I enjoy being able to determine my schedule.
9) I prefer having set times to begin and quit work.
10) I want to be my own boss.
11) I enjoy working for others who are responsible.
12) I need a regular salary or income I can count on.
13) I enjoy the thought of working on commission.
14) I would like a job I could stay on for 40 years.
15) I need to make a major change every three or four years.
16) I want to have to continue learning to stay on top.

17) I want to develop a skill and have little demand for furthering my education.
18) I enjoy working with my hands more than my brain.
19) I enjoy using my brain more than physical work.
20) I enjoy seeing the results of my labor immediately.

Ask yourself these questions in determining what kind of job you should seek. You must get to know yourself.

Frankly, career planning does not mean you must know what you want to be doing twenty years from now — or even five years, for that matter. I've had enough different jobs (some of which I thought I'd spend my life with) that I've finally learned that as I change, my desires change. I've finally determined that my primary career goal is to continue growing and always remain flexible to take advantage of important career opportunities as they become available.

This may shock you but I've had these different jobs in my first twenty years after graduation from high school. They are as follows:

- Gas station attendant
- Farm hand
- Janitor in a factory
- Paint mixer in a paint factory
- Soldier (working as a crane operator, carpenter, bridge and tower builder)
- Box packer
- Photographer
- Ditch digger (field tile)
- Self-employed farmer
- Carpenter
- Sanitation engineer (Garbage man)
- Building mover
- Railroad switchman
- Maintenance man
- House painter
- Delivery man

- Cross-country auto delivery
- Truck dock worker
- Insurance salesman
- Salesman for educational course
- Sales & motivational trainer
- Owner/manager of two computer stores

Now, I realize this list might seem ridiculous and maybe unbelievable. Those who have remained faithful at their first jobs for 20 years might think me somewhat unstable. Once, when I was conducting a seminar for a national company, a participant asked me how I could teach a seminar about career goal setting when I had worked at so many different jobs. I replied, "I don't think it's wrong for a young man to work at many different jobs in his pursuit of becoming the person he desires to be. In fact, I encourage it!" I'm confident that I'm successful today largely because I've learned to work with people in many different occupations and environments. I can relate to people in almost any walk of life.

I did have one job that I thought would last a lifetime — being an insurance agent. I really threw myself into that job for four years and never even dreamed of doing anything else. I changed companies once, after two years, to become more professional. The most difficult decision I've ever made was to leave the insurance field. I was that committed.

Surprisingly, I left because I wanted to pour myself into something I was enjoying even more. You see, I'd sell an insurance policy to a business owner and then spend the next several hours helping "brainstorm" to find ways to improve his business. I realized I was having more fun and providing more benefit in that function than in the role for which I was being paid. Once I realized that, I knew I had to leave.

I had been a serious student of the insurance business those four years and my efforts were just beginning to pay off. I earned over $4,500 by selling one policy (a tidy sum for the 1970s), and knew I'd soon be earning as much as $20,000 for one policy. I knew if I were ever to quit, I should quit before my success became my prison. Don't laugh, but many people are imprisoned by their great incomes.

I've since realized that my primary career goal is to become the person I want to be. I do have income objectives and minimum accomplishment levels at which many of you would laugh; but, my primary objectives are to build character qualities into my life and to enjoy life while growing at what I'm doing. Within a few years, I'll be earning over a million dollars a year, but right now I can't tell you for sure what I will be doing. I do know, however, what principles I will be applying, and I do know I'll be working hard and enjoying it.

I've shared my story with you here to show that you don't need to have all the answers now to get to where you want to be. It's like taking off on a trip from Miami to Boston without knowing the condition of the roads or the weather. You can be confident that you can adjust when necessary. Zig Ziglar taught me that if I wait until all the lights are green before I leave on my trip, I'll never leave.

The biggest problem in visualizing your career at a young age is that you are too prone to sell yourself short. Your potential is virtually unlimited! You cannot know all the answers now — you don't even have half the questions. Don't be discouraged. This is what makes life exciting.

List as your career goals the skills you now know you'd like to develop and the knowledge you'd like to gain. List the things you know you want to achieve, and develop a plan to make it happen. If your desires change, then adjust your goals and plans accordingly. It's that simple! Remember, you'll always accomplish more over the long haul "on purpose" than by "accident." Purpose to be a "meaningful specific" instead of a "wandering generality." Here are questions to stimulate your thinking regarding your career goals.

1) Do I enjoy my present occupation? Am I pleased with the company for which I am now working?

2) Will what I am doing now assist me to achieve many of my career objectives?

3) What skills do I plan to develop over the next several years?

4) Is there another line of work in which I would prefer to be involved?

5) Are my present talents and experiences being put to good use?

6) Should I consider joining any professional organizations?

7) Can I list all the jobs I've had and then list the benefits I've obtained from each?

8) In what ways do I expect to improve myself to advance in fulfilling my career objectives?

9) What education do I plan to obtain in the future to improve myself (books, cassettes, seminars, college courses, etc.)?

10) What do those who are close to me say I ought to be doing? (Often they recognize my talents more than I do.)

In closing, let me strongly encourage you to further your reading on each of these subjects by obtaining additional books which have been written to deal more specifically with each topic. I've attempted to be brief, and certainly there is a lot more to be said about each of these categories.

· Six ·

Is Your Goal Properly Set?

Improperly set goals are, without a doubt, the primary reason that individuals who do set goals fail. An attainable goal must meet certain criteria. I call these, "The Ten Requirements For Getting The Gold Out of Goals."

You've heard Yosemite Sam say, "Thar's gold in them thar hills!" Well, I believe there is gold to be found in goals. The ten requirements your goal must meet to get to that gold are:

1) Your goal must be WRITTEN.

2) Your goal must be SPECIFIC.

3) Your goal must be PERSONAL.

4) Your goal must be MEASURABLE.

5) Your goal must be DESIRABLE.

6) Your goal must be BELIEVABLE.

7) Your goal must be WORTHWHILE.

8) Your goal must be REALISTIC.

9) Your goal must be CHALLENGING.

10) Your goal must be REVIEWED REGULARLY.

You will readily agree with some of these, and you might question, or argue, the value of others. Many are related to each other. Let's closely examine each requirement so we can more fully understand their value.

Your Goal Must Be Written

None of the other nine on the list will be challenged as much as this one, so I thought I'd begin here. The question many ask is, "Why on earth must a goal be written down when it is firmly implanted in my mind?" Many people hate the thought of having to write down their goals.

Before we begin to examine why a goal must be written, let's first consider why a person would not want to write it. I can think of a few reasons. First, writing it down makes a goal become something of a commitment. It may come back to haunt you, especially if you don't even come close to attaining it. Second, it takes time to write it down, precious time you just don't think you have. Of course, if you don't have the time to write it down, when are you going to find the time to do whatever is necessary to attain the goal? Third, you're not sure you really want to do anything about it at this time. It makes sense, however, that you will be more likely to work toward something with a plan in hand, than to expect simply to arrive one day. Finally, many just really don't believe it to be all that important.

I recently had a young man in one of my seminars who really fought me on this one. He was not prone to writing any of his goals, and just couldn't see any value in doing so. Later, during the seminar, we were discussing ideas that should be presented to the management of his company concerning positive changes. Someone came up with an idea that excited him. He interrupted and said, "Yeah, be sure and tell them that!" I replied that I would. Being afraid that I might forget, he said, "Write it down." I replied, "Why, I don't need to; it is an important enough issue that I'm certain I will remember it." He then said, "No, you've convinced me — write it down." It wasn't until I stopped speaking long enough to write it down that he felt comfortable.

I've heard Nido Qubein say, "The palest ink is more enduring than the strongest memory." Thus, we have the primary reason for writing our goals down: so we won't forget them! Today, maybe you can't imagine how you could forget a particular goal, especially if it is foremost in your mind. How do you know what you will be thinking about next week after you've been confronted with a new set of problems?

Mary Lou Retton won the gold medal for women's gymnastics during the 1984 Olympics. I don't know if she had written down the goal of winning the gold medal. I will concede that it's possible to accomplish such a feat without writing it. Still, think about the circumstances. She was working toward that goal, with great intensity, almost every waking moment of her life. She had even left home to train for it. She wasn't about to forget her goal. So, if your goal is something you're that committed to, you might not need to write it; but, why would you not want to?

The saying, "out of sight, out of mind" applies here. When I was 20 years old and was spending my third tour of duty in Vietnam, I made a mistake that has forever embedded in my mind the necessity of this requirement. To make the tour of duty in Vietnam more palatable, each soldier would receive a one-week R & R (Rest and Recuperation). We could visit any one of several countries for this vacation. My first two R & R's had been interesting and enjoyable. I had visited Japan and Taiwan and was looking forward to visiting Australia for my third one.

A soldier had to take his R & R within a particular period and could not have less than 30 days remaining on his tour of duty. Knowing that much of the enjoyment of a trip comes from anticipating it, I decided to wait until I was close to the end of my tour. Then, when I returned from R & R, I wouldn't have long to wait until I'd be returning to the United States.

That strategy seemed to make sense — until one day I realized that I had less than enough time to request and receive my R & R before I would arrive at that magic 30 day mark. I was devastated — how could I have allowed such a stupid thing to happen? By that time, Vietnam had become very unappealing to me. How could I not have remembered to take my week off and take advantage of a free plane ride to visit Australia? There was only one answer. I hadn't written it down on paper! I had intensely desired to go, but hadn't planned for it.

While in Vietnam, I kept track of the time until the end of my tour of duty, using my short-timers calendar (a chart comprised of 365 blocks stacked in a pyramid fashion). Each day I would color in another block and look at how little time I had left in the country. These calendars served as inspirations, especially to soldiers coming down to their last 60 days. At one glance, I could see how long I'd been there and how little time I had left. Thus, one thinks it impossible that I couldn't realize how little time I had left. I always knew to the day how many days I had left before I would take that freedom bird back to the United States, but I hadn't written down when I would need to request my trip in time to receive it, and return with no less than 30 days remaining. That failure to plan cost me a free trip to Australia.

I am convinced to this day that if I'd planned it and written it down, I'd now be sharing many experiences about Australia. Instead, I only have a goal to visit there. Because I am still somewhat upset at myself over this one, my goal is to visit Australia on an expense paid trip. I passed up a free trip—I still want it and, this time, will plan to get it. Needless to say, I've written it down this time.

Your Goal Must Be Specific

When I was first introduced to the necessity of goal setting, I'd written down on three sheets of paper all the things that I wanted to become, do, have, etc. One day I was sharing that information with the person who had encouraged me to make this list. He noticed "Be a good father" as one of my goals. He said, "That is not a goal." I replied with some concern to show that I indeed, thought it was. He challenged me by asking, "What do you mean by 'good father'?" I said, "You know — a good father." He assured me he didn't know and challenged me that I probably didn't either. That hurt — especially when I realized he was right.

The goal was too general even to be considered a goal. I established a set of criteria of what I needed to be doing to be a good father. You, of course, might have a different list, but I'll share mine with you.

Note: Before you read my specific list as to what makes a good father, you might make one yourself. (If you are a mother, make a list describing a good mother.) It might surprise you to find that it's not as easy to define as you might think.

A GOOD FATHER IS ONE WHO DOES THE FOLLOWING:

1) Takes time to get to know his children. (The average father in America spends less than 15 seconds daily with each of his children, getting to know them.)

2) Teaches his children scriptural principles of living. (Everyone has opinions how one ought to live, but only God, the Creator, has the best plan in His Word, the Bible.)

3) Lives, as an example, the kind of life he expects his children to follow. (We cannot say, "Don't do as I do — Do as I say!" and expect long-term results.)

4) Loves his children and tells them and demonstrates his love. (Love is something that is caught — not just taught!) Any father can give without loving, but he cannot love without giving. This giving must be a giving of himself. A child will not remember or value the gifts he receives, as much as he does the time his dad spends with him.

5) Prays with and for his children. (Our children will have more love and respect for us when they can see the love and respect that we have for our heavenly Father.)

6) Demonstrates his love for their mother. (It has been said that the greatest gift a man can give to his children is to love their mother.)

7) Expects immediate obedience from his children and follows through consistently to make sure he gets it. (Children need to know their boundaries; they feel insecure without standards.)

8) Protects his children from harmful influences. (Peer pressure can only become the predominant force in a child's life when the generation gap has been built. A father must know the people and things that are influencing his children — and provide direction as it relates to them.)

9) Assists his children to develop habits that will serve them all the days of their lives. (A good habit is as difficult to break as a bad one.)

10) Disciplines his children consistently when they deserve and need it. (This is not an easy task but certainly a necessary one.) God clearly teaches, in His Word, that the Father who loves his child disciplines that child.

11) Concentrates on the character development of his children. (What lies in a child's past and in his future are tiny matters compared to what lies within the child.)

12) Teaches his children in a way that causes them to become excited about learning. (It is a sad commentary when a child's desire for learning is only strong enough to make the grade to graduate.)

13) Practices humility before his children. (Sadly, many adults cannot recall ever having heard their father say, "I'm sorry.")

14) Provides for the necessities of his family. (Most of us have provided well in the area of material necessities and have neglected other equally important ones.)

15) Communicates well with his children. (If a child is afraid to talk with his father, that father hasn't shown compassion, empathy, and understanding to that child.)

16) Teaches his children to respect authority and the property of others.

Once I made that list, I could say that my goal of being a good father was now specific. It could still have been more specific, but at least I was moving in the right direction. Yet, until I developed an action plan to make it happen, it could not meet all the remaining requirements that a goal must meet.

Your Goal Must Be Personal

Let's face it — none of us really likes being told what to do. When it comes to goal setting, we especially don't like other people setting goals for us that we perceive to be unrealistic. Few things are more discouraging than to make an optimistic projection of next year's production, only to find that your employer has set an even higher goal for you! Working like a dog to reach someone else's minimum expectation is no fun. What gratitude can you expect if you should fall short of the goal?

Yes, working to achieve an impersonal goal is neither exciting nor wise. Thus, since you can't do your best to reach someone else's goal, why not make his goal yours? Any goal can become yours if you so choose.

The following principle has served me well in personalizing goals that are forced upon me.

I ask myself if it is important for me to work at making this goal a personal one. What's in it for me? What are the benefits of success? What are the consequences of failure? What are my alternatives if I choose not to make this goal personal? The answers to these questions help me to decide whether I will put forth the required effort.

I decided a long time ago that life is too short to live halfheartedly. A job worth doing is worth doing right — the first time. Therefore, if I don't want to do something, I probably won't. That may sound selfish at first, but I don't think it is. I will give of myself and will do my best to reach someone else's goal, but only after I make it my own. I can make any goal mine if I choose to make it mine.

Jesus taught this principle in His message commonly called "The Sermon on the Mount." In **Matthew 5:41** Jesus said,

And whoever compels you to go one mile, go with him two. (**NKJV**)

Judson J. Swilhart, in his book: *How to Treat Your Family As Well As You Treat Your Friends*, says the following about that passage:

> *[This passage] is an interesting one because it again deals with issues that have been faced primarily in childhood. So, it brings to the surface all those old feelings from childhood. How do you handle a situation where somebody forces you to do something you do not want to do? Verse 41 says that you should not only do what they want, but should do more! The people in those days understood the principle in context of the Roman soldiers who sometimes imposed upon the local folks. They would make them carry their heavy armor for them. So Jesus says, "Look, if some Roman soldier comes along and makes you carry his armor for a mile, you willingly carry it two miles." I'm certain the Roman soldier's attitude was one of disregard for the people and a lack of concern for their plans at the time of forceful imposition. What could be more difficult? They didn't want the Romans there in the first place. They didn't like being forced out of their routine. But Christ says to do even more.*

Here is how I apply this principle. If I am handed a goal that I think is unrealistic or even unfair, I determine that I will not only do it, but will do more. Sometimes, I can do twice as much. In other cases, I might just multiply the goal by 120%. At any rate, I decide that I will do more — even if I originally thought the goal to be unrealistic. I reason like this: if the person who gave me the goal has enough confidence to believe I can do it, then I ought to believe in myself to an even greater degree. Thus, I ought to be able to put a plan together to do 120% at least! I make that my minimum objective.

You might say, "That is crazy! How can I reach 120% if I think 100% is ridiculous?" That is a good question. The answer is simple: If you will determine to go the "extra mile," you will have more self-respect and enjoy the task. Anytime I find myself doing a job halfheartedly, I ask myself whether I ought to be doing it at all. If I decide that I should, I then buckle down and give it my all. The job goes much faster, and I enjoy myself more. I don't care how dirty or mundane the job is — this principle works. I've applied it when I was hauling garbage, when I was working on construction, and when I was cleaning up after other people. I have applied it in all types of situations, and I can tell you it works. Goals are accomplished much easier when they become personal.

Visualize this scene. You're a teenager playing a game of basketball, when a Roman soldier comes along and selects you to be the lucky one to tote his armor a mile. How would you feel? What would your attitude be while carrying that heavy load? Would the event make or ruin your day — especially if when you returned, your buddies had finished their game and gone home? I think you would agree that it might easily ruin your day. You'd probably go home and kick the cat — and anything else that got in your way.

Now let's change the scenario. You've just returned from hearing Jesus speak these words. You don't like His principle, and you don't even believe it makes sense, but you are willing to try. You're playing that same ball game, but this time when you're selected, you decide you'll go two miles. After the first mile the soldier tells you that you are free to return. You say: "Thank you, but if you don't mind, I'll just continue for another mile." Shocked, he emphasizes that you've completed your obligation and you may now put down the armor. But, after you've explained that you would really like to go the second mile, he agrees. (He thinks you're crazy, but he agrees.) Now, let me ask you, what kind of attitude would you have during this second mile? Would it be improved? If so, why? How about your attitude during the first mile? Would it have been better as well, knowing that you would be going on and doing even more than was expected, or required? You bet it would because you would now see yourself as completing this chore because you wanted to — not because you were being forced. You would not only be in charge of the situation, but more importantly, you also would be in charge of your will!

You see, in reality, we always have choices. We can refuse to do anything we wish not to do. Of course, we might suffer consequences. In this day, it probably wouldn't be the lashing of a whip; it might be the loss of a job. But so what? If we aren't going to give our best, then we ought to be working elsewhere anyway. Don't you agree? Would you want your employee giving less than his best? Giving less than 100% isn't fair to an employer.

Take advantage of your resources. The person who set the goal, undoubtedly, believes it to be realistic. If you work hard to make the goal realistic, but are unable to come up with a satisfactory plan yourself, go to that person and say:

"I wonder if we could schedule some time to get together and discuss the goal assigned to me. I'm excited about it and very anxious to see it happen. I appreciate the confidence you have shown in me by setting it as high as it is. Can we get together and discuss it in detail?"

If the person who set the goal asks what you wish to discuss about it specifically, say something like this:

"Well, I believe in the old saying that we should plan our work, and work our plan. A plan is like a blueprint. Once we can see how something goes together on paper, we can expect it to become reality. I've been working for a while on this, and I can't seem to make everything fit. I'm sure that you could share some insight with me that I'm not considering, or where I'm falling short with my projections. You must have had a pretty good basis for coming up with your projections, and I'm sure you could help me. Could we meet together sometime soon?"

Also, consider additional resources available to you. Surely, someone in your field has done more in a similar set of circumstances that you're now hoping to do. Then tap his reservoir of knowledge and experience. He may have written books on the subject or even may be available for you to contact personally. If no one is available, then look into other fields where a similar circumstance exists, and learn from that. There is always an answer — a way for you to realize any goal you truly want.

Your Goal Must Be Measurable

This requirement is related to being specific. One way to help make a goal specific is to make it measurable. We don't have trouble with this requirement if our goal is to lose ten pounds. We can measure that. However, some things are not quite as easy to measure.

What if your goal is to be happy, increase your love for someone else, or have a good attitude? How does one measure those things? Kenneth Blanchard discussed this matter in the film adaptation of the book he coauthored, *Putting the One Minute Manager to Work.* He was called into a bank and given the assignment to improve the friendliness level in the bank. He asked the bank president what was meant by "friendliness" and was given the answer "friendly." Upon being pressed further, the bank president gave Ken Blanchard the assignment to define it himself. They discussed this matter with the customers and found that customers felt "friendly" had to do with non-business related conversation and interaction. With this definition in mind, they observed the bank personnel and found the bank to be only 5% friendly. They then had the information necessary to help the bank in becoming more friendly.

When you're attempting to make a goal measurable, consider the following categories:

- Quantity
- Distance
- Time
- Cost
- Quality

If you consider it long enough, you can always measure your goal by one or more of these five categories.

First, figure out what it is you are going to measure. Are you going to focus on a positive or a negative? Be careful if you determine to focus on a negative, because it's difficult to refrain from moving toward that on which you focus. As Denis Waitley says so often, "It's impossible to move toward the reverse of an idea." Thus, if you focus on the measurement of mistakes, and not on the positive activity it takes to avoid them, you might find yourself with an increased level of mistakes.

Second, focus on and measure the important. I had a boss who wanted me to focus on being out of the office between 8:00 A.M. to 5:00 P.M., the time he considered the prime selling time. He had read that salespeople in their offices during the daytime are wasting time and losing sales. Because he had chosen to measure my value by the amount of time I spent in my office, he didn't notice that I was outselling his other 10 salespeople put together. Another item he was focusing on was the number of appointments I kept. The other salesmen averaged 10 to 15 appointments each per week; I averaged three. He was frustrated with my performance — because of what he was focusing on. That is, until I asked him what was really important to him. He said, "You know that, Gene. The most important point is the sales you make and the profit picture." I then asked him what his "bottom line" was concerning my production. When he told me, I could see his bottom line was less than mine. So I asked him if he would measure me on that factor alone, and forget the rest. He agreed, and that seemed to improve our relationship. (Now, I might mention that I was a commissioned salesperson responsible for producing more profit than his other salespeople combined. I got him to agree that we needed to arrive at a "win-win" solution, and that was the foundation for our conversation.)

Your Goal Must Be Desirable

You may have an excellent plan of action — one that specifies in minute detail everything necessary to guarantee success — but if you don't have the desire to carry it out, you won't accomplish our goal.

Many goals require changing certain habits: eliminating destructive habits, adding good ones, or simply modifying some. Changing habits can be a frustrating experience, requiring discipline that can come only from desire. The objects of the desire can be many. You might want the result of the goal, or you might want the character qualities attained by the accomplishment. You might simply want a smile of approval. At any rate, without desire you will not be willing to pay the price, endure the frustration, or make the necessary sacrifices.

Desire creates enthusiasm, and enthusiasm creates energy. This energy is necessary both to give you the desire and the means to tackle those difficult and mundane tasks. Sometimes this desire is the only thing you have going for you. Let me illustrate, with a painful personal experience.

In 1982, I was preparing to leave on my first of two summer Canadian fishing trips. I was to drive 1,700 miles to Northern Manitoba to a secluded spot for the trip of a lifetime. I was planning to drive my 1974 Dodge Charger, which had 120,000 miles on it. (I was a confirmed Dodge Charger lover — I drove one from 1969 until 1988.) I could tell the timing chain was loose on this engine and knew it might slip off any day. I wasn't about to let something like that happen in Northern Manitoba, where gas stations are sometimes 300 miles apart.

I priced what it would cost to have someone else fix my chain compared to what it would cost if I bought the parts and fixed it myself. (I had never changed one.) I figured I could save about $100, which would look better in my tackle box, once it had been converted to fishing lures. Thus, I purchased the parts and commenced to tearing my engine apart at 3:00 P.M. on a Sunday afternoon.

If you've changed timing chains, you know what was in store for me. I had to begin by taking my radiator out and the fan off. I disconnected the air-conditioner, removed the alternator, the power-steering unit, and several other parts to get to the water pump. My attitude was great. I was focusing on the $100 worth of lures I planned to purchase as my reward, and more importantly the fish I expected to catch with them.

I experienced many little difficulties, but by midnight I was ready to begin putting it all back together again. Around 2:00 A.M., I noticed I had an extra bolt. I looked for the hole it should go into for about 15 minutes, but I couldn't find it. Obviously, the bolt was meant to go through the water pump, but all holes seemed to be filled with a bolt already. Being an optimist, I figured that I should go ahead and put the engine back together. I knew that only three possibilities existed:

1) The bolt was really not very necessary. Sure maybe six were used initially, but five might hold just as well.

2) The bolt would prove necessary evidenced by water pouring out on the garage floor when the engine was started. In such event, I could simply spot the hole by following the stream of water, and then replace the bolt.

3) (This was the only bad option of the three.) This possibility was the same as the second option, except that I would not be able to find the hole or place the bolt in the hole once I found it. In this event, I would need to tear the engine down again.

Can you guess which possibility proved to be the correct one? That's right, number three. By 3:00 A.M. the car was all back together again (except for the one bolt), and I started it. I heard water hitting the pavement. That ruled out number one. When it took me another ten minutes to even find the hole (with water coming out of it), I suspected that I could be in trouble. Sure enough, I was.

By 6:00 A.M., I had the engine dismantled and was cleaning the parts again. I knew I'd have to purchase another gasket and finish it that night after work. By 8:00 A.M., I began to clean up so I could resume being a salesman that day. At 6 P.M., after a long day at work, I changed clothes again and went back to finish my car. By 9:30 P.M. I had the car on the road.

Does that sound like a long ordeal? Well, I guess it was — 21.5 hours. But I completed the task only because of the intense desire I maintained all along the way. I had many desires, but none stronger than the one I had to complete that job myself. I was discouraged at 3:00 A.M. when I first determined the extent of my mistake. But, I simply erased all the events up to that point, faced the present situation and tackled it as if nothing had happened. Although I had less energy, at that point, I still had enough to do what had to be done. I determined I would not sleep until that car was fixed. My desire to fulfill my commitment to myself kept me going.

Your Goal Must Be Believable

Each of these requirements is vitally important, but I cannot emphasize this one enough. Napoleon Hill, in his best selling book, *Think and Grow Rich*, said,

Whatever the mind of man can conceive and believe, it can achieve.

Your goal must be believable. Zig Ziglar says,

You must see the reaching.

There is something almost magical about this act we call believing. Read the book, *The Magic of Believing* by Claude M. Bristol. He'll convince you that the very act of believing can make things happen.

The act of believing is so powerful that it can seal your success by itself, if you act upon it. Medical wisdom has been confounded many times because a patient believed he would recover, though all the doctors gave him no hope at all. Monumental tasks have been tackled and conquered by those who believed it could be done when everyone else said it couldn't. Perhaps, you will be blessed by Edgar Guest's poem, as I have.

IT COULDN'T BE DONE

SOMEBODY SAID that it couldn't be done
But he with a chuckle replied
That "maybe it couldn't," but he would be one
Who wouldn't say so till he'd tried.

So he buckled right in with the trace of a grin on his face.
If he worried he hid it.
He started to sing as he tackled the thing
That couldn't be done, and he did it.

Somebody scoffed: "Oh, you'll never do that;
At least no one ever has done it;"
But he took off his coat and he took off his hat,
And the first thing we knew he'd begun it.

With a lift of his chin and bit of a grin,
Without any doubting or quiddit,
He started to sing as he tackled the thing
That couldn't be done, and he did it.

There are thousands to tell you it cannot be done,
There are thousands to prophesy failure;
There are thousands to point out to you, one by one,
The dangers that wait to assail you.

But just buckle in with a bit of a grin,
Just take off your coat and go to it;
Just start to sing as you tackle the thing
That "cannot be done," and you'll do it.

Edgar A. Guest

Yes, this world is full of those who say, "It can't be done." I used to feel sorry for them but I don't anymore. I've come to believe that this is what they want to believe. After all, if you think something can't be done, you're not going to be held responsible for having wasted your time in attempting to do it. And it is a waste of time if you really don't think it can be done. Why don't you think a thing can be done? Is it simply because you have not yet done it? Or is it because nobody has done it before? Has it been proven to be scientifically impossible? Or is it just because you haven't taken the time to figure out how it could be done? Is it something that requires luck or chance, as in a random drawing where you only have one chance out of several million? If so, that is not the type of goal I am suggesting you set. This book is to help you in achieving goals over which you **can** have control.

Let me relate another story. In 1979 on one of my fishing trips to Canada, we were ready to return to the camp to pack up and go home. I decided to make "one more cast." My buddy, Dave, asked me: "Gene, do you really expect to catch the big one on that cast?" I replied, "If I didn't believe that I wouldn't waste the effort." Well, I didn't catch the "big one" I was hoping for but it wouldn't have surprised me if I had. Often I've caught the big one on my last cast.

How can believing have anything to do with catching fish? Isn't that a game of chance, as well? I'll tell my story, but suggest again that you also read Claude Bristol's *The Magic of Believing* regarding this issue. At an early age I became a firm believer in the power of belief as it relates to success in catching fish. I used to go fishing with my stepfather. It would utterly amaze me how he could catch trophy fish one right after another. I would fish within a foot of him, using the same bait, fishing with the same tackle, casting in the same manner, and I wouldn't get even a bite! I was frustrated to say the least.

Though I enjoyed what few successes I had, I developed a dislike for fishing. My interest wasn't revived until I was 22 years old, when an Army buddy invited me to go fishing with him in the Florida swamps. On that first afternoon, I hooked nine largemouth bass, and landed only one. I was hooked that afternoon, too. It was my first experience using artificial lures. I improved my skill until some three years later when I hooked nine and landed them all. Obviously, my confidence had improved!

Two weeks before Dave questioned my insistence in casting one more time, I had caught *five* smallmouth bass, four three-pounders and one two-pounder, in only *four* casts — all at 3:00 P.M. (usually a bad time for catching fish). I was using a Rapala with two hooks. The guy in the canoe with me wasn't catching a thing. The day before Dave posed his question, my first cast netted a three-pound bass, followed by five more before noon. None of my five friends with me even got a hit, although fishing in the same area. These are some reasons for knowing that my belief can make a difference when I go fishing.

Belief won't help me to catch fish where none are present, and I never catch everything I really want to, but I do experience better than average results. I can't explain it any other way — can you?

What about the power of charms, good-luck pieces, four-leaf clovers, old horseshoes, a rabbit's foot, and the other trinkets in which thousands of people believe? Claude M. Bristol says in *The Magic of Believing:*

> *By themselves, they are inanimate harmless objects without power, but when people breathe life into them by their thinking they do have power, even though the power isn't in them per se. The power comes only with the believing —which alone makes them effective.*

In Alexander the Great's day, an oracle proclaimed that whoever loosened the Gordian knot would become ruler of all Asia. Alexander, as you may remember, cut the knot with one stroke of his sword and rose to tremendous height and power. Napoleon was given a star sapphire when he was yet a child, with the prophecy that it would bring him luck and one day make him Emperor of France. Could it have been anything but the supreme belief in the prophecy that carried these two great men to fame? They became supermen because they had exceptional beliefs.

A cracked or broken mirror isn't going to bring you bad luck unless you believe it, and if the belief is fertilized, nurtured, and internalized then the broken mirror will bring you bad luck. The subconscious mind often brings to reality what it believes.

I caution you, be careful what you make the object of your belief or faith. Belief, itself, is not to become a god. When I talk about making a goal believable, I am really referring to a plan so clearly laid out that you "can see it." Believing a thing is possible is different from believing it will definitely come to pass. I am referring to this latter belief.

How does one make a goal believable? One does it by the development of a plan and a dedication to carry out the plan. The plan must be based upon a solid foundation of sound information. Wanting a goal to happen and knowing it can happen is not enough for success. You should be doing everything within your power to make it happen.

When your plan is prepared and you are committed to carrying out your plan, then you've met this requirement. I actually take it a little further. I work like it all depends upon me, and then I trust God like it all depends on Him. I expect to be blessed only when I have truly given it my best while trusting God — even if my best would not ordinarily be good enough. Hebrews 11:6 teaches that it is impossible to please God without faith. It is God who sees our faith and our dedication and then rewards us accordingly.

Belief is the hand that lays hold of God's grace and power. One does not have to read far in the Bible before seeing the importance God places on our believing and trusting in Him.

Your Goal Must Be Worthwhile

You can devote your entire life to various goals and purposes, far more, in fact, than I can even list in a book twice this size. But only you can, and must, decide if a goal is worthwhile to you.

Would you be willing to count a billion dollars if someone would give it to you in one dollar bills on the condition that you personally counted each one? Do you have any idea how long that would take? Approximately, 60 years, counting at the rate of eight hours per day, 365 days per year. First, you must consider if you will live long enough to complete the task. Then you must decide if you give your life for this, will the cause still be valid 60 years from now? People give their lives for causes every day — you might decide to do so also. Would you take the project on hoping to spend the money yourself when you were done? That wouldn't be worthwhile at all.

How does one decide if a goal is worthwhile? First develop the action plan, and then, upon evaluating the necessary action, make your decision. You can't know if a goal is worthwhile until you know what price you must pay to obtain it. Even then, because some things are easier to talk about than to do, you might not really know the price until you begin performing the actual activity.

What is worthwhile to one person might not be worthwhile to another. I know men who have earned millions of dollars in activities that I wouldn't touch with a ten-foot pole. I, myself, have a goal to earn a million dollars a year before I am 46 years old. However, I wouldn't compromise the principles I believe in to achieve my goal. **Proverbs 16:8** teaches:

> *Better is a little with righteousness, than vast revenues without justice.* (**NKJV**)

Mark 8:36 also indicates the importance in determining priorities. Jesus said,

> *For what will it profit a man if he gains the whole world, and loses his own soul?* (**NKJV**)

Some goals just aren't worthwhile. When evaluating the value of a goal in contrast to the price, consider the time frame. If you have to sacrifice for two years, to flourish over the remaining 40, then it might be worthwhile. I cannot choose for you, only you can.

Also, evaluate how the goal coincides with your other goals. Will it supplement them or conflict with them? Will it prove to be a hindrance to accomplishing these other goals? Will it require resources already committed elsewhere? These factors must be considered.

How will your goal affect your relationships with other people? Maybe some relationships will die because of your pursuit of this goal, either because of an ideological conflict, or because you just no longer have time to spend developing them. Maybe others will be jealous and attempt to discourage you, and you'll find they're a hindrance to you. If pursuing this goal will hinder relationships, you need to consider if the goal is still worthwhile.

What might striving for this goal do to your devotion to God and your family? Will it draw you closer to them, or will it alienate you? The Bible clearly teaches in **Matthew 6:21,**

For where your treasure is, there your heart will be also. **(NKJV)**

You cannot invest time, money, or other resources into something without becoming devoted to it. Therefore, consider how such a devotion might conflict with other devotions.

Your Goal Must Be Realistic

Is your goal realistic? Is it practical to assume that it can be achieved based on the current facts? Too often we say, "Yes, it is realistic" long before it is. A goal only becomes realistic when a plan has been developed to bring it to pass. Otherwise, the goal is only wishful thinking.

Beware of the two extremes. Either we think a goal is realistic when it's not, or we give up on an idea instead of working to make it realistic. With the first extreme, we waste our time and resources while working on a project destined to fail. With the second, we waste our human potential. Avoid both extremes!

Don Hutson said,

There are no unrealistic goals — only unrealistic time frames.

While I don't agree wholeheartedly with his statement, I think it has much merit. Earning a million dollars this year may be unrealistic; but, earning a million dollars in my lifetime is not unrealistic. With the proper planning, eight years from now, earning a million dollars in one year may be realistic. It could be realistic for you too, if you have the desire and are willing to prepare and plan.

Remember Napoleon Hill's statement,

Whatever the mind of man can conceive and believe, it can achieve.

Is your goal based on an idea you really believe can be made to work? If so, prove it by planning it on paper! Sure, you may not have all the answers, but you can have a plan that you are confident will produce the answers. This plan will help make your goal realistic.

Several years ago, all runners faced the unrealistic goal of breaking the four-minute mile barrier. Many believed it to be totally impossible. After all, nobody had ever done it! Finally, Roger Banister broke the barrier. Runners everywhere began to realize that the four-minute mile was realistic. After all, if Roger could do it, then why couldn't they? Within six months the barrier had been broken by almost thirty additional runners.

When I took a speed-reading course, I became frustrated during the second lesson and complained that I wasn't getting anything out of the material I was supposed to be reading. I scolded myself, "Gene, quit complaining about what you're not getting and start looking for what you can get. Then you can build on that. If a million other people can do it, so can you!" Concentrating on the fact that a million other people had successfully built this skill into their lives helped me realize how realistic the goal actually was.

Your Goal Must Be Challenging

Elton Trueblood said,

> *Make no small plans; they have no power to move men's hearts.*
> *Unless our proposals are bold, they will be ineffective.*

Yes, goals must be big and challenging, or they will not give you the power and desire to accomplish them.

I've already discussed the danger of making a goal too big. You don't want to set goals that require miracles to accomplish. But if a goal is too small, you won't get excited enough about it to act. In short, the goal must be big enough to generate the enthusiasm needed to produce the energy to activate you. If your goals are not big enough to make others laugh, and some scoff, they are probably not big enough to make you act. Enthusiasm produces the energy necessary to act when you should.

How big is big enough, and how big is too big? That may seem like a difficult question, at first, but it really has a simple answer. Set as big a goal as your heart desires, making sure it demands a stretching on your part, and then work to develop the plan to make it happen. If your plan comes together, and you feel really good about it, then your goal is probably not too big. You can check with other people in your field to evaluate your plan. If you can't seem to put together a satisfactory plan, and you've spent the time and done your homework, then perhaps your goal is too big.

Your Goal Must Be Reviewed Regularly

Many a goal has been set, and an action plan developed, only to end up in a filing cabinet. There it remains until the file is pulled to set next year's goals. Or, it might be looked at quarterly to see how it compares to reality.

The point is simply that goals must be reviewed regularly if they are going to work for you. I've mentioned this before but it bears repeating here:

Only losers don't keep score!

Think about that for a minute. Losers, in the true sense of the word, don't like to keep score because it continually reminds them of their failures. On the other hand, winners want to know the score even when they are losing so they can make the necessary adjustments.

The score serves as a measuring stick to compare where you're with where you want to be. A regular review will help you to figure the score. Often, goal setters fail to review their goals until it is too late to make the proper adjustments to guarantee success.

I almost made that mistake in 1981. I had set a goal to earn $40,000 in commissions during the year. My commissions had been only $23,500 in 1980, my first year in that business. I believed it was realistic to expect growth and, therefore, the $40,000 should be attainable. I hadn't yet thought through the entire process of goal setting and didn't yet understand the importance of this requirement.

In fact, it wasn't until the last day of July (7 months into my goal) that I decided to review how I was doing. I was shocked to find that my year-to-date commissions were only $14,000! I was only on schedule to have a $24,000 year. In fact, even that might be optimistic since December was always a very slow month.

I was forced to face some hard facts. Either I would have to lower my goal, making it more realistic, or I would have to develop a better plan. I decided I still wanted to earn the $40,000 and would, therefore, work on a better plan. I needed to develop a plan that would allow me to increase my monthly income from $2,000 per month to a whopping $6,500 over the next four months! I stayed up all night and developed such a plan.

When I retired for bed the next morning, I said to myself, "Gene, it's a piece of cake; it's in the bag; no sweat; you've got it made!" I knew that all I had to do was walk through my plan and keep on track by meeting all of my sub-goals. I determined to review my goal at least weekly, keeping accurate score. I did just that and earned over $28,000 in commissions during the next four months. By year's end, my 1981 earnings were over $43,000!

What did I learn from that experience? I learned that regular review can do two things for us. First, it will help us to maintain focus. Remember the saying, "out of sight, out of mind"? That can easily apply to focus, especially when we get extremely busy. Second, regular review will serve as a motivating factor. Just as sporting teams often play their best when the game comes down to the wire, so can we when we've set deadlines along the way. Each large goal should be broken down into sub-goals, or manageable parts, with each one having a deadline. These deadlines should be placed on our calendars, and checked off as they are met.

Summary

I've discussed the ten requirements that every goal should meet. I'm sure you now realize the purpose for the action plan. It would be impossible to make most goals meet these ten requirements without such a plan. Having the goal properly set means you will have the vehicle in place that can be used to transport you to your desired destination.

In order to assist you in arriving at that destination, I've written the rest of the book. As you continue reading you'll learn about obstacles, solutions to those obstacles, proper perspectives and principles to have, how to maintain self-control, and make wise decisions, and how to manage yourself in relation to time.

· Seven ·
Nothin's Easy

This may seem like a strange title, especially for a chapter in a book on goal setting. It might even seem pessimistic to some of you. I hesitated to write this chapter, knowing that some of you need all the encouragement you can get. In the next chapter, I will discuss in some detail many of the obstacles we all are apt to encounter as we attempt to realize our dreams.

I often approach projects saying to myself, "No problem — it's a piece of cake!" Believing that to be true, especially with the aid of a carefully developed plan, I'll jump into a big project without fear and trepidation. I'm never in a project very long, however, before I'm talking to myself again, saying, "Nothin's easy!"

The only real problem I ever have is with my attitude. If I truly expect a task to be easy, I'll let my guard down and won't be mentally prepared to deal with the obstacles. I'll be easily disappointed and frustrated when I encounter them. My attitude will suffer and I may even decide to give up.

Twenty years ago, before I realized this principle, I'd find myself continually feeling persecuted, asking God, "Why me?" It seemed as though everything would go wrong whenever I attempted to do anything.

Here's an example. Once, when the brakes needed replacing on my car, I decided to do the job myself. I went to the auto parts store to purchase the new brake shoes, only to find that my model was sold with at least two optional sizes. I guessed at the size and guessed wrong. After returning the wrong size shoes, I experienced the dilemma of finding the proper tools — which wasn't easy. Once I had the proper tools, I began work. Soon I experienced a rusted bolt and a rounded head on the bolt. Then I had to purchase more tools to remove the bolt through other means. You get my point? All in all, the bottom line is that I often have to spend six hours to do a two-hour job!

I recall once in 1971, I decided to replace my own rear shocks instead of paying Sears their five dollar labor charge. That simple little job took me over five disgusting hours lying under the car on a very hot day. The bugs were terrible, my arms were worn out, and my knuckles were more red than white when I finished. I'll never do that again!

I could think of a hundred other examples like this, and I suspect you can too. We've all found that nothin's easy, haven't we? Life seems to be even more difficult when we expect it to be easy. Interestingly enough, this seems to contradict another principle I teach which says that we tend to get out of life what we expect to get.

Let me attempt to reconcile these two principles. You do tend to get what you expect to get. If you expect to be successful — to complete your task, to make friends easily, to land a job you really want, or to have a good day — you probably will. Remember, you cannot move towards the reverse of an idea. You cannot consistently act in a manner which is inconsistent with the way you see ourselves.

If, on the other hand, you expect every operation to be without its share of problems — for everything to go smoothly — you are headed for frustration and disappointment. Life just doesn't happen that way. If everything were easy, everyone would be successful. While it's true that some obstacles are only imagined and, therefore, a result of negative expectations, there are still many real obstacles. You'll read about those in the next chapter.

When we understand that these obstacles exist, and are even to be expected, we aren't as likely to be floored when they are manifested. Instead, we can have the wherewithal to buckle down and plow through. I simply say to myself, "Nothin's easy!" I don't waste much time wishing it were, or complaining because it isn't, but I make a fresh evaluation of where I am, and go from there. It never does any good to cry over spilt milk!

I have an engineer friend who told me once that he always considers a "probability factor" in his equations when putting together a major plan. He recognizes that there will be problems. He doesn't always know what they will be, but they will show their ugly heads sooner or later. We might be wise to approach our goals in the same manner.

These problems, obstacles, or setbacks provide us with a tremendous opportunity for growth. Remember it is during the tough times that we grow most. If we will but persevere, we'll not only increase in strength of character, but we'll add extensively to our own sense of self-worth. Ultimately, our successes will provide great encouragement to assist us through the tough times.

I'll never forget one night soon after I began writing this book. I began typing on my IBM Personal Computer about 6:00 P.M. on Friday evening and finally finished the chapter at 2:00 A.M. Saturday morning. I was totally exhausted and with great excitement I attempted to save my file. To my astonishment, the computer beeped at me and flashed the following message:

UNABLE TO SAVE BECAUSE OF INSUFFICIENT DISK SPACE

My computer did not have a hard disk drive, only two floppy drives. I had never encountered this problem before. I exchanged the floppy diskettes, inserting one with ample space to save the file. I couldn't believe my tired eyes when the computer failed to respond to my commands. It was "locked up," as they say in computer talk. I was devastated! I hadn't saved the file since 10:00 P.M., and my last four hours of precious creativity was annihilated. I called my friend who had sold me the computer, and the software, to see if there was a solution. He sleepily informed me that there was none.

I don't know how you'd feel, or what you'd do, but I know I couldn't have felt much worse at the time. I had no notes, and I was quite proud of the work I'd just lost. I didn't have a lot of confidence that I'd remember the next day what I'd just written if I yielded to exhaustion, and went to bed as my body was demanding. Thus, I made the decision to begin again and redo the four hours of writing I'd just lost.

I made sure that I would not lose it all again. I stopped writing every time the screen was full and saved the file to disk. I was amazed at how well I was able to recall the material almost word for word. Soon it was 6:00 A.M. and I saved my last screen to the disk. I even laughed when the computer once again gave me the message:

UNABLE TO SAVE BECAUSE OF INSUFFICIENT DISK SPACE

I realized that I had forgotten to replace the almost full diskette when the problem had occurred at 2:00 A.M. I should have copied that file to a diskette with more available space. I could laugh though because now all I stood to lose were those words that appeared before my eyes on the screen. I simply got a piece of paper and a pen and wrote the words down. Once I restarted the computer, I copied the file to the new diskette and retyped the final words.

It seems as though I've had far too many experiences like the one I've just described. Perhaps you have also. Fortunately, I seldom make the same mistake twice. I've learned a great deal from my mistakes and that education is very valuable. The value of the education, however, still pales in significance to the value of understanding this principle — "Nothin's easy!"

I recall hearing Charlie Tremendous Jones speak several years ago in St. Louis. His speech lasted for three hours and he kept us in stitches most of the time. At one point during his speech, he informed us that what he was about to say was the most important thing he would say all night. He strongly encouraged us to lean forward in our seats so we wouldn't miss it. He continued for several minutes, building our desire to learn this tremendous truth he was about to share. When he had us anxious as we could be, he said,

NOTHING WORKS!!!

He then repeated "Nothing works" several times until we had it firmly implanted in our minds. As he gave his examples, we laughed ourselves silly. He then helped us to understand that if everything worked, there would be no need for us. It is because nothing works that we have purpose.

His book, *Life Is Tremendous,* is a masterpiece. It's easy reading, and it's fun reading. The average reader can easily complete the book in two hours, and the investment is well worth it. I first read the book in 1971, and some of the things I learned from the author still impact my life.

I've heard people in churches I've attended say, "Living the Christian life is not easy." Perhaps you've heard someone say that too. Or, perhaps you've even said it yourself? I always respond by challenging the speaker with the message that the non-Christian life isn't easy either. In fact, when the two life-styles are compared, there is no comparison. I'd far rather face the trials of the Christian life with a God and Saviour who loves me, and promises me power and wisdom, than to live the non-Christian life without Him.

Think about some of the issues of life in general.

- *Being a child is not easy! Being an adult is not easy!*
- *Being a single adult is not easy! Being a married adult is not easy!*
- *Raising children is not easy! Being childless is not easy!*
- *Being unable to buy a house is not easy! Buying and maintaining a house is not easy!*
- *Earning a good living is not easy! Unemployment is not easy!*
- *Maintaining good health is not easy! Attempting to get well is not easy!*
- *Obtaining an education is not easy! Being ignorant is not easy!*
- *Living life is not easy! Dying is not easy!*

Although nothing in life is easy, let me say that some things do get easier with education and experience. The education may have to come as a result of your own mistakes and the experience may be miserable, but things can get easier. Most jobs and projects are easier the second time through, and get even easier each time thereafter. That's the good news!

Don't let the fact that nothin's easy keep you from attempting great things, but instead determine to do that which is necessary to overcome the tough times. They will come. Obstacles are a part of reality. They won't keep us from successfully arriving at our goals **unless we let them!** Determine now never again to let them make you turn back. Success can be yours!

The next chapter is the longest chapter in the book. While reading it won't be easy, it will be necessary. You need to be aware of what you're up against. I learned years ago the 4 P's of success. They are:

PREPARATION PREVENTS POOR PERFORMANCE

The purpose of the next chapter is to assist you in developing your action plan. It is difficult to develop a plan to handle an obstacle you're not aware even exists.

·*Eight*·
Obstacles & Roadblocks

Obstacles and roadblocks are only problems to those attempting to accomplish something in life. If all you ever hope to do in life is meander around as a wandering generality, then obstacles will be meaningless. Picture two people entering a forest. One has an objective to make it through the woods to the other side in the quickest time; the other doesn't care if he ever makes it. They encounter a fallen tree across the path. The person with the objective has to either crawl under it, climb over it, or quickly go around it. The other person, on the other hand, will probably react differently. He might turn around, walk in a different direction, or stop and rest. The fallen tree presents "no big problem" because he didn't need to go that way anyway.

As you work on your action plan, you should consider possible obstacles, roadblocks, and other deterrents. Some would say this is the negative chapter of the book, the "doom and gloom" of it all. Still, I'm convinced that your chances of accomplishing your goal will be infinitely better if you first consider the potential obstacles and roadblocks, and then develop ways to remove or to go around them. I will list many obstacles you are likely to encounter along the road to successfully accomplishing your goals and will deal with these in some detail. Many books could be (and have been) written on each of these subjects. In some cases I will simply refer to other chapters of the book, and in others I will recommend that you read other books for greater detail. I have divided the obstacles and roadblocks into seven categories.

1) Poor Attitudes and Poor Thinking
2) Poor Habits
3) Poor Influences
4) Poor Information
5) Poor Resources
6) Poor Plans
7) Poor Situations

Now, let's look at each of these categories in some detail. As you think about each potential obstacle, realize you may be affected either directly or indirectly by the obstacle. A poor attitude, for example, may be your poor attitude, or it may be the poor attitude of someone with whom you work which is the obstacle in fulfilling your goal.

Poor Attitudes & Poor Thinking

Obstacles and roadblocks within the human mind are the most difficult, and yet they are also the obstacles over which you have the most control. Realize that you not only have to be concerned about your attitude, but also about the attitudes of other individuals who help you reach your goals.

Fear

Fear is the greatest obstacle we will ever encounter. Fear has the power to paralyze, or to enrage a person so frightfully that he drives off a cliff. Many people are so filled with fear that they go through life running from things that aren't even after them.

Let's analyze fear. The function of fear is to warn us of danger, not to make us afraid to face it. Many never face their fears but, instead, allow them to dictate the direction of their lives. These people live sad lives indeed! Recognizing a fear produces caution. Perhaps the fear is warranted, and turning away or carrying out a protective measure is wise. Or perhaps the fear is totally unwarranted and founded on misconceptions formed many years ago. Thus, we should be thankful for fear, recognize it for what it is, deal with it, and then act accordingly. Fear makes fools of two kinds of men: the one who is afraid of nothing, and the other who is afraid of everything.

Fear, like fire, can be either a friend or an enemy. Both can serve to protect or to destroy. A key word here is balance. Fear must give us a healthy respect for things or situations that can cause us great damage, and yet, not be so great that it keeps us from facing fears and dealing appropriately with them.

I'm thankful that I learned many years ago to examine and fight the fears that were limiting me. I grew up afraid of many things, and I paid dearly for those fears. When I began to challenge those fears (one at a time), I discovered what an opportunity for joy and exhilaration they provided. I've climbed a high voltage tower to overcome my fear of heights. I did not have sense enough to fear the electricity. I've walked miles in swamp water to overcome my fear of water snakes, and canoed in violent waters to overcome my fear of drowning. I've parachuted from an airplane and bungy jumped to challenge my fear of the feeling of falling. I tackled my fear of standing before a crowd by taking a public speaking course. You might not evaluate all my reactions to those fears to be balanced, but then again, they were my fears and my decisions. I needed to swing the pendulum an equal distance to get balance.

Fear usually produces the thing of which it's afraid. If you fear being rejected by someone, you will probably act in such a way to produce the rejection you fear. If you fear being dog-bitten, the dog may sense it and bite you. If you fear being taken advantage of in a business deal, then you're certain to be. Fear selling a prospect, and you probably will not even call on him. Fear stumbling in a sporting event, and you very well may stumble. Your mind often fulfills that which you visualize.

If you're not afraid to face the music, you may someday lead the band. People who do great things in life have the courage to attack their fears with action. They're courageous. Courage is not the absence of fear, but the conquest of it. There is no shame in being afraid. There is shame in allowing fear to keep you from growing or doing what you should. Someone once encouraged me not to be afraid to go out on a limb, for that is where the fruit is. I will grow and reap benefits if I stretch by challenging my fears. I have followed that advice often and can't think of one time I regret having done so.

Fear falls before the fortress of faith. In fact, the greatness of our fears show the smallness of our faith. A preacher once said, "Fear not tomorrow; God is already there." The more I thought about it, the more I realized how silly I am to be afraid today of something over which I have absolutely no control. God doesn't give me the grace today for tomorrow's problems. He will do that tomorrow. I'm responsible to deal with the problems to the best of my ability and I trust God to do what I cannot. He is a God that can control circumstances I cannot control; therefore, I can trust Him to withhold or allow them to occur as He sees fit. If disaster strikes, He can use even that to "work together for good," according to His Word (See Romans 8:28). In 2 Timothy 1:7, the Apostle Paul said,

> *For God has not given us a spirit of fear, but of power and of love and of a sound mind.*

This verse has been extremely helpful to me.

I recall the first time that verse bailed me out, so to speak. I was changing the universal joints on the driveshaft of a friend's car. As I was lying under his car, which was not jacked up, it began to rain. It was an extremely tight fit for me, but something was about to happen to make it even tighter. The hard downpour appeared to form a wall around the car, and I began to suffer from a spell of claustrophobia (fear of tight or enclosed places). I began to think, "What will happen if the tires lose their air?" Of course I knew what would happen; I'd be crushed. My chest was already enlarging as the fear entered my body, and I felt trapped beneath this car! Despite this stressful moment, I was ashamed to admit my fear to my friend standing in his nearby garage. So I didn't admit it; I decided to deal with it. God reminded me that He's given me a spirit of power and sound mind, not of fear. I quoted the verse to myself and talked to myself about it. I literally talked myself out of the fear by focusing on the fact that God had given me a sound mind, and my fear had come as a direct result of not using it properly.

Most fears fall into one of three categories. They are:

- Fear of pain

- Fear of failure

- Fear of rejection

I'll discuss each of these in detail.

Fear of Pain

Have you ever been afraid of pain? Of course! Hasn't everyone? Even if it was only being afraid as a child of the pain of a spanking, we have all experienced the fear of pain. Did you ever notice that the pain, when it did occur, was seldom as bad as the fear had been? I learned this lesson in high school. We boys had a contest to see who could get the most "whacks" from teachers during one semester. I might not have been the brightest kid in school, nor the most talented in sports or music, but this was one contest I could win! And, win I did. I received whacks from every male teacher I had, including the one most feared by all. I learned that the pain was always short-lived, and the respect I perceived I gained from my peers by being able to grin and bear it was worth the pain.

My mother, bless her heart, had always been somewhat afraid to allow my brother and me to play football. She was afraid we might get broken bones or something worse. Her fear transferred to me and, thus, I was also afraid to play. Then, one day I played a game of barnyard football. In barnyard football, nobody wears protective gear, and no holds are barred. I was tackled hard and got up smiling, "That ain't so bad!" In fact, the more I played, the more I enjoyed it. I began to play as often as I could. The day after I broke my nose, I was still anxious to carry the ball into a crowd of bigger guys. It was "mind over matter." Experiences like these now help me to identify with a scene in Rocky III. Rocky, while being hit really hard by Clubber Lang, responds, "Go ahead, hit me. My mother hits harder than that. You ain't so bad! Go ahead, hit me! Hit me again! Again!" After having been beaten to a pulp in their first fight, this was the event he had feared so much. He could now relate the pain directly to the fear that had been plaguing him.

Fear of Failure

Remember, failure can reap so many benefits that, even if it does occur, it is not so bad. The easiest way to deal with this fear is to develop such a great action plan that the fear will die. Again, fear falls before the fortress of faith. When you can see the accomplishment of your goal as simply a matter of walking through your plan, the fear of failure will become insignificant.

You should try to find what your fear is based on, whenever you sense it. It may be that you have an inadequate plan. Maybe the risk seems too great or the consequence of failure too severe. Perhaps you are too proud to face failure. Maybe you fear failing because you sense you will only get one opportunity, and you do not want to "blow it."

Once, in my sales career I was about to drown financially even as several great prospects lay in my path. I was very inexperienced in selling this service and that fact, combined with my lack of self-confidence, seemed to spell certain doom. I felt I would someday be prepared, but I was not yet. Finally, realizing that my fear of failure was contributing to my failure, I became desperate and began calling on these prospects anyway. I at least wanted to go down swinging! I picked up the phone and called the prospect I perceived to be the largest of them all. I set the appointment, met with the prospect, and within 20 days closed a sale netting me over three thousand dollars in commission! Over the next two years I was to earn over forty thousand dollars in commission from sales made to that one company. Can you believe it? If I had allowed my fear of failure to continue prohibiting me from approaching that company, I would have continued to have the failure I feared.

Fear of Rejection

We have probably all been afraid of rejection at sometime in our lives. We may even have experienced some rejection, and not having especially fond memories, have no desire to repeat the experience. Anyone who has ever been turned down for a date, a job, a position on a team, a part in a play, or even a marriage proposal knows the pain rejection brings.

Thus, the fear of rejection may be, in part, a fear of pain or a fear of failure — or both! Many people feel they could never be salespeople because of their fear of the rejection they perceive they would have to endure. I find it interesting that I, as a salesman, seldom feel rejected. I dislike rejection as much as the next person, and feel I had more than my share during the first 20 years of my life. As I look back on it now, I believe that most of the rejection I felt was due to my lack of self-confidence and poor self-image. I have not really felt rejected very often for the past 20 years.

Salesmen are taught not to take rejection personally. They are told that their offers or products are being rejected, not them. Since my product, as a public speaker, happens to be me, how can I not take it personally? It's simple! I can take it casually because I realize each person, no matter how good, experiences rejection. Even, Jesus Christ, God in the flesh, was rejected. St. John 1:11 tells us,

He came unto his own, and his own received him not.

Even a president, elected by a landslide, is also rejected by millions of people. Everyone will be rejected at various times in his life. The key is to seek to understand rejection and deal with it.

Had I not learned this lesson, I probably would not have married my wife. After allowing someone for whom I cared deeply to marry another without attempting to sell myself, I determined not to allow that to happen again! I had to fight for Saundra, and only through dogged determination did I find the endurance to remain in the battle. The story I am about to tell may sound humorous now, but I assure you it was not funny at the time.

At one point during our courtship, Saundra rejected me and told me, over the phone, that she thought it best that we not see each other again. I was living a thousand miles from home and had to decide whether to pursue the relationship. I would either stay and attempt to win her, or move back to my home state. This was back in 1970, and I was only 22 years old.

This is how I decided: On a very hot July 4th in Orlando, Florida, I decided to visit a friend in Christmas, Florida — 17 miles away. I was lovesick, and to get my mind off Saundra, I decided to do something physical — run all 17 miles. I was not in shape and had never run more than three miles at once in my life (years before). I took off running and, to my amazement, I ran five miles before I had to stop to walk. I was wearing a pair of cutoffs and a $2 pair of loafers. When I had gone ten miles, I was exhausted, extremely thirsty, and the buzzards were flying overhead. I could visualize myself crawling in the desert moaning, "Water...water." Then I got a great idea. I decided to make this journey a test, to see how much I wanted to continue my relationship with Saundra. If she was worth fighting for, I would stay with it — do or die. The buzzards would have to pick my body out of the ditch. If she was not worth it, I would give up and hitch a ride.

Let me tell you, it was a long 17 miles! When I got there, I didn't even attempt to visit my friend. I crossed the road and stuck my thumb out to hitch a ride home. I knew that I wanted her to be my wife enough to risk more rejection. Interestingly, the first car stopped and gave me a ride. The older man said, "I don't usually pick up hitchhikers, but you don't look like you could hurt anyone." He was right.

I returned home that day determined, more than ever, to win her. I had already convinced myself — now, I simply had to convince her. I have discovered since that the person from whom I most have to fear rejection is me. If I can accept myself while realizing that others may not (for whatever reason), the fear of rejection will have very little control over me.

To learn more about how to deal with the fear of rejection, do the following:

- List the fears that you have.
- Select the one fear you would most like to conquer.
- Determine how you developed this fear.
- Decide how this fear has hurt you, or hindered your progress.
- Decide which opportunities this fear might cause you to miss.
- List the benefits you will receive by overcoming this fear.
- Consider how others have successfully dealt with this fear.
- Decide how important it is that you gain victory over this fear.

Pride

Pride has one positive side and several negative sides. Here, I will discuss only the negative that keeps us from doing things that might otherwise help us to attain our goals.

As a teenager, I didn't know that pride had a negative side. I was "poor, but proud," as the saying goes. I had not yet recognized, nor experienced, the damage that pride can cause. It can keep us from doing that which we ought and, by that, keep us from accomplishing that which we might. The Bible contains very clear instruction regarding pride:

> *Pride goes before destruction, And a haughty spirit before a fall.*
> **Proverbs 16:18 (NKJV)**

> *Likewise you younger people, submit yourselves to your elders. Yes, all of you be submissive to one another, and be clothed with humility, for God resists the proud, but gives grace to the humble. Therefore humble yourselves under the mighty hand of God, that He may exalt you in due time.* **I Peter 5:5,6 (NKJV)**

Pride is manifested in many ways. We may begin to think we are "too good" to do a particular thing. I, of course, do not mean "good" as in moral excellence, but as in elite. Know the value of your time and treat it as valuable, but don't refuse to do a thing because of pride. I once took a job as a sanitation worker (garbage man) largely because someone attempting to influence me thought I was "too good" to do it. He thought that kind of work was only for what he called a "lower class" of people. I resented his teaching, and took the job to display my resentment. I don't ever want to allow pride to keep me from doing anything that is honest.

Another manifestation of pride is refusing help from another. We respond with, "I don't want charity!" Or we think we already know it all and, therefore, refuse to accept advice from another. These manifestations, also, must be seen as obstacles or roadblocks. A foolish man does not accept wise counsel or help from another in time of need. I used to be guilty of this form of pride. When I learned what the Bible teaches concerning giving and receiving, I changed my mind. I found that there are blessings from both giving and receiving. The blessing for giving is greater. If I want others to receive when I give, then I should receive when they give. Don't rob others of a blessing by refusing to allow them to give to you.

Prejudice

Another mental obstacle or roadblock is prejudice. I despise this obstacle, possibly more than any other. Maybe because I felt "looked down on" for much of my childhood, or maybe because I recognize some prejudices reside in me, as well. Note the following account:

Once a survey was conducted of people's attitudes toward other groups. Participants were given a list of various races, religions and cultures, and were asked to check each item with a plus (if the attitude was favorable), a minus (if unfavorable), or zero (for neutral or unknown). Among the many groups listed were some fictitious names: Melonians and Waluvians. It was amazing how many reacted negatively to these. They could have put "zero" but they did not. Apparently they thought: "Here are some strange names — thumbs down on them, whoever they are!"

Now, that is prejudice, pure and simple, and we are all guilty to some extent. You must recognize it and deal with it accordingly. You might begin by trying to determine why you have the prejudice. At any rate, don't allow it to be an obstacle or roadblock to the successful completion of your goal.

I like the story about a black man who wanted to join a fashionable church and was told by the minister to go home and think about it. The minister suggested that he might be happier among his "own people." The black man returned sometime later and said, "You were right, I've decided not to join. I talked it over with God and He told me to give up trying to get into your church. He said that He, too, has been trying for several years without success."

Selfishness

Let's face it, by nature we are selfish. Even our goals may reflect more of what we want to "get" instead of what we want to "give." Most have not accepted that we get more from life by focusing on giving than by focusing on getting. If selfishness is the reason for our refusal to do something, then we ought to change "I won't" to "I will."

A wealthy woman was once asked to help the people in the slums of her city. She refused, saying that she did not want to set foot in such filthy places. One day, she dropped her diamond wedding band in the mud. Without a moment's hesitation, she put her hand into the mud and picked up the ring. "It is not fear of filth," said her friend, "that prevented you from helping the unfortunate in our city, but an unwillingness to put yourself out for anyone but yourself."

That story illustrates one way in which selfishness can be an obstacle. This next parable shows a different perspective on how destructive selfishness can be.

A selfish man was bequeathed a rice field. The first season the irrigation water ran through his field and made it productive and fruitful, then overflowed into the neighbor's field and gave him blessings as well.

When the next season arrived, the selfish fool said to himself, "Why should I permit all the waters to flow through my field into his? Water is wealth, and I must keep it all for myself." He then built a dam that prevented the water from flowing into his neighbor's fields. The result was that he had no crop that year. The irrigation water brought blessings only as it flowed. When it became stagnant it bred a marsh and swamp.

Thus, we see, selfishness can become an obstacle in two ways: It can make you unwilling to help another at some expense to you, and it can make you unwilling to help another at no expense to you. In the first case, you lose a blessing by not giving. In the second case, you lose in two ways. You do not receive the blessing, and you may inherit a tragedy. It's like the saying, "You cut your nose off to spite your face."

Discouragement

Any section on negative attitudes would be lacking if it didn't include a discussion on discouragement. Discouragement is not something we look forward to, but we all encounter it occasionally.

Discouragement is an attitude disease that takes away our "want to" by causing us to lose our visions of purpose or faith that a task can be accomplished. Often, long-range plans are laid to rest in an early grave because of improper reactions to short-range frustration. Since we know that these short-range frustrations will occur, we must prepare beforehand to deal with them. We cannot be "on top of the world" when we are "under the circumstances."

The obstacle of discouragement can be a tough one to hurdle. Often, it is difficult or even impossible to do it alone. Discouragement can often be seen ahead of time, and dealt with before becoming a serious problem. Any action plan not including a way to deal with discouragement will prove to be of little value.

Inflexibility

I have already discussed our natural resistance to change in the third chapter of this book. You might find it advantageous to review that material again to decide if, and why, you remain inflexible.

Self-Pity

You've heard of pity parties. This obstacle, related to both pride and discouragement, can immobilize you. We get engrossed in self-pity by feeling so sorry for ourselves that we don't change our situations. Self-pity usually rears its ugly head immediately after a tremendous disappointment.

In my Army days, I spent 27 months in Vietnam, 14 of them as a Specialist E-4. That might not sound so bad, except I expected I would be promoted to E-5 at least eight months before I was. I truly worked hard every day, while other guys, who seldom worked, but patronized the sergeant by supplying his beer, were promoted in an average of five months. Each month, when the promotion list came down without my name, I would have a pity party. Then, I'd overcome this discouraging attitude by convincing myself to work just one more month before sinking into a level of mediocrity. This "one more month" mentality kept me going. In the end, I finally reaffirmed in my mind that persistence does pay. I knew the tide would eventually turn, that I could not be turned down forever. Although it was never easy, I had to fight self-pity if I was going to accomplish anything. After all, what future is there in quitting?

Hatred

Hatred causes far more harm to the person harboring it than to the one at whom it is directed. If allowed to remain, hatred becomes an attitude that affects almost everything we attempt to do. Hatred affects our health.

If you despise someone so much that it affects your ability to function normally, then you must forgive him. The Lord Jesus said of those crucifying Him, "Father, forgive them; for they know not what they do" (Luke 23:34). We must realize that the people who have offended us are no smarter than those who crucified Jesus. Jesus forgave them because He loved them. I admit that sometimes I forgive simply because forgiveness is the best thing to do.

Don't allow your hatred toward someone else to hinder you from accomplishing your goal. It doesn't matter who he is or what he has done — you cannot allow him to hurt you anymore. Forgive him.

Pessimism

Few attitudes are as damaging to goal accomplishment as pessimism. A pessimist is one who burns his bridges before he gets to them. You've heard it said, "Whether you think you can, or you think you can't, you're right!" Because this is true, the pessimist does what he expects — he fails! So, eliminate pessimism.

There are three kinds of people in the world: the wills, the won'ts, and the can'ts. The wills accomplish everything; the won'ts oppose everything; the can'ts fail in everything. Many attitudes discussed to this point fall into the "won't" category. This one, pessimism, is in the "can't" category.

I will deal with the "won't" category first. When you decide, for whatever reason, that you will not do something, you limit your options in finding a solution. Now, I will be the first to say that there are many things we should not do, under any circumstances. We should decide just what we will not do, and carefully evaluate why.

Therefore, there is certainly a place for saying, "I will not!" You should decide that you will not be immoral to accomplish one of your goals. Yet, on the other side of the coin, many of us are too quick to say, "I won't," without a reason for such a decision. Your refusal may be simply a matter of pride, prejudice, selfishness, a preconceived misconception, or inflexibility on your part.

The "can'ts," love to say, "I can't," for whatever reason. We've all had to deal with those guilty of this. We might not like to admit it, but sometimes we too are guilty. "Whether you think you can, or you think you can't, you are right!" Since this is so true in the negative sense, we must reckon with this obstacle or roadblock.

Henry Ford knew how to overcome the "I can't" obstacle. He decided that he wanted his engineers to build an eight-cylinder engine. They said that it could not be done. He told them to build one anyway. After weeks of trying, they reported that it still could not be done. He sent them back to work toward the same objective — to build a working eight-cylinder engine. Well, you know the rest of the story.

The greatest achievements of mankind have been accomplished by two types of men: Those who were smart enough to know it could be done, and those too dumb to know it couldn't. I can't count the times I've seen someone do something he wasn't supposed to be able to do, primarily because he had not yet been told it couldn't be done.

Have you ever had (or almost had) an accident while driving because you switched lanes with a car beside you that you couldn't see? Though you looked in all your mirrors, you still had a blind spot. Blind spots don't just appear when we're driving cars. They appear in many areas of our life. Just as blind spots can destroy our cars, they also can destroy our goals. Businesses fail, relationships wreck, and roadblocks occur because we don't consider these blind spots. By definition, we cannot see these blind spots. Otherwise, they wouldn't be called "blind," would they? Thus, we must enlist the help of others to point them out for us.

Attitude Regarding Past Failures And Negative Experiences

Another obstacle or roadblock will be your remembrance of past failures or negative experiences. This will be especially true if you've already failed at what you're now hoping to achieve. Just as success breeds success, failure breeds failure — if you allow it!

The key is to ask yourself questions. What valuable experience have you gained from the failure or negative experience? What didn't work? What were some of the benefits? Seldom is any experience totally negative. While past failures can contribute to undermining your self-confidence, that need not be the case. Even a drop of water continuing to fall on a slab of concrete will eventually either wear it away or cause it to crack. I am a firm believer that failure plus failure plus failure can, and often does, equal success.

Other questions you might ask yourself concerning your past failures are as follows:

- What caused the failure?
- How could it have been avoided?
- How can I minimize the damage caused by failure?
- Whom do I know who has succeeded in accomplishing this task?
- How can that failure help improve my chances for success?

Distractions

How often are you distracted? Quite often, I suspect, if you are anything like most people. Most of us cannot listen to a speaker for more than a few minutes without our minds wandering. We are easily distracted, especially if we're doing something we're not crazy about anyway.

One of the biggest obstacles or roadblocks you will face as you attempt to reach your goals, is "distraction." Many things — good and bad — are vying for your attention. We should always remember that *good is the enemy of best.*

If you allow something (even a good thing) to take your attention away from doing the best thing, you will be stymied. To accomplish your goal, you must set your eyes on the objective, and don't allow yourself to look aside, and thereby loose sight of your goal.

Insincerity

So often, we say things we don't really mean. We join organizations, we agree with people, and give money to causes — all because we don't feel comfortable saying "No." If you're insincere about accomplishing one of your goals, you won't accomplish it. In reality, you'll have to make your goal meet on of ten requirements — making it a personal goal. It's not difficult to be sincere when we really want something.

Isolation

Lord Tennyson said,

> *No man is an island unto himself.*

Yet, many of us fall into the trap of isolationism. Isolation can be an obstacle in many ways. If we isolate ourselves from others, we won't benefit from many things others can offer us. Isolation can cause us to have improper perspectives. The strength of two together is more than twice the strength of one. Just as a rope can become unbreakable with enough strands intertwined together, so a person who has woven his knowledge and skills with many others can be unbreakable.

Unrealistic Expectations

Did you ever attempt to do something and knew you would fail, even before you began? Either you, or someone else, had placed unrealistic expectations on you. Yes, it's possible to expect too much from yourself. So much, in fact, that you're doomed before you begin.

Many a son has experienced what it feels like to be up to bat in a baseball game when his father is sitting in the stands expecting a home run. Encouragement is a good thing, but placing the burden of an unrealistic expectation on someone is not. If you feel like you're defeated before you even begin, you will not accomplish nearly as much.

I once watched a Disney movie in which a boy was attempting to climb a rope. He continued to fail, day after day, though he had a lot of motivation to accomplish the task. Finally, one day his brother explained that if he would quit concentrating on the top but, instead, concentrate on one pull at a time, he would be successful. When he followed that advice, he accomplished his goal. Until then, he had been expecting that he must reach for the top — something he did not really believe possible. We rise, or fall, to the level of our expectations.

Pigeonhole Thinking

Pigeonhole thinking occurs when one is so shortsighted that he only sees one solution to his problem. We have all seen pigeonhole filing systems before. They are used at motels (to put keys in), at small post offices (to separate mail), or on desks (to separate objects and papers). While they might serve a very useful purpose for filing, pigeonholes can be limiting in solving problems.

We all have been guilty of this at times. My daughter, Kim, helped me remember this obstacle while we were returning from church one Sunday morning. I just had spoken on the subject of goal setting, and she thought she would take advantage of the situation to inform me of one of her new goals. She proudly announced, "Dad, I have just made a goal. My new goal is to persuade you to buy me contact lenses to replace my glasses." Now, I surely understand her reasoning. Only 12 years old at the time, she figured if she were to get them, I would have to buy them for her. While that may have been true, I cautioned her not to be guilty of this pigeonhole thinking. What she really wanted was contact lenses. There might be several possible solutions, and they all should be considered just in case the first one to come to mind wasn't the best one.

Sometimes we are blind to the fact that we are guilty of pigeonhole thinking as such. This type of thinking especially reigns true when we isolate ourselves, and do not work with counsel in attempting to solve our problems. I'm sure you've heard about the five blind men who described an elephant after feeling it, each from a different angle. Several people can come up with several solutions after pondering a problem for just a few minutes.

Tradition

Webster's New Collegiate Dictionary defines tradition as "the handing down orally of customs, beliefs, etc. from generation to generation," or "a long-established custom that has the effect of an unwritten law." Thus, tradition falls into the same category as the "We've always done it this way!" syndrome. While traditions can become very precious, they also can become very stifling when allowed to hinder progress.

Some become so wrapped up in tradition that they allow it to repel and eliminate any good idea with which it might be in conflict. I have discussed the subject of *change* in chapter three, and much of that information can apply here. Like many of these obstacles, tradition can be either good or bad, depending upon the situation.

Poor Self-Image

Few things will hinder you more than having a poor self-image. Remember, a person cannot act in a manner inconsistent with the way he sees himself. Thus, if you or any other person on whom you depend, has a poor self-image, you should begin working immediately to improve it.

Poor Habits

Whenever you attempt to accomplish anything extraordinary, realize that one of the greatest obstacles you will face is the habits you have that are inconsistent with the goal itself. Habits are said to be either the best of servants or the worst of masters.

The worst boss anyone can have is a bad habit. Bad habits, like chiggers and cockleburs, are easy to get but difficult to shake off. A man could live twice as long if he did not spend the first half of his life acquiring habits that shorten the other half. First we make our habits, then our habits make us.

A habit is like a cable. We weave a thread of it every day until it is extremely difficult to break. (Note that I said "difficult" — not "impossible.") In reality, the best way to break an old habit is to form a new one in direct contrast to the old one. Did you ever attempt to move toward the reverse of an idea? It is very difficult. For example, I want you not to think of a green cat. What happened? A green cat, although unusual, is difficult not to think of when you try, isn't it? The same is true of life when you attempt to change or break a bad habit by focusing on not doing it. Anyone who ever dieted has learned this important lesson. Determine not to eat something you love, and the desire to have it becomes even stronger!

Did you ever analyze how much of your life you live habitually? Most guess, and I agree, at least 75%. Some guess as high as 95%! Think about it. From the time you rise in the morning until you go to bed at night, you do a multitude of things without even thinking about them. Ever stop to think about which shoe you put on first each morning? How about the system you use in preparation and dressing? When you get into the car to drive, do you think about how to start the car or any of the other functions involved in driving? Once you had to — when you were first learning. You were very careful to make sure you did everything correctly and made no mistakes. Now driving has become a piece of cake.

As we analyze how this process occurred (getting to the point where we live at least 75% of our days habitually), let's think about how habits are developed. The process follows this flow:

Thought — Desire — Action — Habit — Way of Life

You meet an idea, you think about it, you desire it, and then you act upon it. All habits begin this way. Once you have acted upon it, you repeat the action many times until the action becomes routine. You don't even need to enjoy the action the first few times if the desire is strong enough. The habit of smoking is a good example. Few people enjoyed their first cigarettes. Yes, the thought finally works its way into becoming a habit, and the habit determines our way of life.

To control our lives, we must consciously build the habits we want to be present in our lives. We also must consciously decide to rid ourselves of the destructive habits which keep us from our objectives. What habits do you have that are inconsistent with your goals? Write them down as obstacles with which you must deal.

Among the bad habits preventing goal achievement may be the following:

- Poor sleeping habits
- Poor eating habits
- Poor personal hygiene habits
- Sloppy dress and grooming habits
- Lazy work habits
- Inadequate study habits
- Excessive entertainment habits
- Immoral habits
- Vices
- Poor communication habits

Let's look at these briefly, one at a time.

Poor Sleeping Habits

Too much or too little sleep can be detrimental to successfully completing your goal. You need to know your body, the amount of sleep you need, and plan accordingly. You cannot shorten the time for sleep on your schedule just because you want to, if your body will not allow it.

Too much sleep harms your success in two ways: You will be more sluggish, and you will have less time in which to accomplish your goals. Too little sleep eventually causes you to be less alert than you should be and become less enthusiastic than you'd like to be. If this occurs over a long enough period, you will suffer "burnout."

Poor Eating Habits

Some of us eat to live, and some of us live to eat. Living to eat will eventually cause us problems that will become obstacles to reaching some of our goals. A very high percentage of Americans are overweight. Are you among them? If so, chances are that your eating habits have contributed to this problem.

Eating the right kinds of food, in the correct amounts, with proper preparation, at the appropriate times enhances your weight and energy level. This, in turn, will ultimately determine how easily you can accomplish some of your goals. Poor eating habits contribute directly to your lack of needed energy. Try carrying a 20 pound attache case around all day to see the effect an extra twenty pounds has on you. Then you will understand why I refer to poor eating habits as an obstacle or roadblock. Twenty extra pounds might be an obstacle to running in a marathon; 50 could be a roadblock.

Poor Personal Hygiene Habits

Some of you might be surprised to find this listed as an obstacle or roadblock. It shouldn't be — but it is! I am amazed at the number of people who fail to shower every day, or at least every other day. Some simply have reading problems. They read the deodorant cans too fast and thought they said every 24 days instead of every 24 hours. Then, they have the audacity to wonder why they get turned down for jobs and have a difficult time making friends.

Poor personal hygiene habits can cause you other problems. They ultimately lead to poor health and disease, which can shorten your life. Obviously, early death can be a roadblock in goal accomplishment. Even if you don't die early because of neglect in this area, you may lose time off work for sickness and doctor visits.

Sloppy Dress And Grooming Habits

Sloppiness can often be an obstacle that hinders us from becoming what we could be. Among other things, sloppiness tells others that we respect neither them nor ourselves. Some argue they can't afford nice clothes. Maybe so, but everyone can afford to dress neatly in clean clothes. Almost everyone can afford a comb and an occasional haircut. Sloppy dress and grooming will turn others off, and in turn, greatly diminish your chances for success in many areas.

Many good books have been written on this subject. You may be amazed, as I was, at the tremendous effect your dress and grooming can have in helping or hindering your success. I recommend John Malloy's book, *Dress for Success.*

Lazy Work Habits

Laziness not only prevents people from setting goals, it also prevents them from attaining goals they do set. Laziness causes us to work only halfheartedly at whatever we're attempting to do. Therefore, the cost is seen in time and quality. Sometimes, the objective is never completed at all. It seems to me that the only thing lazy people do well is complain and blame others for their misfortunes.

Inadequate Study Habits

Reading and studying may be required to accomplish your goals. Amazingly, most people have never learned how to study. You may have attended 12 to 16 years of school and still not learned sound principles and techniques for studying!

While inadequate study habits may not prevent you from successfully reaching a goal, they can certainly slow your progress. Even if you have already graduated from all the courses you expect to enroll in, you should still work to improve inadequate study skills. Only the person who continues to be a student can be assured of continued growth.

Excessive Entertainment Habits

These habits can cost you plenty in terms of two of your most valuable resources: time and money. Unless you already have an excess, you'd be wise to take care how you spend your time and money. A few years ago a study reported that the average home had a television turned on over 2100 hours each year. The average person spent less than five hours per year reading a book.

I am not encouraging you to do without entertainment — only to enjoy it in moderation. At the very least, make a conscious decision to figure out how much you can enjoy and remain consistent with your other goals.

Immoral Habits

Can immorality be considered an obstacle or roadblock to success? You bet it can! Ask candidates for public office who had to withdraw from the race when immorality was uncovered. Immoral behavior and habits such as dishonesty, promiscuity, pornography, vulgarity, drug abuse and stealing, to name a few, can be detrimental to success.

These habits will undermine and destroy the very foundation on which you are building. Not only will you not realize the fulfillment of your objectives, you may lose what you had to begin with if you do not conquer these immediately.

Vices

Among some vices that may hinder you in attaining your goals are smoking, drinking, and gambling. Some of you may think that I've left teaching and have gone to meddling or preaching. I understand. I ask you to hear my full argument.

Smoking, drinking, and gambling probably will not keep you from accomplishing many of your goals. That is, unless of course, your goals include quitting smoking, drinking, or gambling. I do strongly believe that they affect your ability to realize your full potential in attaining your goals.

If, for example, you smoke because you do not possess the self-control to quit, then your resulting loss of self-confidence affects other areas of your life. Also, these, and other vices, may be offensive to those with whom you associate. You must decide whether these are habits that present true obstacles to your success.

Poor Communication Habits

The ability to communicate well is vital in attaining a high level of success in most walks of life. This is true whether we're talking about communication in marriage, at work, with friends and neighbors, or with simple acquaintances. Poor communication habits in speaking, listening, grammar, and timing can be corrected.

Many a relationship has been hindered, or severed, because something was not communicated properly. You've heard it said that, "It is not always just what you say, but how you say it." Just as having good relationships can be valuable in helping you reach your goals, damaging them can be tragic.

Poor Influences

No man is an island unto himself. Each of us is subject to outside influences daily. Some of these influences are positive, and of course, some are negative. Negative influences undermine our chances for successfully attaining our goals as surely as a landslide on a mountain road.

People

The people we meet often affect how we live more than we realize. We like to see ourselves as individuals, independent of others' opinions and whims. Few people enjoy being told what to do. Although we often rebel at others trying to tell us what to do, we still allow those others to influence us greatly, either to our benefit or detriment. Each of us is constantly changing, and it is impossible not to be influenced by those with whom we come into contact.

Note that this influence occurs both consciously and subconsciously. Consciously, we decide whether to accept or reject what we perceive to be negative influences. Subconsciously, we do not have that luxury. We accept or reject these influences without even realizing it. I might consciously reject another's life-style even though I subconsciously envy it.

Also note that you, and you alone, bear the responsibility of whom you allow to influence you and whether that influence is positive or negative. First, you decide those with whom you will associate, realizing that birds of a feather flock together. Probably you will conform to the standards and mentality of a group before you influence them to conform to you. I said, "probably," not "always." For that reason you must be very selective of your peers. Peer pressure is real, like it or not.

Second, you bear the responsibility of determining how you react to the influence. A son of alcoholic parents does not have to drink; it is his decision to make. A peer group may attempt to influence you to do many things contrary to your chosen goals. You decide.

Among the people who influence you are family members, people at work (employers, supervisors, co-workers, suppliers, customers), professionals (ministers, physicians, attorneys, accountants, government officials, etc.), friends, acquaintances, and neighbors. As a child, you were also influenced by teachers, neighbors, baby-sitters, and visitors to the home. Although this list is not all-inclusive, it may help you to realize the scope of those who influence you.

Places

Certain places can influence you. Undeniably, particular environments are designed to influence you. Factors like lighting, music, furniture, and pictures all influence you to act in a manner desired by the designer.

You also tend to act a certain way when you are in familiar surroundings. People are inclined to repeat themselves and their activities at places where they have been before. While this may not present a really strong obstacles, it is still worthy of consideration. To walk into a bar when attempting to quit drinking, even if just to visit with friends, may not be wise.

Things

If you're avoiding a particular activity, you might want to remove things that remind you of the activity. Things, when used as props, can serve either as positive or negative influences. Set a picture of a log cabin on your desk if you are working extra to earn money to build it. Also, don't keep your golf clubs nearby if you're tempted to chuck it all and go play golf.

Among the things that influence, none carries more weight than televisions and VCRs. Although you can decide whether to watch a particular television show or video tape, you cannot always know ahead of time what the viewing will entail. You cannot watch those things and not be influenced by them. Sad to say, most of the influence is negative. While I don't advocate getting rid of all television sets, I do encourage and challenge you to be very careful what you watch. Anyone who denies that the programs influence his thoughts and actions is really mistaken.

Radios and stereos can also be a powerful negative influence. While these fantastic inventions may be used to bless our hearts, they are often real tools of destruction!

A sincere friend once argued that he didn't think music was influential in molding the mood and thoughts of its listeners. He thought it was merely reflective in nature, reflecting the mood and thoughts of the writers and musicians. While I will agree wholeheartedly with the "reflection" idea, I will continue to stress that the "reflection" screams and grabs for attention — thus, it is influential.

Another category of influence is games. Many games on the market today, including video and computer games, project a very strong influence on young minds. A *60 Minutes* television report interviewed parents tearfully testifying how the game *Dungeons and Dragons* had negatively influenced their children. Some of their children had committed suicide, while others had become killers, all as a direct result of playing the game.

Books, magazines and newspapers influence. If not, why would advertisers spend millions of dollars to share their messages? You must guard what you read because we often seem to believe the axiom that says, "If it is in print, it must be true." Ridiculous as this may seem, we often accept the written word as truth without questioning it. A book is more effective in convincing a person who reads than a verbal argument. A book will allow you to change your mind without backing you into a corner and embarrassing you. You can "save face" this way. Don't allow this fact to keep you from reading because "leaders are readers."

Events

Events might, at first, seem like an unusual category of influences. Certain events do affect our lives both positively and negatively.

Sporting events certainly come to mind. The frame of mind you have when your team is in the heat of battle is a direct influence on you. A victory can cause a joyous mood, and defeat can turn your attitude sour. If you're not careful, we can allow a terrible disposition, after a loss, to carry over into other areas of our lives. If we feel our team were cheated, we may be furious or vengeful.

I find it easy to refrain from spending very much time viewing sporting events, except during a championship series when one of my favorite teams is competing. Every March, I spend many hours watching my favorite college teams participate in the NCAA Championship Tournament. Then, In October, it's the baseball League Championship Series and the World Series. I'd say I allow sporting events to influence how I spend some of my time. If that time keeps me from accomplishing a more important objective, then the sporting event has influenced me negatively.

Parties, also, often provide influence possibly inconsistent with particular goals and objectives. If they provide environments in which you lose self-control and act shamefully, then their influence is unhealthy.

Beliefs

Each of us has beliefs that are formed by a cast of experiences and information received throughout his life. Someone once said, "Talk is cheap. What we do with our lives tells the rest of the world what we really believe." Our beliefs determine, when the chips are down, what we are going to do.

Therefore, it might be wise to examine your goals to see whether any of them conflict with your beliefs. You cannot strive to accomplish something contrary to your true beliefs without it undermining your level of success. Of course, it also might be very interesting, while you are at it, to figure out why you believe what you do. Are your beliefs well-founded, or are they somewhat shallow? Are they only as solid as the last speaker you heard, or do they have a firm basis to maintain them?

When I speak of beliefs, I'm referring to the philosophies, religious convictions, and superstitions you hold. While you might be surprised to learn that I include superstitions in that category, I suspect you'd be surprised to learn that an estimated twenty million Americans carry rabbits' feet or other good luck charms. Superstitions still play a significant part in the way many people think and act. Therefore, beliefs may become an obstacle, or even a roadblock.

I took my son on a Canadian fishing trip soon after his tenth birthday. It just so happened that the last day of the trip fell on Friday the 13th. I assured him that I always consider Friday the 13th a lucky day, in contrast to "unlucky" anyway, and expected him to get a big one that day. Of course, I expected to get a big one myself, too. He caught the largest fish of the trip right off the bat — an 18 pound Northern Pike, 39 inches long! Now, every time Friday the 13th rolls around, I hear him telling others he caught his biggest fish on Friday the 13th. I'm not worried about that particular superstition plaguing him.

We're constantly making decisions based upon bad information; therefore, we must rethink each option before we automatically dismiss it. Even if your decision to refrain from a particular action in the past was a correct one, many changes may have taken place. New information often warrants a new decision.

Satanic Oppression

It may surprise you that I include satanic oppression in a list of things that undermine your chances for attaining your goals. It shouldn't, because Satan is alive and well on planet earth today. Though we may chuckle when we hear a little boy give the excuse, "The devil made me do it," we cannot ignore the fact that Satan and his army are powerful foes to be reckoned with. One cannot accept that God is real and the Bible is His written Word, without accepting the existence of Satan.

Consider the following Bible verses about Satan's influence and attack on mankind.

Therefore humble yourselves under the mighty hand of God, that He may exalt you in due time, casting all your care upon Him, for He cares for you. Be sober, be vigilant; because your adversary the devil walks about like a roaring lion, seeking whom he may devour. Resist him, steadfast in the faith, knowing that the same sufferings are experienced by your brotherhood in the world. But may the God of all grace, who called us to His eternal glory by Christ Jesus, after you have suffered a while, perfect, establish, strengthen, and settle you. To Him be the glory and the dominion forever and ever. Amen.
1 Peter 5:6-11 (NKJV)

But I fear, lest somehow, as the serpent deceived Eve by his craftiness, so your minds may be corrupted from the simplicity that is in Christ. **2 Corinthians 11:3 (NKJV)**

For such are false apostles, deceitful workers, transforming themselves into apostles of Christ. And no wonder! For Satan himself transforms himself into an angel of light. Therefore it is no great thing if his ministers also transform themselves into ministers of righteousness, whose end will be according to their works.
2 Corinthians 11:13-15 (NKJV)

But even if our gospel is veiled, it is veiled to those who are perishing, whose minds the god of this age has blinded, who do not believe, lest the light of the gospel of the glory of Christ, who is the image of God, should shine on them. **2 Corinthians 4:3-4 (NKJV)**

And you He made alive, who were dead in trespasses and sins, in which you once walked according to the course of this world, according to the prince of the power of the air, the spirit who now works in the sons of disobedience, among whom also we all once conducted ourselves in the lusts of our flesh, fulfilling the desires of the flesh and of the mind, and were by nature children of wrath, just as the others. But God, who is rich in mercy, because of His great love with which He loved us, even when we were dead in trespasses, made us alive together with Christ (by grace you have been saved), and raised us up together, and made us sit together in the heavenly places in Christ Jesus, that in the ages to come He might show the exceeding riches of His grace in His kindness toward us in Christ Jesus. For by grace you have been saved through faith, and that not of yourselves; it is the gift of God, not of works, lest anyone should boast. For we are His workmanship, created in Christ Jesus for good works, which God prepared beforehand that we should walk in them. **Ephesians 2:1-10 (NKJV)**

I find it interesting that I almost did not think to include information about Satan in this section concerning obstacles. I find it most interesting considering I truly believe Satan would be pleased if I'd omit mention of him. I'm certain he chuckles at the way most of us ignore him and, thereby, allow him to roam and do his bidding as he pleases.

When I refer to Satan, I am also referring to his mighty host — an army of a multitude of demons. Satan is only one being and can only be at one place at a time. Chances are he will not give most of us his personal attention unless we are about to accomplish, or have just accomplished, a great thing to the glory of God. Otherwise, we are simply not important enough to warrant the presence of the Prince of demons. Each of us, however, does have to deal with his army, his influence, and the effects of his working in this world.

Several years ago, a friend told me that he had decided to quit attempting to do anything for God because of this obstacle. He told me that his life ran smoothly until he attempted to do something for God, then all hell broke loose. Fights would erupt within his family, equipment would break down and need costly repairs, and everything seemed to go wrong. It was obvious to him that Satan, and his army, are alive and well on planet earth.

While I agree with my friend's assessment, I disagree with his solution. God tells us to:

> *Resist the devil and he will flee from you. Draw near to God and He will draw near to you.* **James 4:7b-8a (NKJV)**

Read Ephesians 6:10-18 to learn about how to:

> *Put on the whole armor of God, that you may be able to stand against the wiles of the devil.* **Ephesians 6:11 (NKJV)**

I realize many of you may be reading about this for the first time. It may, or may not, be a subject you want to learn more about. I suggest you learn more about it, but only from proper sources. Study the Bible with the aid of a good concordance. *The Open Bible*, which comes in several versions, has an excellent aid in the front, and a three hundred page encyclopedic outline on almost every topic, including this one. Many good books discuss this subject. These books can be found at most large Christian bookstores. One I will strongly recommend now, however, is *Satan Is Alive and Well on Planet Earth* by Hal Lindsey.

The key word in handling satanic oppression is "balance." Just as we are not to ignore the presence and influence of Satan and his host, we are not to become too preoccupied with him. God is mightier than Satan and will help us to withstand him. Someone told me concerning a business situation, "If you understand the rules, you can better play the game." That applies here as well.

It might be beneficial to know a little about the way Satan works in our lives. I'm convinced he works differently with Christians than he does with non-Christians.

Concerning Christians, Satan will do whatever he can to hinder any ministry they might attempt to have in others' lives. Satan doesn't really care if we achieve great things, only that God does not receive the credit or glory for it. I'm convinced that he might help us to accomplish anything by which we might become so enamored with ourselves and our possessions that we forget God and our need for Him. Also, Satan recognizes that we hate to go backward or lose something we have gained. Therefore, he might use the fear of losing to entice us to ignore God's principles.

If we do achieve things that could give us greater influence and respect, and we do give the credit and glory to God, then Satan will make it his purpose to bring us down — usually through immorality. Doing so, supposedly, will bring shame to God and His family.

Also, Satan works in the lives of Christians to get them so preoccupied that they have little time for God. Activities are not necessarily bad in and of themselves. In fact, they might even be good. Since "good" is the enemy of "best," Satan and his cause will still benefit.

Now, let's consider the ways Satan works with *his* children, non-Christians. (Lest you become offended at my referring to non-Christians as Satan's children, please read St. John 8:37-47. Some erroneously teach that all are God's children. This is simply not true. All are God's creation. According to the Bible, only those who believe on the Lord Jesus Christ are "born-again" into God's family and become God's children.)

If you understand that Satan neither enjoys losing numbers from his family, nor enjoys anything that pleases God, you will understand why he works night and day to prevent it. Someone once asked, "Why does the devil want to damn someone to Hell?" The answer is quite simple. It's his major way of hurting God. You see, God loves each individual and has demonstrated that love by giving His Son, Jesus, to pay for his sins by His death. He, thereby, freely offers to each one the gift of eternal life in Heaven. If Satan can keep someone from trusting Jesus Christ as his Savior, Satan can truly hurt God.

When I was a child, my younger brother would attempt to hurt me by threatening to mistreat one of my pets. Satan can only hurt God by bringing hurt to those whom God loves. Since God loves all men (not just those who are born-again into His family), He does not want to see any *perish* (go to Hell).

Satan, therefore, does all within his power to blind the minds of the natural or unsaved man to the glorious truth of the gospel (good news) of Jesus Christ. Satan knows that one day he will be cast into Hell and he wants to cause as many as possible to spend eternity there with him. He may attempt to get men to live as ungodly as possible and by that become alienated from the gospel message. Or, he may try to get them to live generally good life-styles and by that feel no real need for a relationship with God. The first group might believe that God could never love them, as ungodly as they are. The second group might sense that God has already issued them a free pass into Heaven because of their goodness. The truth is that you can be neither good enough to earn, nor bad enough to lose, eternal life. Eternal life (becoming a child of God) is not based upon how good one is. It is based on how good God is, and on the payment He has already paid for sin. No one can ever merit eternal life, neither can anyone ever be so bad to be refused it. The sin of man can never exceed the love of God. Still, Satan attempts to withhold this truth from his children. He literally, blinds their minds.

Therefore, remember that Satan may prove to be one major obstacle, especially if the goal you're working toward is meant to glorify God in any way. You're no match for Satan, but God is more than Satan's match, and He can give you the strength and wisdom to defeat satanic oppression. Christians can take great comfort in the following verse which supports this fact.

> *You are of God, little children, and have overcome them, because He who is in you is greater than he who is in the world.* **I John 4:4 (NKJV)**

The Nature Of Man

Just as Satan might be an obstacle you'd never think of, so the nature of man could be also. Yet, this shouldn't be too surprising when you really get honest with yourself.

I used to believe that "all people are basically good." I thought that all we really needed to do was show them we trusted them, and they would respond in the manner we expected. No matter how bad a track record someone had, if I would but trust him, he would not disappoint me.

I lived according to that philosophy, and fortunately for me, I never got burned too badly because of it. Maybe I didn't because I learned the truth before it was too late. I now read often about people who are taken advantage of, robbed, and even murdered because they learned this lesson too late. The truth is that people are basically bad, natural born sinners. The Bible states it this way:

> *There is none righteous, no, not one.* **Roman 3:10 (NKJV)**

> *But we are all like an unclean thing, And all our righteousnesses are like filthy rags.* **Isaiah 64:6 (NKJV)**

> *All we like sheep have gone astray; We have turned, every one, to his own way.* **Isaiah 53:6 (NKJV)**

> *The heart is deceitful above all things, And desperately wicked; Who can know it?* **Jeremiah 17:9 (NKJV)**

> *For all have sinned and fall short of the glory of God.* **Romans 3:23 (NKJV)**

Actually, now that I understand the nature of man, I more readily can accept inconsistencies and shortcomings in myself and others. I do not expect good or bad necessarily; I recognize that is determined largely by the maturity level and character qualities of each individual. If a man works with God's help to control his sinful nature, he can bring it into subjection and live a moral life. Each man still encounters a daily battle to determine whether he will do right or wrong. Total victory over immorality is never guaranteed, nor is it something to be taken for granted.

If you do not consider the basic nature of man an obstacle, you may often find that you are frustrated with yourself and others. The best that you can do is to combat this errant nature by developing godly principles and habits in your life and the lives of those with whom you work. The Bible sums it up when it states, "It is better to trust in the LORD than to put confidence in man" **(Psalm 118:8). (NKJV)**

Poor Information

You might wonder why I would include information as an obstacle or roadblock. Information, like the other obstacles, can either work for us or against us. Some problems regarding information are as follows:

- Insufficient Information
- Inaccurate Information
- Excessive Information
- Disorganized Information
- Conflicting Information

Lack of knowledge or proper understanding has sunk more than one good plan. Remember the Titanic? The builders of the Titanic said that it could not be sunk. We all should learn something from that tragedy. We seldom know it all. The enemy of learning is knowing — or, at least, thinking we already know.

Therefore, you should gather all the information you need to make wise and correct decisions regarding your action plan. Just as an incorrect road map will lead you astray, so will a plan built on either *insufficient* or *inaccurate* information. Also, just as it is important to have sufficient and correct information, it is equally important to know where you are on the map. The best map in the world will not help you if you don't know where you are on that map.

Excessive information can be tedious and time consuming. You don't have to know everything about everything to put your plan together. Gather information only as necessary, and use it accordingly. I've often seen individuals bogged down in a mire of information they felt might be necessary — just in case. It's a wonder some of these ever go on vacation without first checking to see if all the traffic lights along the route will be green. Again, the key word is "balance."

Disorganized information is not much better than having no information. What good is something if you can't find it or, if you find it and can't make heads or tails out of it? Record keeping plays a very important role in goal accomplishment. Only losers don't keep score. Information must be properly organized to be useful.

Conflicting information presents a dilemma. I welcome it when I am attempting to make a tough decision, and I despise it when I am attempting to make a quick decision. Every situation has two or more sides, and looking at the problem from different perspectives is indeed wise. How often have you purchased an item to solve a problem, only to find that something else would have worked just as well — at less expense?

So, do research, keep records, and have information organized and accessible. You don't need to be a walking encyclopedia to succeed with your goals — just know how to obtain the information you need, when you need it!

Poor Resources
Financial Obstacles
Lack of Money

Would you believe that some people actually consider the lack of money an obstacle or roadblock to accomplishing some of their goals? Of course I'm being sarcastic. Each of us has probably felt at one time or another that limited finances were the only real obstacle to achieving his goals.

Interestingly enough, while we might not say, "If only I had ten thousand dollars, I would have it made," we might say, "If only I had one of those (referring to an item we would like to purchase), I could get the job done." Thus, whether we have thought we needed the money, or simply the item the money could buy, we have felt the money pinch.

As a salesman, one of the first things I learned was that people do not need money to make a purchase. What they need is a way to get the money. I've made many a sale by helping the prospect find a way to obtain the money needed to purchase the item or service I was selling.

A few years ago I was driving around listening to a cassette by Dr. Robert Schuller called, *Possibility Thinking,* when one of his phrases hit me between the eyes! I was under great financial pressure at the time and had sold most of our possessions that were worth selling in an attempt to meet our financial obligations. Dr. Schuller's words, "People don't have money problems, they have idea problems!" came alive to me, and I immediately changed my thinking on the matter. At once I began to realize that every money obstacle I had could be solved by a good idea.

Lack of Credit

Someone once said that the only thing worse than not having money is not having the credit with which to obtain it. While I don't agree that credit is necessary, I do recognize that the lack of credit can present a real obstacle to some people — if they're depending on it.

Actually, credit can be an obstacle either way. Borrowing makes the borrower servant to the lender, which may not be desirable. So, whether you borrow and cannot easily repay, or you attempt to borrow and cannot qualify, you can find the going rough. This is especially true if you haven't planned for it. Amazingly, you often have to prove you don't need the money in order to borrow it — but for good reason. If you've ever loaned money, without collateral, to someone who could not repay, you know what I mean.

Cost of Interest

I knew a tractor dealer who was forced to sell tractors at a loss because of the high cost of interest. One tractor, in particular, was costing him over two-thousand dollars in interest each month! Many companies go under because the owners did not consider the impact interest rates can have on a financed business. An increase of only one percent can sometimes break a business, if things are too tight.

I once agreed to give a friend 120% interest for his help in a financial matter. Before it was over, I had borrowed some $20,000. Each month, I had to decide whether to reduce the debt or to reinvest the money I was reaping. It was not always an easy decision. At any rate, I knew what I was doing and made conscious decisions based on many factors. It worked for me, but I wouldn't recommend it to anyone else. Borrowing can become risky business, and borrowing at high interest rates can be devastating!

Price Increases

Often, as we are developing our plans, we fail to consider inflation. Prices increase over time, and if your goal is long-term, you may have to pay more later. Price increases can cost major builders millions of dollars by the time their projects are completed.

One of your goals might be to take a Hawaiian vacation. Money, for you, might be very tight, but you determine to save "x" number of dollars per week toward this vacation. You look at a brochure, get the pricing, figure out spending money, and then begin working toward the goal. Imagine your shock when you go to book your reservations and find the price has increased several hundred dollars for each of you!

Inflation

Inflation, of course, affects us all. Inflation is a fact of life and you must consider it when setting financial goals, especially long-range goals. Price increases are certainly related to inflation, just as are some of the other considerations I will mention.

Imagine that you want to begin saving now for your baby's college education. How much will it cost? You cannot expect today's tuition rates to remain the same! You might use the past 20 years as a guideline in evaluating how much you will need. I say "20" as an average because your baby will leave for college when she is 18 and will graduate when she is 22. If the average cost for room and board at the college was $800 per year 20 years ago, and it is now over $4,000, then you can consider an inflation factor of 500%. If this rate of inflation continues, then you will need over $20,000 per year for your child to go to college. Don't cringe too much. Some already pay that much today.

Another example of inflation is how much life insurance a man needs to provide for his family. If he wants to leave his wife and children enough to assure them that they continue living in the style to which they have become accustomed, he must consider inflation. Twenty-thousand dollars will not provide the same standard of living in five years that it does this year.

Depreciation

Many fail to consider the continually decreasing value of their possessions. Some items do appreciate, but most depreciate. As I determined the value of my inventory in my computer store, I realized that it lost approximately $1,000 in value every week. I determined this by projecting what the total value would be if I simply closed the doors and walked away for a year. I calculated that the value of my inventory would decrease approximately $50,000. Thus, I could have counted on about a $1,000 per week decrease.

Depreciation occurs for many reasons. Technology is constantly improving the quality of what a dollar will buy. Ten years ago, the least expensive car phone was priced at over $2500. Today, I can have my pick of many superior models priced under $150. I recently purchased some older model computer printers (new) for $35 each. I was shocked to talk to someone, soon after that, who had paid approximately $1,000 each for the exact items only four years ago! Though my printers were new, improved technology demanded that I sell them for less than $100. The list of examples goes on and I'm sure you could give many examples yourself. No one can deny that many items can be purchased today for less than they cost several years ago.

Age is another reason for depreciation. Except for antiques, some real estate and possibly a few other items, the value of most things decreases with age. Even if an item is not used, certain parts become useless. I've been told that lack of use is harder on an airplane than daily use.

Lack of interest also causes depreciation. What was a fad yesterday, and sought after by millions, may have run its course. Try getting a premium price on a hula hoop or a pet rock today and you'll see what I mean. Being in the right place, at the right time, has its advantages. Try selling "1987 NATIONAL LEAGUE CHAMPIONS" T-shirts to St. Louis Cardinal fans this year.

The important point here is this: If you're considering the value of depreciating items as assets to help you in attaining your goal, then anticipate the depreciation and plan accordingly.

Equipment Problems

Often we have goals that involve using equipment. Our goals may require the use of automobiles, computers, typewriters, televisions, cameras, watches, calculators, flashlights, telephones, fishing poles, boat motors, or any of thousands of other things. Too often, we neglect to seriously consider the problems they can bring into our lives, just when we need them most.

Breakdowns

If it has moving parts, receives electrical current, or simply stands in one place (like a sign, for example), it can break, wear out, or become obsolete. An Indianapolis 500 race was lost on one of the last laps because a six-dollar part failed. I have seen whole construction crews come to a standstill because one little part on a piece of equipment failed.

Wouldn't life be much easier if we knew what, when, and where something was going to break down? Trouble is, life doesn't work that way. The rate of breakdowns can be decreased by proper care and maintenance, but can never be totally eliminated. Again, be prepared. Some breakdowns can be costly; others can be fatal. Remember the Challenger disaster caused by a bad seal? Breakdowns can be obstacles we should anticipate.

Improper Equipment

Just as you wouldn't drive a tractor to your vacation spot one-thousand miles away, you shouldn't attempt to accomplish major goals with the wrong equipment. I will agree that improvising is sometimes necessary. Proper tools, however, are designed for specific tasks, and we should consider this when developing our action plans.

When I sold knives door-to-door, I was taught to explain the reasons for accidents. One of the three major reasons was failure to use the proper knife for a specific job. Many of my prospects who had cut themselves in this manner, readily agreed to the importance of having a proper knife for each type of job. The same is true in whatever you are doing. I have seen and used wrenches as hammers, scissors as wire cutters, and screwdrivers as punches.

When the wrong equipment is used to do a job, several things can occur. The equipment can be broken, the item on which you're working may be damaged, the job may take longer, and someone may get hurt — to name a few. Therefore it is important to plan to use the right equipment whenever possible.

Improper Use of Equipment

Most equipment comes with an operator's manual written for a reason (not just to fill a manufacturer's obligation). Many a manual never gets read. Often the people who use the equipment are not the same people who pay for it. Thus, reading the manual is not seen as "all that important." If proper maintenance procedures are not followed, the equipment may see an early grave.

Just as some equipment is used to perform functions for which it was never designed, it often has important features that are never used. As funny as it may seem, some people continue to work harder than necessary simply because they don't understand their equipment. I heard about an Indian who had inherited a new Cadillac. He was seen, soon after that sitting in the front seat while it was being pulled through town — by horses. Know how to use your equipment properly.

Inadequate Equipment

Equipment costs money, something most of us do not possess in great quantity. Not having the equipment we need to do jobs right can cost even more in loss of time and often quality. In reality, the by-products of being too slow and having inferior quality are a poor reputation and loss of business. It pays to invest in the proper equipment!

Not Enough Time

Read the chapter, "No Time To Spare," and you will find many interesting hints to help you with this obstacle. However, there are occasions when there just is not enough time to accomplish a particular goal. If you wait until 7:50 A.M. to get out of bed to go to an 8:00 A.M. interview, you probably will not have enough time. If you wait until you're 40 to begin attacking the four-minute mile barrier, you may be too late.

The element of time, or our use of it, can be an obstacle in at least three ways. First, we may take it for granted and therefore, not make the most of it. Second, we may give up our goals when we're intimidated by the shortness of it. Third, we may underestimate how much can be done during any particular time span.

Time is a constant, and our use of it is a variable. Time can be made to work for us or allowed to work against us. As with most of these obstacles, we ourselves, decide.

Manpower

Too often, we underestimate the manpower required to do a certain job. We attempt to do too much with too few, and get burned in the process. Or, on the other hand, we may overestimate the manpower necessary, and this, also, can be costly. This is especially true with employers and organizers. Send too few to do a job, and they will all be standing around waiting for additional help. Send too many, and you will be squandering another resource — money.

Improper use of manpower is also an obstacle in using each person's strength and minimizing his weaknesses. If fulfilling your goals requires the building of a team, then you must become good at recognizing your people's strengths and weaknesses and using them accordingly.

A third consideration is hiring the wrong people to do a particular job. Too many fail in accomplishing their goals because they place trust in untrustworthy people. Thoroughly check out the references of those who will be helping you to reach your goals. You can fail because you use unqualified people, and you can fail because you pay too much for overqualified people.

Inadequate Support

If the support is removed from under a porch roof, what will happen? Of course, the roof will collapse! The same is true with you, if you need support. You should know yourself. Do you have a pioneering spirit? Can you go it alone, when working on a goal, or do you need support? If you need support, and it disappears, how will you replace it? Will that present an obstacle to you? If so, decide now, as you develop your action plan, how you're going to deal with it.

All too often, failure is blamed on someone else not supporting some activity; or someone supported it for awhile and then dropped his support. Realize in advance this may happen, and be prepared mentally for it. Don't allow someone else and his support to make or break you.

Inadequate Ability Or Skill

People frequently attempt to accomplish things without the proper ability or necessary skill. This is a real obstacle and should be considered before beginning a project. This obstacle can stop us dead in the water, or it may not even be manifested until after we think we've completed the project.

You might disassemble an engine to repair it, and then forget how to put it back together. Or after you put it back together, thinking you have it repaired, you drive 20 miles from home only to have it blow a gasket.

The point is this: Decide ahead of time which skills and abilities are necessary to accomplish your goal. Then, either develop those skills yourself, or acquire the services of someone else who possesses them.

Physical Impairments Or Handicaps

Physical impairments and handicaps should be evaluated as potential obstacles to goal achievement. The illness or injury of someone on whom you depend can directly impact your ability to realize your goals. Although many physical impairments are unavoidable, they should not be unanticipated. Take necessary steps both to prepare for the unavoidable and to prevent the avoidable.

Handicaps are a different matter. While handicaps usually mean that a people cannot function normally in particular areas or situations, they can be reckoned with and compensated for. I know of people with great physical handicaps who accomplish more than the average person. Often, a handicapped person is more motivated and more determined than the average person, and is a great person to have helping you. Still, make sure you consider, in your action plan, a way to deal with the handicap, or it may become an obstacle.

In either case, realize that we do not enjoy perfect health all the time; therefore, we must develop action plans that neither expect nor demand it. One of the things that makes a planner valuable is that he expects problems, and develops a plan to deal with them. When someone on whom you depend becomes sick or has an accident, you need to respond in a proper manner toward him and your problem. Be understanding and empathize with him. If you have anticipated and prepared for this potential obstacle, then its appearance will be merely an inconvenience (if that) rather than a roadblock.

Insufficient Energy

Energy is required to fulfill almost every goal. Whether it is human energy, electrical energy, horse power, or another form of energy, energy is a vital force. Be sure to take precautions to assure that the energy you need is available when you need it.

I have flown into the wilderness in Northern Canada, slept in tents, and still had the use of a propane stove and freezer. With the availability of our modern technology, we can have energy, in one form or another, in just about any place in this world. We can be toasty warm on the North Pole, and cool as a cucumber in Ecuador. Batteries, generators, engines, and even the sun can provide all the energy we need — if we will plan for it.

Poor Plans

Opposing Or Conflicting Goals

This category may present one of the bigger obstacles. Goals can conflict with one another, and there is not always a simple answer. As a young athlete, you may want to be a heavyweight wrestler and a competitor in marathon races. The weight you need to wrestle will slow you down as a runner. You may want to take six weeks of vacation next year, while at the same time enjoy your most productive year ever. This, of course, is possible, but these goals could conflict with one another.

Many a businessman faces his intense desire to provide the best for his family with the demand that he spend a lot of time with them. He is needed at home to provide encouragement, guidance, love, and domestic support. He finds it difficult to walk the tightrope and find the proper balance. Often, he is labeled as a workaholic. I have felt, and continue to feel, the tremendous pressure that these two conflicting goals place on me. I often feel I work extra hard today so I can vacation 20 weeks a year tomorrow. In reality, I don't really desire to vacation 20 weeks every year, but I would like to be able to go when and where I want to, without being too concerned as to what it costs. How about you?

Poor Situations

Natural Disasters

Natural disasters such as tornados, hurricanes, floods, and earthquakes cannot be predicted with accuracy, but they can be considered and prepared for, to some degree, with proper planning. If you want to build a house in Florida, for example, the building code requires you to have hurricane clips attached to the trusses. This requirement came, no doubt, after many roofs were lost to strong winds. If you build a hotel on the beach, it is wise to prepare for high tides.

No matter where you live, consider the possibility of these obstacles, and determine if they can keep you from achieving your goal. People are always more capable of handling these things if they've thought about them. Planning can make the difference between a total loss, and a partial loss.

Tragedy

A tragedy, by definition, brings with it obstacles and roadblocks. The tragedy may be fire, robbery, illness, death, or any number of things. We must realize that tragedy can strike at any time and be as prepared as possible to deal with it.

Businesses prepare for this, for example, by purchasing insurance policies. If a partner dies, a buy-out agreement goes into effect, and the money to purchase the remainder of the business is made available by means of a life insurance policy for the surviving partner. We purchase auto insurance, homeowner's insurance, disability insurance, health insurance, etc., to cover financial needs caused by tragedies.

Certainly making a will is preparation for a tragedy such as premature death. How sad when parents are killed in an accident, and no will has been drawn up to name the preferred guardians. Prepare for tragedies. Ignoring them will not prevent them from happening.

Bad Weather

Weather frequently represents an obstacle. At times, it's too hot, and, at other times, it's too cold. I've worked on construction jobs when we had to show up for work and wait until it was at least 15 degrees before we could begin work. Besides the temperature, we must contend with rain, snow, and hail. These can, and will at times, present obstacles with which you must contend. Unless the weather is perfect, outdoor projects are affected by the weather. I'm not one to spend much time being too concerned about the weather. In fact, I seldom even notice it unless it's at an extreme. I've driven cars without air conditioners when it was 114 degrees, and the wind was like a heater in my face. I've taken ice water showers in an unheated room during the winter. My point is, weather doesn't have to stop you.

If I plan an outdoor event, I consider the weather. Considering the time of year, what fluctuations should I expect? If it should rain, what will I do? Is it possible to change, at the last minute, and have the event indoors? If this becomes necessary, what additional costs will be involved? Could the weather make it difficult for people to attend the event? Should this occur, how will I notify them of any changes, such as postponements?

People Problems

Strained Relationships

Strained relationships can hinder accomplishing goals. Gaining support is difficult from those we have offended or didn't consider. Dealing with these people can become a time-consuming process. They'll go out of their way to slow us down until we mend the wounds we've caused.

Even if you have great relationships with those with whom you work, you may still encounter problems because they may be bickering among themselves. A team must be of one accord to work properly.

Enemies

You may be the nicest person, but chances are you still may have enemies. They may not want to kill you, but they may enjoy undermining any opportunities you have for successfully accomplishing your goals.

They may have any of the attitude diseases, such as envy, selfishness, revenge, pride, greed, me-first-itis, or jealousy. They may not even personally know you, just know of you. You must realize they may exist and not be too shocked when they appear. Taking common-sense precautions doesn't hurt. You can purchase insurance to cover some of the damage they may cause, and you can build in safeguards to protect you against others.

A wise man takes time to know his enemies and those he should distrust. At times I do business with people I don't trust if I'm confident it's still in my best interest to do so. (I'd rather do business with those I know to be dishonest than with those who are dishonest without my knowing it.) Unfortunately, enemies are a reality and we must therefore know how to cautiously deal with them.

Competition

Although, I believe your biggest obstacle is you, I do acknowledge that you must consider what your competition is doing. You must be aware of their strategy, and develop a better plan to overcome any losses that could occur as a result.

Age

Strange as it may seem, even your age can be an obstacle or roadblock. No matter what your age, there will be some things for which you will be considered too old, or too young.

Some of these obstacles occur because of restrictions that others have placed on a particular activity. Others will occur simply because of the changes in you that age brings about, or has not yet had the time to cause. Many of these barriers are being challenged all the time, and many fall as we progress or regress depending on your point of view.

I also might mention that it's not just your age, but often it's the age you appear to be. You might be the correct age to "qualify" for a particular activity, but run into problems because you don't appear to be your age. Often, there might not be a qualifying age at all, but because of your deceptive appearance, you might have certain expectations placed on you for which you are not prepared. As an example, appearance of age and the maturity of the mind do not always correspond.

Simply be aware that this is another category that could present you with an obstacle or roadblock.

Distance

Even in this jet age distance can be an obstacle to accomplishing some of your goals. This obstacle is usually solvable, but the solution may not always be a simple one. Modern technology has done amazing things for us in this area. We can now communicate from almost any point on, or above, the globe with someone else at almost any point. Via many means of transportation, we can move almost anything anywhere. The real questions regarding the problems that distance invokes are "How?" and "How Much?"

Interruptions

Many a day has been cut short because of interruptions. Interruptions occur from many angles and in many ways. They occur from within (others in your office, etc.) and from without (the telephone). By definition, interruptions are events that stop you when you're in the middle of accomplishing something and hold you in abeyance until you eliminate them.

Interruptions can constitute 25 percent, or more, of your day if you don't work to control them. They present obstacles to accomplishing goals both by breaking your concentration and by taking valuable time. To become the best you can be, you must learn to control these interruptions and keep them to a minimum.

Rough Terrain (topography)

I enjoyed, a few years ago, the TV commercial which advertises the United Parcel Service. It showed a truck driving across the desert, a U.P.S. delivery man poling a raft down a river, and another carrying his package in a mountain cablecar. Then, as the commercial ends and we're being told that U.P.S. delivers in "tough places" (referring to these just mentioned) and "easy places," the scene is shown of a truck turning a corner in a major city, with cars packed, like sardines, in several rows of a major traffic jam. It's funny, of course, because as anyone who's ever driven in a traffic jam knows, that isn't easy.

I don't know what your goals are. I do know that there may be somewhere the topography does play an important part. The mountains presented themselves as obstacles to the men who first built a railroad from the East to the West. These men had to decide the best way to deal with those mountains. In some cases they went around, in other cases they went through. When they came to rivers, they built bridges called trestles.

Many a person has lost his job because he arrived to work late one too many days. Wise is the person who expects the unexpected when it comes to driving in traffic regularly.

Rules, Regulations And Established Standards

When I think of rules, regulations, and established standards, I first think about our federal government. The governments with which we must all deal provide their share of obstacles for each of us. Before you can build anything today, you must first get approval from some government agency.

Rules, regulations, and established standards are not solely the property of government agencies. Almost any authority in our lives have a few of its own. We may have even set a few ourselves, with which we must now contend. You must know what they are, why they exist, and how to deal with them. If penalties exist for failure to comply, know the extent of those penalties. (Sometimes it's beneficial to ignore the rule and simply pay the penalty.)

Animals, Birds, Insects, And Other Vermin

Depending on your goals and objectives, these creatures can be a real pain in the neck, so to speak. It could be mice, squirrels, or insects in your house; or it might be moles ruining the appearance of your yard. You might find, as I did once, that bears can put a damper on a fishing trip simply by stealing a duffel bag full of food.

Weeds, Trees, Thistles, And Thorns

This category is somewhat related to the previous. Just as wildlife can spoil your goal, so can plant life. Take a few seconds to consider whether these can be a problem to your achievement of a particular goal. They need not be planned for beforehand.

Summary

This chapter covers many obstacles. Perhaps, just a writing this chapter has presented my greatest obstacle to finish the book, it may have been your greatest obstacle to completing your reading of it. (The chapter actually is more than three times the length I anticipated it being.)

Let's face it, there are many obstacles to being successful. It it were not so, everyone would be easily successful. While the obstacles may be seen as the "bad news," the next chapter will present the "good news" — there's always an answer! Read on.

·Nine·
There Is Always
An Answer

You have just read at length pages about obstacles and roadblocks, and we did not even cover them all. That is the bad news. The good news is "solutions" to these obstacles and roadblocks exist!

It's one thing to be faced with a tough problem. It's quite another to be faced with a problem for which you don't feel an answer even exists.

The point I want to make in this chapter is that answers always exist to our problems. They may not be easily seen, but we must develop the confidence that they do exist, or we don't stand a chance. I often enjoy responding to a failure, by saying, "Well, it looks like I need to go to Plan B!" There are actually times I have to move to plan C, then D, and so on.

Let's examine the steps to finding answers to our problems, troubles, obstacles, and roadblocks. The steps are:

- Have a proper attitude.
- Face the problem head on.
- Expect to succeed!
- Seek to understand the problem.
- Make a list of possible solutions.
- Continually work on improvement.
- Learn creative alternatives.
- Practice offense and defense.

Have A Proper Attitude

One thing we must all accept if we are ever going to realize our potentials is that problems, even tough ones, are inevitable. Actually, we should be thankful that this is so because they are necessary. Yes, I said "necessary"! There are many benefits to be gained as a result of facing problems, and even failing; we would be foolish to attempt to run from them all, or wish them away.

Since problems always will be with us, and are even necessary, doesn't it make sense to develop appreciation for them? I don't like problems any more than any other sane person, so I have enjoyed learning how different an effect a positive attitude can have when it comes to solving them. I know people who spend more time complaining about their problems than it would have taken to solve them.

Some time ago I was scheduled to speak on the subject of Getting The Gold Out of Goals. My wife asked me if I had a practical formula that others could use to get gold out of goals. I realized that I did not, but told her I would come up with an answer in the near future.

Several weeks later, as I was retiring to bed at about 1:00 A.M., it dawned on me that I had never come up with that formula. I jumped out of bed, turned the lights on, and wrote the letters G-O-A-L-S down, as you see them below.

G
O
A
L
S

I knew if I was going to come up with a catchy phrase, the **G** would have to stand for the word "gold" or "golden." The **O** would stand for "opportunities." It only took a couple of minutes before I had the rest. It read "Golden Opportunities Always Look Super." How does that sound to you? I looked at it for a couple of minutes, feeling pretty good about my creativity, until it dawned on me that, even though it sounded pretty good, it just wasn't true.

Golden
Opportunities
Always
Look
Super

Think about it for a moment. The real golden opportunities aren't the ones that always look super. In fact, the opposite is most often true. It is the obstacles and problems, the things that everyone says can't be done that present us with our real golden opportunities. Thus, I marked through the formula I had just made, and came up with the slogan below. You see, whereas pessimists see obstacles as stumbling blocks, optimists see them as stepping stones.

Golden
Opportunities
Appear
Like
Stumbling blocks

History is full of people who have responded to problems with the proper attitude, and demonstrated how truly valuable those problems can be. Consider Wallace Johnson, builder of numerous Holiday Inn motels and convalescent hospitals. He said,

> *When I was forty-years old, I worked in a sawmill. One morning the boss told me, "You're fired!" Depressed and discouraged, I felt like the world had caved in on me. It was during the depression, and my wife and I greatly needed the small wages I had been earning.*

> *When I went home, I told my wife what had happened. She asked, "What are you going to do now?" I replied, "I'm going to mortgage our little home, and go into the building business."*

> *My first venture was the construction of two small buildings. Within five years, I was a multimillionaire!*

Today, if I could locate the man who fired me, I would sincerely thank him for what he did. At the time it happened, I didn't understand why I was fired. Later, I saw that it was God's unerring and wondrous plan to get me into the way of His choosing!

Consider for a moment the benefits of problems. It is trouble that gives a person an opportunity to discover his or her strength — or lack of it. The difficulties of life are intended to make us better — not bitter. When things get rough, remember, it's the rubbing that brings out the shine.

When the Confederate Army retreated after Gettysburg, General Lee wrote to Jefferson Davis a remarkable letter, saying:

We must expect reverses, even defeats. They are sent to teach us wisdom and prudence, to call forth greater energies, and to prevent our falling into greater disasters.

Thomas A. Edison's laboratory was on fire. As he helplessly watched it burn, taking his costly experiment up in flames, he called his son Charles. "Come!" he said. "You'll never see anything like this again!" Then he called his wife. As the three stood gazing, Edison said, "There go all our mistakes. Now we can start over afresh." In two weeks he started rebuilding the lab; shortly thereafter he invented the phonograph.

Obviously Edison had learned the important lesson that much can be gained through troubles, if we will but maintain the proper mental attitude in the face of them. Unfortunately, there are those who have not grasped this lesson.

A young man was trying to establish himself as a peach grower. He had worked hard and invested his all in a peach orchard which blossomed wonderfully — then came a frost. He did not go to church the next Sunday, nor the next, nor the next. His minister went to see him to find the reason. The young fellow exclaimed: "I'm not coming any more. Do you think I can worship a God who cares for me so little that He will let a frost kill all my peaches?"

The old minister looked at him a few moments in silence, then said kindly: "God loves you better than He does your peaches. He knows that while peaches do better without frosts, it is impossible to grow the best men without frosts. His object is to grow men, not peaches."

Yes, God is in the business of growing people. He is much more concerned about building character in lives than he is in handing us everything we desire on a silver platter. In fact, the two never go together. We might learn some things from prosperity, but we learn many more from adversity. Instead of praying for God to change our circumstances, we ought to be praying for Him to help us change to be able to meet and handle those circumstances.

Interestingly enough, while I was in the process of writing this book, my own business caught fire. The two illustrations you've just read encouraged me greatly as I stood in the cold one winter night waiting to see whether my computer store would survive a fire which had been started in an adjoining building. It did not; the business was totally destroyed. I was under-insured by over $200,000! Thomas Edison's words rang loud in my ears. I told others that I couldn't say that the building contained all my mistakes but it contained a lot of them.

I would have gladly risked my life to save some of my personal possessions which were in the store at the time (including my only copy of this manuscript), but was refrained from doing so by policemen who said I'd be arrested if I attempted to do so. As I stood waiting for everything to be destroyed before my eyes, I took consolation in the words of Job who said,

> *The LORD gave, and the LORD hath taken away; blessed be the name of the LORD.* **Job 1:21b (KJV)**

I told others if Job could say that in view of his great losses, I surely could. I knew God could stop the fire if He chose to do so, and if He did not, He must have something better in mind for me. I've learned to trust Him, and even thank Him for the trials.

Additional consolation came from one of my favorite Bible verses — that of **1 Thessalonians 5:18**, which says:

> *In everything give thanks; for this is the will of God in Christ Jesus for you.* (**NKJV**)

This became a favorite of mine during the mid 1980s when I was going through a period of great financial hardship. I had gotten myself into debt to the tune of some $70,000. That seemed like a lot of money, and I wasn't certain just how we'd ever recover. We actually went almost 18 months without heat or hot water during that time. (This was while living near St. Louis, Missouri.) By applying this verse and giving thanks to God for the hard times, I actually did become thankful for them. I often prayed, "Lord, please don't give me a way out of these hard times until I become the person I need to be, and learn the lessons I need to learn. I thank you for these hard times."

An interesting side note here is that I took a cold shower in an unheated room every day during that 18 month period. That includes one day when the temperature outside was 70 degrees below zero (with the chill factor). Often, I would have to thaw the ice in the pipes by using our hair dryer, just to get the ice water to move through the pipes. Talk about an invigorating shower! I'd enter the shower each day saying, "Gene, it's all mind over matter; if you don't have a mind it doesn't matter!" Once I'd showered, and stepped out of the shower to dry, I'd say, "Gene, if you can handle that, you can handle anything this day has to offer." Then I'd go off and have a great day!

Then, as now, I practiced that a person's circumstances should never be allowed to dictate his attitude. I taught motivational seminars while going through those trials, and shared the truth with those to whom I was speaking. I've always felt my trials actually gave me more credibility, rather than detracted from it. I've listened to a number of speakers who talked about "overcoming" when I didn't believe they ever had.

I've often heard it said that one can usually determine the caliber of a man by ascertaining the amount of opposition it takes to discourage him. Because I believe this, I get excited when I realize how I am no longer fazed by the molehills that used to seem like mountains. I get even more excited when I

Let's face it, living life is much like the ride on a roller coaster. Our circumstances are the ups and downs – exciting us one moment and attempting to make us fear devastation the next. We must not allow our attitudes to become affixed to the rails of that roller coaster but, instead, affix them on something much more stable – the promises of God. (see Philippians 4:4-9)

think about the day when today's mountains will seem like molehills. In fact, I really get excited just thinking about the blessings that are going to come out of my present testings.

We can begin to have proper attitudes by understanding that there is a blessing in every testing. It only remains to be seen. In fact, troubles can be seen as precious gifts in wrappings. You might ask, "Is it really possible to have that kind of outlook in the face of troubles?" Without a doubt! In fact, I believe it is a sign of growth and maturity, when we can see the time it takes to positively respond to a negative situation constantly decreasing. After all, what good does it do to blow our stacks or get bent out of shape? The problem has occurred; now solve it!

The following six points constitute a line of reasoning that has proven very healthy for me. There isn't a problem that I've encountered that couldn't be made easier to deal with by considering these points:

- God loves us and cares for us — even more than we care for ourselves.
- Because He loves and cares for us, we can trust Him.
- God gives no small assignments — we're all important to His plan.
- There isn't a single problem God can't turn into an opportunity.
- We should think of God as a BIG GOD able to meet BIG NEEDS.
- We should learn to accept blind alleys as bold challenges.

Another way to look at this is that every minus is filled with pluses. The bigger the minus, the greater number of pluses. Also be forewarned that every plus is filled with minuses. You'll read more about this later.

Face The Problem Head On

Someone once said, "We might as well face our problems. We can't run fast or far enough to get away from them all." If we continue trying to solve problems by sweeping them under the rug, we may end up in the dustpan of civilization. Most people actually spend more time and energy in going around problems than in trying to solve them. The correct angle at which to approach a difficult problem is the **try**-angle. The best time to tackle a minor problem is before it grows up!

There is a lot of talk about stress these days. People are dropping dead from it all the time. It is my opinion that the stress that kills is not primarily the stress that comes from working too hard to solve a problem, but rather the stress that comes from ignoring, or worrying about a problem. If a problem is real, then it must be dealt with. Ignoring it won't make it go away, and neither will worrying over it. Inaction will not change an emotion, but action will! In other words, any problem worth worrying about is a problem worth doing something about.

Expect To Succeed

Charles F. Kettering, the noted scientist and inventor, believed the easiest way to overcome defeat was to ignore completely the possibility of failure.

In an address delivered at Denison University, Kettering told how he had once given a tough assignment to a young research worker at the General Motors laboratory. Just to see how he would react to a difficult problem, Kettering forbade him to examine notes on the subject that were filed in the library. These notes were written by expert research men and contained statistics to prove that the assignment was impossible. The young research worker did not know this, of course, so he went to work with confidence that he would succeed. He did succeed, too. He didn't know the task couldn't be done — so he did it!

The biggest obstacles we will ever encounter are those contained within our own minds. We would all be wise to do what one man did. He was so upset at his own pessimistic attitude that he literally cut the word "can't" out of his dictionary. I am reminded of a story about Igor Sikorsky. When he was a lad of twelve, his parents told him that competent authorities had already proved human flight impossible. Yet Sikorsky went on to build the first helicopter. And in his American plant he posted this sign:

ACCORDING TO RECOGNIZED AEROTECHNICAL TESTS, THE BUMBLEBEE CANNOT FLY BECAUSE OF THE SHAPE AND WEIGHT OF HIS BODY IN RELATION TO THE TOTAL WING AREA. THE BUMBLEBEE DOESN'T KNOW THIS, SO HE GOES AHEAD AND FLIES ANYWAY.

I have a little bumblebee pin I sometimes wear on my lapel to remind me of this story. In fact, I get charged up and motivated when I am told by others that something I'm attempting to do is "impossible."

I'm involved in selling, so I especially appreciate this next story. Norval Hawkins, the first Ford sales manager, used to tell about a car salesman in South Dakota who was "too dumb to be afraid of tradition."

"Back in those days," said Hawkins, "people didn't drive cars in the winter. They put them up on jacks. Consequently, dealers made no car sales. They just about shut up shop for half the year. But one small dealer in South Dakota kept sending in orders right through the winter. I went to see him. He was a big, awkward, gangling,

> *farmer-like youngster who confessed that he just didn't know he wasn't supposed to sell cars in the winter months!"*
>
> *This gave Hawkins an idea. He challenged his dealer organization to keep after winter sales. Now, January is a peak month for motor sales.*

In fact, as I have already mentioned, the fact that an eight-cylinder engine was ever developed was due to the persistent insistence by Henry Ford that it could and would be done!

There may be times when the situation really looks impossible, but it is still better, even in those times, to remain optimistic than to give up. Have you heard the ancient story of "The Flying Horse?" There once was a man who had been sentenced to death by the king. He begged a reprieve, saying he would teach the king's horse to fly by the year's end. He was granted the year and told he would then be put to death if he had not succeeded. Later, when he was asked why he would make such a deal, the man explained: "Within a year the king may die, or I may die, or the horse may die. Furthermore, who knows? Maybe the horse will learn to fly."

What can we learn from that story? First, the man knew he needed to buy time to find a solution. Without it, he was dead. Next, he realized that there were a number of options available to him. If all those failed, he still had others. As one person said, "It's not over until it's over!"

Seek To Understand The Problem

If you can't state your problem in ten minutes or less, you don't understand it yourself. Until you can understand it, you are probably not going to solve it. Charles Kettering said:

> *A problem well stated is a problem half solved.*

The biggest problem we have in stating a problem is in recognizing what the problem really is. In fact, what we usually look at is not the problem at all, but the manifestation of the problem. An example is a headache. The headache might be evaluated to be the problem, when it is really only the manifestation of the problem. The real problem might be an improper diet, stress, or any number of other things. It is not always easy to see the "root" problem.

Whenever we seek to find the source of problems, we tend to look at other people. We will be several steps ahead if we will but look in the mirror. We may not like to face the facts, but we are usually the roots of most of our problems. Actually, we ought to be thankful this is so, because it is certainly easier for us to change ourselves than to change others. I have found it helpful to begin my search for the root cause to my problem by asking the following questions:

- What kind of an attitude have I had toward this person, or situation lately?

- Have I attempted to do my very best in this area, or have I neglected my responsibility?

- Have I sought additional information or have I been satisfied with things as they were?

- Have I been less than thankful?

- What might God be wanting to teach me through this?

- What character quality needs improving as evidenced by my initial response to this problem?

- Have I wronged someone else in this situation?

These are the kinds of questions I ask. They are tough ones, but I have found if I am willing to face up to them, I become a better person for it. I was once told if I could kick the person responsible for most of my problems, I would not be able to sit down for three weeks! These questions can teach me much if I will take the time to concentrate on them. Part of the problem today is that we have a surplus of simple answers and a shortage of simple questions. We spend our time looking for answers when we should begin looking for the right questions.

Obviously, there are problems for which you cannot be blamed: acts of nature, the death of loved ones, the economy, depletion of the ozone, etc. You didn't cause those. I can accept that, but let's look at what you are accountable for — your response to those problems. Those events occur in each of our lives and we can do nothing to change them — we can only accept them. All that I am saying is that we must accept the fact that we are the ones responsible for our own attitudes.

If you want to go to the root of the problem, you must look at who you are. You see, who you are mentally and spiritually determines how well you respond to problems. I cannot expect to respond to a catastrophe in my life with faith in God if I have not cultivated that faith. I cannot expect to withhold my anger when being mistreated if I have not cultivated patience in my life.

Notice, I headed this section by saying you should seek to understand the problem. I didn't necessarily say that you would always be able to understand its source, nor its purpose. In some cases it might be many years before you know why you had to suffer through a particular problem — if ever.

Just recently I heard a story over the radio about a man who was suffering from a rare disease, and needed a blood transfusion from another person who had suffered from, and conquered, the same disease. After a diligent search, another man was found who had been afflicted with the same disease some 15 years earlier. He said he was thankful to give blood, and to finally know part of the reason for his suffering many years ago. His suffering then made it possible for another man, now, to continue living.

Make A List Of Possible Solutions

No matter what the obstacle, there is a solution for it if we will but look. The problem is that most people prefer to complain than to look for solutions. Someone once told me:

Don't tell others your problems because 80% don't care, and the other 20% are glad you have the problem.

Although I don't agree with that statement completely, I find that it is largely accurate. Those who really care about your problems, and want to see you solve them, are very few indeed. If you sit around waiting for someone else to come to your aid, you will waste valuable time, and your hopeless expectations will lead only to disappointment.

If you have a problem in common with someone else, it may be that you can solve it better together. Likewise, a friend can often be counted on to help. However, don't ask a friend if he is willing to help — unless you really want to know. Some people would rather think they have many friends than to test them and find out for sure. This is a delicate matter, and one in which I am certainly no expert. I only ask for help in solving a personal problem when I am at the end of my rope and believe many will suffer if I don't. I also make it a rule not to ask anyone else to do anything for me that I would not be willing to do if the situation were reversed. That demands honesty on my part.

Notice, I used the term "end of my rope" regarding the time when I begin to look elsewhere for help. I seldom get to the end of my rope. Oh, I probably stay pretty close to it because of who I am, but I always know that an answer exists. When I have to ask for help regarding a personal matter, I know it is because I have failed to place into action the proper solution at the proper time.

So, the real question is: "How do I find the solution?" The answer is really quite simple: "Look for it!" Begin by making a list on a piece of paper with the numbers 1 to 25 down the edge. At the top of the paper, write the words "Solutions to *(name of problem)*." Now, begin writing a brief description of possible solutions to your problem beside each of the numbers. Don't attempt to classify or qualify them at this point. Just write the ideas down as they come to you. I am confident if you will force yourself to make it to 25, you will be amazed at the number of great ideas you have come up with. I used to say 10, and 10 may do it — but I am sure 25 will. Now, once you have made your list, attempt to determine which are your five best ideas.

Spend at least one hour developing each of the five ideas. Begin a file on each one of them, if necessary. Allow your mind to run wild as you think of ways which would make each one work. Concentrate on only one at a time. After spending an hour on each one, you should have a pretty good feel for which you think are the best two or three.

Now take the best three to a couple of friends whom you greatly respect and admire. Get their initial reactions to the ideas before you show them the plans you have begun to develop. After receiving their feedback, reveal what you have developed, and see if the three of you agree on the best solution. Work at it until you come to an agreement. Once you agree, return to your study and continue to develop your action plan.

You might find the following list of guidelines helpful in providing direction in dealing with your problem:

- When a crisis develops, take a few minutes to collect your thoughts.
- Don't waste time and energy trying to blame someone for the problem.
- Define the problem in writing.
- Evaluate the seriousness of the problem.
- Decide if it's serious enough to warrant changing your priorities.
- Inform your superiors of the problem, if necessary.
- Inform staff members of the problem.
- Gather information pertaining to the problem.
- Ask staff members to suggest solutions.
- Review past experience with similar problems.
- Decide what kind of action, if any, will alleviate the problem.
- Work out an organized plan to deal with the crisis.
- Assign staff members to handle details of your plan.
- Evaluate the result of your plan.
- Record your solution for future reference.
- Assign someone to develop a plan to prevent the problem from recurring.

Continually Work On Improving You

This may seem like an old story by now but the single most important thing you can do to solve your problems and deal with obstacles and roadblocks is to improve the person you are. After all, you are the one person who cares the most about solving your problems, the person most responsible for them, and the person in the best position to deal with them. You are also the person who will most benefit from the solution, since removing these roadblocks and obstacles will help you.

Self-improvement can begin with a list of character qualities toward which you want to work, for example:

- Alertness
- Compassion
- Confidence
- Courage
- Courtesy
- Creativity
- Decisiveness
- Diligence
- Discernment
- Discipline
- Discretion
- Earnestness
- Efficiency
- Enthusiasm
- Expressiveness
- Fair-mindedness
- Flexibility
- Forgiveness
- Frankness

- Frugality
- Generosity
- Gratefulness
- Honesty
- Hospitality
- Humility
- Loyalty
- Neatness
- Objectivity
- Patience
- Persistence
- Persuasiveness
- Punctuality
- Purposefulness
- Respectfulness
- Resoluteness
- Resourcefulness
- Sensitivity
- Sincerity

Self-improvement can also be accomplished through improving personal skills and attributes, including:

- Communication Skills
- Negotiating Skills
- Speaking Skills
- Vocabulary Skills
- Reading Skills
- Memory Skills
- Appearance
- Time Management Skills

Study The Creative Alternatives

All too often, when we have problems, we also encounter the obstacle of "Pigeon-Hole Thinking," as discussed in the last chapter. The solution to that is to become creative.

As an example, many years ago I wanted to purchase a Kroy Lettering Machine. This is a piece of equipment that places type on a piece of Scotch tape-like material, allowing me then to place that type on paper. It is sort of a poor man's typesetter. Because I was doing a lot of speaking and wanted to make nice-looking handouts and transparencies, I determined that the Kroy machine was the solution. Unfortunately, the machine was $900, and I didn't have the money.

At first, I was creative and solved the problem this way. I went to the dealer and explained to him that I wanted to purchase the Kroy but couldn't afford it at that time. I suggested that I rent one from him for a week for $50, plus the price of the necessary supplies. The benefit for me, of course, was that I could get a lot of work done that should last me for some time, and I could get it done for much less than the $900.00. (In fact, I was able to rent the $2,000+ model for the $50.) The benefit for the dealer was that he was getting paid for a demonstration of his product.

During the week that I had the equipment, I used it to make every conceivable word and phrase I thought I'd need for some time. The work I did lasted me for several months. The day came, however, when I determined I really needed to buy one. I still lacked the necessary funds, so I turned again to creativity to solve my money problem.

First, I found a used Kroy machine in the paper with a lot of extras for $800. By asking questions, I learned that the person selling it needed the money to purchase a particular Radio Shack computer. He said he would be willing to trade the Kroy for a computer. I then found that model computer in the paper for $875. The seller said he couldn't trade it for anything because he needed the money to purchase an IBM PC for his service station. I asked what the IBM PC was going to cost him and he told me the best deal he had been able to arrange was $1,675. Therefore, I asked him if he would be willing to give me the Radio Shack computer and $800 for a new IBM PC. He agreed.

Next, I went to a consultant I knew who sold IBM PCs and told him of my plight. He agreed to give me an IBM PC in exchange for $800 and some advertising in a local magazine. To obtain the ad space for the IBM consultant, I traded a reading course to the magazine publisher for their managers. I then traded the reading instructor sales training in my own course in exchange for his teaching the advertising people.

I'll tell you, it was an exciting moment when I delivered the Radio Shack computer and picked up my Kroy machine! This is an example of what I mean by creative alternatives. I became so excited about this deal that I then set my sights on obtaining an IBM PC for myself. Within a short period of time I had my computer and six or seven other companies had what they wanted. We were all happy.

When you want to buy something, but money is an obstacle, consider renting, leasing, borrowing, trading, or hiring.

Practice Offense And Defense

Several times I have felt that I needed to raise several thousand dollars within the next couple of days. Now, I realize that money is a relevant thing and "several thousand dollars" may seem a lot to you, or it may seem like a drop in the bucket. In my case, it often has seemed like a lot.

When I am faced with such a situation, long-range planning is not in order. Whatever I am going to do, I must do it quickly, and be successful. It was a real benefit to me when I realized the value of considering both offense and defense. I consider offense to be the art of raising the money. Defense, on the other hand, is reducing the need for as much money.

To raise the money, I go on the **offensive**, asking myself these questions:

What do I own that I can immediately sell to bring in some money?
- Look in my closets, garage, shed, etc. for clues.
- I will want to sell something I do not need any longer.
- If I need do it, it must be something I can easily replace.
- If I have to replace it, I will want to do so at low cost.
- I must also think of whom I know that would want to buy the item.
- The offer must be attractive to make the prospect act now.

What skills do I have that I might be willing to pre-sell at a discount?
- What are these skills worth at fair market value?
- Whom do I know that could benefit from these skills?
- Can I make time in the future to provide this service?

What possessions or equipment do I have which could be rented out?
- Whom do I know that could benefit from the use of these?
- Can I do without them from time to time?
- Could a mutually beneficial schedule be worked out?
- What would the value be to my prospect?
- What amount should I ask, allowing for a prepayment discount?

What liquid assets do I possess that I have not yet considered?
- Do I have any account receivables which are collectible?
- Do I have savings? How about bonds?
- Can I borrow quickly on my life insurance policy?

These are some examples of what I refer to as offensive moves. I have been saved from an embarrassing situation more than once by asking myself these questions.

Now for some **defensive** moves. In an attempt to reduce my need for as much money, I asked myself these questions:

Why do I need the money at this time?
- Whose deadline is it anyway?
- Can it be changed?

What alternatives might be acceptable in lieu of cash?

If it is someone else's deadline, is there a reason for it?

What are the real needs involved?

If I am making a purchase with the money, can I get by with less?
- Is it possible to simply purchase an option?
- Is there a layaway plan available?
- Can I receive terms?
- Would the other party accept a nonrefundable deposit?
- Are there other suppliers who will work with me?
- Is this really the best time to make the purchase?
- Can I renegotiate for a lower price?

What are the real consequences if I do not get the money?

Ask Yourselves These Questions

I refer to the following list of questions on a regular basis to provoke my thinking concerning problem-solving and making improvements. Perhaps these questions will assist you as well.

- What do I want to improve?
- What is my objective or goal?
- Why have I not accomplished it already?
- What are the obstacles standing in my way?
- What is the current situation?
- Who or what caused it?

- When, why, where, and how was it caused?
- Who is responsible for solving the problem?
- Who can better solve the problem?
- What benefits are to be gained from solving the problem?
- Who will gain the greatest benefit?
- Are the benefits worth the cost?
- How do I think the problem can best be solved?
- How long should it take to solve the problem?
- Can improvements be made by doing any of the following?
    Increase or decrease size?
    Increase or decrease numbers?
    Increase or decrease speed?
    Increase or decrease weight?
    Increase or decrease softness or hardness?
    Increase safety and decrease danger?
    Increase activity?
    Increase strength?
    Decrease expenses?
    Decrease boredom?
    Decrease failure?
    Improve appearance?
    Improve efficiency?
    Improve quality?
    Reduce rejects?
    Change the shape?
    Change the direction?
    Change an emphasis?
    Change the color?
    Change the location?
    Change personnel?
    Change the schedule?
    Change the price?
    Change the material?
    Change the objective?
    Change the position?
    Change the timing?

Can any of the following changes help?

- Condense?
- Expand?
- Automate?
- Computerize?
- Self regulate?
- Elevate?
- Lower?
- Strengthen?
- Make more quiet?

- Streamline?
- Tighten or loosen?
- Recycle?
- Refine?
- Invert?
- Make more flexible?
- Stiffen?
- Rotate?
- Insulate?

Can improvement be made by doing any of the following?

- Make something more difficult to obtain?
- Make something easier to obtain?
- Divide the workload differently?
- Develop a better marketing strategy?
- Emphasize a different aspect?
- Advertise?
- Make something more — time, labor, or money saving?
- Reduce necessary maintenance?
- Increase necessary maintenance?
- Delegate more selectively?
- Offer training classes?
- Offer greater incentives?
- Promise severe penalties?
- Provide greater organization?
- Identify materials, etc.?
- Use audiovisual equipment?
- Change the measuring stick and method of testing?

While these questions, and lists, are not meant to be all-inclusive, they are representative of the kinds of questions you should be asking. Most of us feel we have all the answers long before we recognize that we do not even have all the questions. The important thing to remember is that questions can help us obtain better answers.

God, the possessor of true wisdom, can also help us obtain better answers, as evidenced by the following verses from the book of Proverbs. God liberally offers us wisdom and insight in dealing with our problems:

Trust in the LORD with all thine heart; and lean not unto thine own understanding. In all thy ways acknowledge him, and he shall direct thy paths. **Proverbs 3:5,6 (KJV)**

Wisdom is the principal thing; therefore get wisdom: and with all thy getting get understanding. **Proverbs 4:7 (KJV)**

My son, attend to my words; incline thine ear unto my sayings. Let them not depart from thine eyes; keep them in the midst of thine heart. For they are life unto those that find them, and health to all their flesh. **Proverbs 4:20-22 (KJV)**

The integrity of the upright shall guide them: but the perverseness of transgressors shall destroy them. **Proverbs 11:3 (KJV)**

Where no counsel is, the people fall: but in the multitude of counsellors there is safety. **Proverbs 11:14 (KJV)**

The way of a fool is right in his own eyes: but he that hearkeneth unto counsel is wise. **Proverbs 12:15 (KJV)**

He that handleth a matter wisely shall find good: and whoso trusteth in the LORD, happy is he. **Proverbs 16:20 (KJV)**

Hear counsel, and receive instruction, that thou mayest be wise in thy latter end. **Proverbs 19:20 (KJV)**

·Ten·
The Action Plan

Dreams, without action plans, are just that — dreams. Until we've developed action plans, it is impossible to be assured that our objectives are meeting the ten requirements for classifying them as "goals." The action plan is simply a blueprint or map that shows how to get from where you are to where you want to be.

How Does One Develop An Action Plan?

As you begin to develop an action plan, you must realize that planning takes time. It may take days, weeks, or even months to develop some action plans. For example, think about the time it must have taken to develop the plan that put Neil Armstrong on the moon. It actually took hundreds of man-years! The plan to build the Empire State Building took many people several years to develop. The time you spend in planning reaps large dividends by reducing the time and other resources needed for execution. It may mean the difference between success or failure. The time necessary to develop your plan depends upon a number of factors:

1) How familiar are you with the problem itself?
2) Have you dealt effectively with this or similar problems before?
3) How important is the project or goal?
4) Who else has been successful accomplishing this task? Is their research and knowledge available?

One thing to remember as you develop your plan is that direction is more important than speed. All too often someone heads off in a wrong direction at a fast rate of speed only to find himself worse off than when he began. It behooves us to put our plan together with correct information.

An action plan should include the following:

- The goal, clearly stated
- A list of the benefits you expect to receive
- A list of the obstacles you expect to encounter
- A list of the possible solutions to those obstacles
- A list of the resources you have and will need
- A schedule of deadlines for the manageable parts or subgoals
- A listing of consequences and rewards should you fail or succeed

Some goals require a more detailed plan than others. A goal to visit an out-of-town friend for the weekend, for example, might only take five minutes and one sheet of paper to plan. A plan to design and build a new house on a three-acre plot within five years might easily take several months and a hundred sheets of paper to complete.

The amount of research necessary will also vary. A phone call to your friend might provide you with all the information you need to put the first plan together. The plan for the house, on the other hand, could require that you view dozens of model homes, making note of the features you really like. You might also need to research neighborhoods to decide in which area you want to live (considering your shopping, schooling, and church needs). You'll want to research contractors to find a good one, and price materials to determine the cost of everything. Then, of course, you'll have to develop a plan to pay for it all. That may require researching additional income opportunities.

To illustrate how to develop an action plan, I'll discuss three goals I've tackled myself. These goals were:

1) Immediately increase my monthly income from $2,000 to $6,500

2) Lose 52 pounds in 89 days

3) Take a family trip around the United States

4) Step 8,000 steps in less than 50 minutes

Goal – Increase Monthly Income *From $2,000 to 6,500*

This was the single most important event to occur among my goal setting experiences, as it taught me the value of developing a good, solid action plan. I have made reference to it in an earlier chapter so I will just review it here.

The date was July 31, 1981, and it was time for a serious evaluation of my annual income goal. Seven months were gone, and for all practical purposes, only four remained. My goal was to earn $40,000, and I had earned only a little over $14,000 to date.

It was quite obvious that something had to be done. I needed either to lower my goal, or improve my plan to make the goal a realistic one. I had been earning only $2,000 per month, and needed to average $6,500 for the next four months to make it. The product I was selling could not be expected to produce an income for me in the month of December.

After giving it some serious thought, I asked myself the question, "Do you still want to earn $40,000 this year?" "Sure!" was my reply. I snapped back, "Well, you had better get to work on a better plan!" This internal discussion motivated me to start working on a better plan that night about bedtime. In fact, this motivation to come up with a better plan kept me up all night.

When I finally retired to bed at 6:00 A.M., I said to myself, "Gene, that was eight of the most profitable hours you have ever spent. It's like money in the bank; no question about it!" Yes, I had come up with a plan that I was very pleased with. I knew that all that remained now was simply to walk through the plan.

For the next four months I did exactly that — simply followed my blueprint to the letter. I earned $29,000 in those four months, and finished the year having earned more than $43,000. On the last day of October, I calculated

I had earned $11,900 in one month! I realized that if I had to work that hard for $11,900 every month, it would not be worth it. I would not work that hard for $140,000 per year. However, it had been worth it for that one month. I was well on my way to accomplishing my goal.

But something far more important had happened. I had become a believer in the value of taking the time to develop a proper plan to realize my goals. I had learned that goal setting without the proper planning is only wishful thinking.

Now, whenever I am tempted to become discouraged about realizing a particular goal, I remember that incident. I also remember the quote from Robert Schuller, "People don't have money problems, they have idea problems." My problem is not that I don't have the time, money, manpower, prospects, or resources to meet some need; I just haven't come up with the right idea yet.

I'll not attempt to rewrite or duplicate the plan I developed that night. Quite frankly, I don't remember the specifics that well. I do recall that I simply evaluated those activities which had rewarded me most, and I increased them while reducing those activities that had rewarded me least. In one night, I planned four months worth of work. I planned my work and then over the next four months I worked my plan. It served me well!

Goal – Lose 52 Pounds In 89 Days

Perhaps you also have a goal to lose weight. If so, you might find my experience in this area particularly helpful.

Let's face it; losing weight is hard to do. (By conservative estimates, more than one-third of the adult population in America is overweight.) There are literally hundreds of diets, and thousands of people attest to having tried them — most without achieving any real success. Many of these self-proclaimed "professional" dieters would acknowledge that they are fighting a losing battle. They are worse off today than they were years ago when they first began dieting. Not only are they heavier, they are far more discouraged.

Some, in fact, are so discouraged that they have given up hope of ever winning the battle — they hope merely to maintain the status quo.

While I do not claim to be an expert concerning proper eating habits, nor concerning the best ways to exercise, I do believe I know a lot about the subject of losing weight. I can testify to having lost over 400 pounds. Now, I realize you might be trying to picture me weighing 400 pounds more than I do today. Notice that I did not say I ever weighed 500 or more pounds at any one time. In fact, my top weight has been 224 pounds — at least 50 pounds overweight for my height. On numerous occasions, I have lost 30 or more pounds.

At times I even kidded myself that I was not overweight — I was just too short. However, I have always known it is easier for me to lose weight than to grow taller. Thus, whenever I become too heavy and decide to do something about it, I develop a plan of action to assure myself of taking the weight off. I have found it fairly easy to lose weight by developing a good action plan, and then focusing my attention on sticking to it.

While a large percentage of the American population needs to lose weight, many who don't need to lose weight believe the answer to be a very simple one. They say it's simply a matter of "will power." They often look at overweight people as being obese slobs without any self-control. I suspect that it gives some a sense of pride and superiority to think that they do not fall into that category. However, the truth is that we all have areas in our lives on which we need to focus. I, personally, would far rather have to work hard at bringing my eating habits into check than to have to constantly work to cover up my immoral habits.

I know there are some of you who are reading this book who can say that your weight has remained completely stable for 20 or more years. Good for you! You find it hard to imagine someone who could gain and lose 30 or more pounds every 18 months. I've had some suggest that I not include this personal information in the book as it might destroy my credibility in the eyes of others. Some readers might, they suggest, decide to ignore this material because I've never set and achieved a goal of maintaining my body weight within an acceptable range. I'm including it, anyway, because it's the truth, and it is not necessarily something of which I'm ashamed. Someday, I will determine to set my goal and my focus on keeping the weight off, and I'll do it.

You also might think this section will be of little value to you because you never expect to have a weight problem. I suggest you continue reading, however, because you'll find the ideas presented herein can prove beneficial when applied to developing an action plan for any area of your life.

The issue of having self-control is much more complex than simply having enough will power. Though we will later discuss the concept of self-control in greater detail, for now let it suffice to say that we need good action plans to deal with the urges that often control us.

It's only when I decide on a plan that I'm convinced will work, and commit myself to it, that I get anywhere. Without this plan and commitment, I allow the emotions of the moment to dictate what I'll do. Someone offers me ice cream and cake, a girl behind the counter asks if I want french fries, or I am offered free soda and donuts to start off a morning meeting — it always happens! If I'm committed to a plan, the decision is easy — I simply say "No, thank you." However, if my plan is simply to watch what I eat today, I'll probably accept whatever is offered, and determine to compensate for it later. We all have the ability to rationalize and justify doing whatever we want to at any given moment, don't we?

In developing an action plan to lose weight, one of the first things we must do is attempt to ascertain the reason or reasons for being overweight. Some of the more common reasons include the following:

- A change in the level of exercise or activity
- Age — the metabolism of our bodies change as we get older
- A chemical malfunction or imbalance in our body glands
- A change in other areas of our lives which prompts increased eating because of nervousness
- A life-style which encourages negative eating habits
- A lack of focus concerning what, when, and how much we eat
- A sweet tooth — the inability to say "no" to certain foods

- A poor self-image — we see ourselves as being "fat" and feel we are trapped in that mold
- We don't care — being overweight is the least of our problems
- We are attempting to use it to frustrate someone else (sort of like cutting off our noses to spite our faces)

Once we've discovered the reasons for our weight problems, we are in a better position to do something about them. We have the same advantage as a military unit which knows in advance the direction of their enemy's attack. We must now figure out if our situation must be changed, or if we must change to cope with them. We are in the best position to know what can be done, and what we are willing to commit to doing. It doesn't make any sense to put together a plan which we aren't willing to keep.

We've all heard the phrase, "Different strokes for different folks." While I will agree it's true that different people prefer to do things differently, I'll say there are both easy and difficult ways to do something. I happen to believe it is much easier to accept the "all or nothing" method. In other words, I think it is much easier to quit smoking by going "cold turkey" than it is to cut down a little at a time. Habits are much more difficult to change, or abandon, when compromise is allowed.

I recognize we live in a world that places a lot of demands on us to compromise. Very little is sacred anymore. The problem exists when we fail to draw lines over which we refuse to cross — or we draw the lines in the wrong places. If we fail to draw the lines, living itself becomes a real chore. We find ourselves having to make so many choices each day, and most of the time we take the easy way out and "go with the flow." The trouble is that the flow is usually going in the wrong direction and we lose ground. If we have drawn our lines in the wrong places, we are constantly fighting tremendous pressure to move or cross over them. When we do, we often feel guilty and lose both confidence and self-esteem. Unless we can acknowledge the compromise as a positive decision, we'll feel that we've failed miserably and ought to abandon ship.

One should, instead, look at one's goal as a balloon, and the activities which will help one to accomplish his goal as the string. One can view the temptations to deviate from his determined course of action as straight pins which will puncture our balloon. Making this practical, let me suggest the following.

Let's say you are 50 pounds overweight. You've ascertained the reasons for this situation and have developed a plan of action to correct them. You can visualize (possibly from your old pictures, or pictures of models) what you'll look like when you lose your weight. You have determined your obstacles, among which are your sweet tooth and many friends who encourage you to satisfy it.

In your action plan, you determine to say "no" to all foods and desserts which contain fat or sugar. The next morning, in a business meeting, someone places a box of donuts in front of you on the conference table. (This always happens to me on my first morning after determining to abstain.) You make it easy to say "no" by looking at it from an "either/or" viewpoint. You visualize the "you" which you desire to become and say to yourself that you can either become that person, or you can have the donut. See the donut as the pin which will pop your balloon. If you reason that you can have both, the donut and the new you, you will probably never make it. Today, it will be donuts which puncture your balloon, and tomorrow it will be chocolate cake, strawberry sundae, etc.

It's easy to do just about anything once you have your "mind set." Remember: "Whether you think you can, or you think you can't, you are right!" If you can develop an action plan so good that you can see the accomplishment of your goal as a simple matter of following your "blueprint for success," you will find it infinitely easier to stay on track.

You might ask, "What happens if I fail?" The answer is simple — start over. Realize that your balloon has been popped, and you must begin once again by blowing it up. The book of Proverbs teaches that "a just man falls seven times and gets up again." Falling down doesn't make you a failure — staying down does. When you fall down, get back up again. Try to determine why you fell, and what you can do to avoid a repeat performance.

It is extremely important that you develop a plan that you can live with. Part of this plan may include habits you wish to develop that will help to maintain your desired weight the rest of your life. Excess weight is one of those pesky little things in life that just keep sneaking up on some of us. Without paying much attention, I can easily gain about two to three pounds per month. That may not sound like much, but it can add up quickly over a year's time. The reason it doesn't seem like much to me is I've proven to myself time and time again how easy it is to take off two or three pounds.

On January 1, 1990, I decided to set a goal to lose 52 pounds by March 31 — 89 days away. Over the previous three or so years I'd spent a lot of time sitting at my desk in my computer store, with very little exercise, and had become quite overweight.

There was little or no pressure on me to lose weight, as my self-image remained healthy. Because I had so many exciting things going on, and had just lived the best year of my life (up to that point), I remained very positive about who I was. It was only when I would look in the mirror that I'd say, "Gene, you need to lose weight!"

At any rate, I determined the first quarter of a new year would be a great time to get the weight off. I've always known I can take it off when I purpose to do so; it's just the getting started and focused that's tough. Since I seem to get extra excited about my goals when I begin a new year, I challenged myself to "go for it!"

It wasn't until later that day, as I was watching a football game on television, that I figured out how I'd begin losing weight. I watched as a well-known baseball manager advertised the benefits of a particular liquid diet drink, I decided to begin with that. My plan was basically simple. I'd have two diet drink meals each day and then top the day off with a reasonable dinner.

I decided that since March 31 fell on a Saturday, and I had almost 13 weeks to lose my weight, I'd break the goal into weekly subgoals of four pounds each. The first week would be a five-day week (which was fine since it is usually easier to lose the first pounds anyway). I mapped out my strategy, determined to do whatever was necessary to be on target each Saturday morning when I awoke.

Perhaps you've heard the joke about the person who went on a 30-day diet and lost a month. Well, I didn't want that to happen to me. I decided to pull out all the stops and make this goal a "do or die" goal. Whenever I get really serious and expect a tough time, I apply the Penalty Principle to my goal. I decided to write a contract agreeing to give my most prized possessions, my personal computer equipment valued at $25,000, to an organization to which I am diametrically opposed. I chose my personal computer equipment because I knew keeping it meant more to me than even eating.

Once I signed the contract, I told everyone close to me about my goal — including the 86 people attending a goal seminar I taught that following Saturday. These people were also diametrically opposed to the same organization and seemed concerned about my goal. They didn't want me to give the equipment to the organization, and they didn't know me well enough to know if I would succeed at losing the weight. My plan seemed quite drastic and very risky to many of them.

Some didn't think I could achieve the goal, and some figured I'd probably compromise if I got close to my desired weight and failed. They couldn't see themselves handing over $25,000 worth of equipment just because they missed success by a small amount. They just didn't know me well enough. You see, I knew I'd give the equipment away if I failed, even by half a pound. It was this knowledge that drove me to success!

Let me add a word of caution here. I don't normally recommend that the Penalty Principle be used to guarantee results. Instead, I believe it should be tied directly to the actions which are believed to produce the results. In my case, I knew I could lose the weight and wanted it badly enough that I was willing to do whatever was necessary. I was willing to risk my most valuable possessions to achieve my goal of losing the weight.

There are several parts to an action plan. I'll continue using my goal of losing weight as an example to describe what a plan looks like. First, the goal must be stated in specific measurable terms. My goal was:

Goal: Lose 52 Pounds In 89 Days

Action Statement

I must focus on eating the proper foods, in the proper amounts, at the proper times, combine this with an adequate amount of daily exercise, and drink plenty of water.

Benefits

- Better health
- Increased energy
- Improved self-image
- Enlarged wardrobe
- Compliments from others
- Encouragement to others
- Greater credibility
- More confidence
- Longer life
- Treating my body like the "temple" God says it is

Obstacles

1) Busy schedule — Often I feel I'm too busy to take the time to eat properly. Fast food restaurants do so well for that very reason. It is extremely difficult to eat properly at these fast food places. Two factors which are affected by a busy schedule are eating the proper foods, and eating them at the proper times. Both aspects are important.

2) Desire for bad foods — Oh, those cravings! Sometimes it just becomes so difficult to ignore them, doesn't it? It's especially difficult to say "no" to something when everyone else is having some, and it's free!

3) Awkward situations—These are situations which cannot easily be avoided. They cannot be dealt with in a plan because they happen so infrequently, and usually without warning.

The day after I began my last diet, my son purchased an ice cream bar from an ice cream truck. He and I had just been in an argument and, as a peace offering, he bought me an ice cream also. He didn't think about my diet and my desire to refrain from sweets and fats, things ice cream is loaded with. How could I refuse? Under these conditions, I couldn't. I just said "thank you" and determined to do additional exercise to counteract my infraction.

4) Friends and family pressures — Did you ever notice how often you get invited to lunch or dinner once you've begun a diet? It never fails for me.

5) Bad eating habits — My bad eating habits include eating the wrong foods, at the wrong time, in the wrong amounts.

Solutions

1) Keep daily records.
2) Make a strong commitment.
3) Maintain focus — concentrate.
4) Develop a track to stay on.

Consequences If I Should Fail

1) I will penalize myself $25,000.
2) Loss of all benefits.

Investment Required

Time - for exercise (4 times weekly /1.5 hrs. minimum)

Schedule Of Manageable Parts (Subgoals)

1) Four pounds per week for 13 weeks (weigh every Saturday)
2) I will do whatever is necessary weekly to be on schedule

Specific Actions

My plan simply included adding to my daily activity the following:

3) Three proper meals
4) Eight glasses of water
5) Deliberate exercise

I eliminated the following from my daily routine: carbonated or sweetened beverages, foods fried in grease, foods containing a high content of fat (butter, ice cream, etc.), or a high content of sugar.

I made these notes to myself to review regularly:

- Realize that I will not starve to death. Most people can go 50 days before they die. True hunger pains won't appear until the fortieth day. The uncomfortable feeling I will get will be my appetite rebelling against my choices.

- I'll design my own diet and change it as necessary. When I've designed my own diet, I have nothing to rebel against and no reason to cheat.

- I'll keep my metabolic rate up. I can do this by eating something early, and regularly, and exercising early each day.

- I'll conquer cravings by focusing on that which I most desire (a thinner me).

- If I must have food, I'll eat a carrot stick, or something equally non-threatening.

- If I really get weak, I'll eat a few bites of that which I desire and then get on with life.

- I'll keep accurate daily records, recording everything I eat and my weight each morning when I awake.

- I'll make the necessary adjustments in my plan as the week comes to an end. To realize my weekly goal, I will ensure that I get the necessary quantity and type of both food and exercise.

These are all things I believed I could live with, was willing to commit to, and could gladly accept as a trade-off to become the person I wanted to become.

The Results

My plan worked, just as I knew it would. I weighed daily and adjusted my eating and exercise accordingly so I'd be on target every Saturday morning. As the weeks wore on, the intake of food decreased only slightly but the amount and intensity of exercise increased greatly. My heartbeat rate improved to the point where it was only 112 after climbing over 8,000 steps in one hour on a step-climbing exercise apparatus. I actually needed to lose eight pounds on my last day. In fact, I lost 8 3/4 pounds with six hours of exercise (three in the early morning and three that night). I spent the last week of March on vacation, but exercised three hours every day anyway. It wasn't easy, but I didn't expect it would be.

One will always encounter plateaus when trying to remove excess weight. The real issue is to focus on the daily activity that will get you to the desired end result. Don't try to mentally take on a month's worth of challenge in one day. It will become discouraging and too overwhelming. You will quit.

Be prepared for the obstacles. Even if you have never noticed them before, once you have committed to a plan, you will be surprised at the number of television commercials or roadside billboards encouraging you to (over)eat. If your friends seldom invite you to their parties, or out to eat, they will now. If you never have been invited to go on a cruise (next week, and free!), you may now. Encouraging, however, is the knowledge that you can easily build the habit of saying "no" once you begin. Most things in life are easy — once you have conquered them in your own mind. This is especially true of losing weight.

Goal – Travel Around The United States

The last goal I'll discuss is a 1990 goal I had to travel with my family around the United States in four weeks. I had always thought it would be great to take such a trip with my children before they flew the coop, so to speak. Kimberly was 15 years old and Joel was 14. My family had never taken a vacation of any kind when I was a child, and this was one of those kinds of vacations I used to dream about back then.

Without going into a lot of detail, suffice it to say that I carefully planned the trip from start to finish. I figured we would drive approximately 9,500 miles in 26 days and the total cost of the trip would be approximately $5,000. Using an atlas, I planned every stop while making sure we would have time to see all the sights we really wanted to. My primary disappointment was that we would not have the time to drive to Alaska.

I evaluated the trip as follows:

Benefits

1) Good overview of the U.S.A.
2) Close time with the family
3) Opportunity to see old friends in other states
4) Opportunity to make some business calls in major cities

Obstacles

1) Busy schedule
2) Automobile too small
3) Fatigue
4) Inadequate finances

Solutions

1) Hire someone to cover for me
2) Block schedule for trip early

3) Buy or rent a custom van
4) Plan rest along the way
5) Plan easy days after hard days

Consequences If I Should Fail

1) Disappointment

Investment Required

1) $5,000
2) 4 weeks of time

In discussing the plan I had written, Saundra and I agreed that we were not too excited about the prospect of sharing all that driving in such a short time. My plan included 13 days of driving distances of 450 miles to 750 miles. After much discussion, we decided to postpone the trip until 1994, after which both of our teenagers would have received their driver's licenses. They would be only too happy to help share the driving. We also decided to plan a six-week trip which also included Alaska. We could take our van on a cruise from Vancouver into Alaska and drive back down through Alaska during the additional two weeks.

The cost of this new plan rose to $12,500. We figured it would be easy enough to raise the extra $7,500, as we would have an additional four years to do so. In discussing this new trip, we figured the "price" required (time, energy, and dollars) would be more worthwhile than the lower amount required for the proposed 1990 trip.

In this case, developing an action plan helped me to realize my goal was not worthwhile to Saundra and me. It could meet nine of the ten requirements but this tenth one was quite important. It was far better for us to realize it during the planning stage than to wait until the execution stage. Don't you agree?

Later, when discussing this "Super Trip" with my teenagers, I learned that they were not at all excited about being gone six weeks. After much discussion, we decided to shelve the trip and take a much shorter one. Perhaps Saundra and I will take this longer trip once the kids have left home.

Goal – Step 8,000 Steps in Less Than 50 Minutes

Perhaps, no other short-ranged goal I've tackled presented me with as much challenge and excitement as this one. It may have been because I was 43-years old and about 30-pounds overweight that I considered it as such.

I was attending a local health club where I have a lifetime membership. My primary purpose for attending was to beat my body into shape, so to speak. I evaluated that the quickest way to burn calories was on the stair-stepping equipment, called the "LifeStep." No other piece of exercise equipment that I know of compares.

This piece of computerized exercise equipment makes a mundane exercise like stair-stepping more interesting. It offers 12 different levels of exercise, each one a little more difficult than the previous one. Level 12 demands that the stepper maintain a speed of 20 floors (160 steps) per minute. It records a running total of the floors climbed, time elapsed, and calories burned. Thus, if a person can begin and continue at that pace for 50 minutes, he will take 8,000 steps in 50 minutes. (The equipment actually shuts itself down after 999 floors, or 60 minutes, whichever occurs first.) To accomplish my goal, I simply continue stepping for another 8 steps in the following 3 seconds after it shuts down.

When I set the goal to go 8,000 steps in less than 50 minutes, I had been exercising on the equipment for about three weeks. I had just accomplished doing the 8,000 steps in less than 60 minutes. When I first set my sights on doing it in less than 50 minutes, I wasn't even sure it would be possible. I knew the LifeStep could record it but wasn't sure my body could perform the task.

I made the commitment to do it and told many of my friends and employees about it. As is often the case, I figured my becoming accountable to them would challenge me all the more. A couple of my employees had tried using the LifeStep and, therefore, knew my goal would not be an easy one.

The action plan for this goal was really quite simple. I exercised on Monday, Wednesday, and Friday mornings at 6:00 A.M. The LifeStep was always my first event because I knew I would need all my strength to accomplish my goal. Knowing that I must begin stepping immediately at the 20-floor per minute pace and maintain it for the full 50 minutes, I decided to get my body used to the pace (100 floors every 5 minutes). My plan was to begin by doing 200 floors on the first day in less than 10 minutes and increase the total by 100 floors each day I exercised. If I could do this, I would accomplish my goal in less than three weeks.

I managed to meet my subgoals each day, although each one seemed to take every ounce of energy I had. I literally staggered away from the machine after each subgoal was met, wondering if I would be able to increase my total by 100 floors the next time. On the seventh day, when I did 800 floors, I knew that the next time I stepped onto the machine would be the day I would go for the goal! There would be no way that I would allow myself to endure the pain for some 45 minutes without gutting it out for another five. Although I was totally exhausted after only 800 floors, I could not get excited about doing those 800 again in order to get to the point where I could go for only 900.

When I arose that Wednesday morning, I was more than excited. While I never looked forward to walking up to that LifeStep and pushing the button to "Begin," all I could envision was the finish line. I approached the LifeStep that morning with a vengeance. When "the smoke had cleared" I had stepped the 1,000 floors in 49:53. I was still 43, some 20-pounds overweight, and still alive! Sure, I felt like I was dying, but I have never felt more alive! I had accomplished what I believe very few can.

In fact, one of my much younger employees made a statement that he felt he could match or beat my personal record. He had been working out at the club as well, and was acquainted with the equipment, having used it for 10 to 15 minutes each time. I offered him a $1,000 bonus if he could beat my goal in less than 60 days. He gave it a valiant attempt but gave up after six weeks.

While this goal required tremendous effort and determination, the obstacles were very few. Other than having to get out of bed at 5:30 A.M. and dealing with my own negative attitude while driving to the club, there were none.

Include These Steps In Your Action Plan

The ideas contained within this chapter can work for you whether you are attempting to lose weight, quit smoking, learn a subject, or achieve any goal you really desire. If you take the time to develop an excellent plan of action, and dedicate yourself daily to sticking to it, you will arrive at your destination. Goal setting is a fantastic tool which will greatly assist you in becoming the person you wish to be. A goal without a plan to bring it to pass, however, is not a goal at all, but only wishful thinking.

Establish "Fail Safe" And "Stopgap" Measures

Perhaps you saw the 1964 movie *Fail Safe*, starring Henry Fonda. I must have seen it more than 20 years ago, but its message has stuck with me. It was about a military jet loaded with nuclear explosives that, due to a computer malfunction, was given the special assignment to bomb Moscow. Several protective measures were taken to assure that the mission would be fail-safe. In other words, it was supposed to be impossible for the mission to fail.

The problem in this case: something went wrong! The assignment was mistakenly given and, because of all the fail-safe measures that had been implemented, could not be recalled. Nothing could be done to abort the mission. While the fail-safe measures had worked to assure that the mission would be accomplished, a disaster had occurred because too little protection had been implemented to prohibit a mistaken assignment.

In order to install "fail safe" measures into our action plans, we must first determine what the potential dangers are that could foil successful completion of our goals.

Here's an example. Let's say I have a goal to travel around the United States this summer in a rented motorhome. I have serious concerns over reliability and safety. I'm concerned that a breakdown could cost a great deal of valuable time, as well as being a considerable inconvenience. I expect to be visiting and staying in some pretty remote areas, and the thought of walking several miles for assistance doesn't excite me too much either.

Applying the fail safe principle, I might want to first make sure to rent the motorhome from a nationwide company that guarantees quick replacement, rather than from a mom-and-pop operation with little or no repair assistance.

Oh, they might agree to reimburse me for expenses, but that is a small comfort when the repair takes several days. Second, I would want to negotiate for a particular low-mileage vehicle. Third, I could take along a small motorcycle, strapped to the back, in case I am stranded in a remote area. Another option is to carry a CB radio on board. There are a number of things which can be done to make the trip more "fail safe."

I've applied this idea to assist me in maintaining my weight. Most of us have clothes in our wardrobes which will allow us to go up or down approximately ten pounds before we have either to do something about our weight or buy more clothes. The last time I was at my desired weight, I purchased many expensive suits that fit perfectly, and had all my other suits altered to fit best at that weight. I then purposed not to purchase suits at a bigger size. As I had to wear suits daily, I considered this a fail-safe measure. It would have been, had I not changed to an occupation which no longer required me to wear suits. It was also one which required me to sit at a desk all day, and therefore, my amount of exercise was reduced, increasing my tendency to gain weight. The idea, coupled with my determination to refrain from purchasing larger suits, did eventually help motivate me to lose the weight once I needed to wear the suits again.

As the film *Fail Safe* shows, we should always realize that few plans, if any, can be totally fail safe. We've all heard about the best laid plans of mice and men. This fact doesn't mean we shouldn't attempt to make our plans fail safe; it simply means that we shouldn't be too devastated when problems we hadn't thought about occur. The best thing to do for such events is to remain confident that we'll be able to make whatever decisions are necessary at those times.

Perhaps you'll think of a stopgap measure. A "stopgap" measure is a measure taken to stop a problem in its tracks. *Random House Dictionary of the English Language* (1969, unabridged) defines it as "something that fills the place of something else that is lacking." *Webster's New World Dictionary of the*

American Language defines it as "a person or thing serving as a temporary substitute."

It is a "Plan B" to be implemented if "Plan A" fails. For example, a backup generator would be a stopgap in case the electricity goes out at a hospital. I have a standby battery power unit that has served as a stopgap for my computers on several occasions when the power went down for a few seconds.

Unbelievably, my stopgap standby battery power unit worked just as I was typing the word "seconds" in the preceding paragraph. I hadn't needed it for a few months. Had it not worked, I would have lost everything I had typed since last saving my work. I would have had to rewrite the last several pages! That is something I never enjoy doing — recreating something I've just written. Once I had to recreate over four hours of writing, beginning at 2:00 A.M.! It was times like that which motivated me to purchase my battery backups.

It's always a good idea to have a "Plan B," and often a good idea to have a "Plan C," depending on how important the project is. Often, in planning the various options, you will decide that one of the options is actually a better plan than "Plan A." It might actually be wise to switch the two and make "Plan A" your "Plan B."

Have A Proper Monitoring And Measuring System

The ability to properly measure your progress, and determine that which must yet be accomplished is extremely important. It is important for the following reasons:

1) Early adjustments can prevent the need for major adjustments later.
2) An improper evaluation can cause great discouragement.
3) Only losers don't keep score.

Let me explain. If we were flying in a spaceship to the moon and were off only three degrees after takeoff, we could easily adjust our course and get back on track. If, however, we waited until much later to check our progress, the necessary adjustment would be much greater. In addition, the fact that we had waited might have added thousands of miles to our journey—thus jeopardizing the entire trip. There might not be sufficient resources to recover.

If we determined that we needed to reach our destination (the moon) by our deadline, we would carefully calculate the distance we must travel each day. Let's say we were supposed to travel 20,000 miles per day. If after one day, however, we had only traveled 14,000 miles, it would be improper to attempt to make it all up the next day. Increasing our speed by that amount might blow our engines. The proper way to make the adjustment would be to divide the number of days remaining into the miles remaining. Thus, the new daily objective might only be 22,000 miles per day instead of 26,000 miles the next day.

While this might seem obvious, it is often overlooked. I've seen many salespeople become discouraged by improperly setting their weekly goals. If they needed to sell $500,000 of product in a year, their initial goal would be $10,000 per week (figuring a 50-week year, with two weeks off for vacation). If after one week, they had only sold $4,000 of product, they would set their goal for the following week at $16,000 in order to get back on track. Let's say during that second week, they only sold $7,000. Using their method of adjustment, their goal for week three would be $19,000. You can see how discouraging this might become. A discouraged salesperson is not too productive.

Annual Goal is $500,000

Weeks to Go	$ To Go	Goal	Actual Sales
50	$500,000	$10,000	$4,000
49	$496,000	$16,000	$7,000
48	489,000	19,000	$?

Using the method I propose, our salesperson would simply divide the amount of sales yet to make ($489,000) by the number of weeks yet remaining to work that year (48) and set his or her next week's goal at $10,188. That's a lot more realistic than $19,000! It is also highly probable that the salesperson will continue to grow and improve as the weeks go by, and sales will increase as a natural result.

Annual Goal is $500,000

Weeks to Go	$ To Go	Goal	Actual Sales
50	$500,000	$10,000	$4,000
49	$496,000	$10,122	$7,000
48	$489,000	$10,188	$?

As I've mentioned before, "only losers don't keep score." When a person doesn't keep score, he or she is almost certain to fail—unless the goal was set way too low in the first place. While there are exceptions, the rule generally holds true. The score, or evaluation, provides both insight and incentive. It provides insight as to how well the action plan is working, and insight as to whether or not changes are necessary.

Break Difficult Tasks Down Into Manageable Steps

Perhaps you've heard the question, "How does one eat an elephant?" The answer is, of course, "One bite at a time."

All too often, our goals look like that elephant and we sit with our forks contemplating just where to begin. The subtitle of this book refers to our goals as mountains and, indeed, some are. Mountains are usually best turned into molehills "one shovel at a time."

Years ago, when I lived on a hill, I used to jog or run three to five miles regularly. It didn't matter which direction I ran — I had a hill to climb in order to arrive at the finish line. Hills that are easy for a car can still seem like mountains to a runner.

In order to make it up the hill, I would begin at the bottom counting cadence to myself. As my left foot would hit the pavement, I would count. Left steps would be 1-2-3-4 and so forth. I would soon tire and change my count to 1-2, 1-2 as I could only project two steps at a time. When I really felt the need to stop and walk, I would reduce the count to one step, one step, and so on. There was never a time when I wasn't able to "one-step" it right over the top of the hill. I could always talk myself into "one more step" until I made it.

Often, that is what you must do in your action plan — break the activity into manageable parts. Any task can become a "piece of cake" if it is broken down

small enough. Once again I'll repeat the saying,

It may be a trial by the mile, and hard by the yard, but it is a cinch by the inch.

Summary

I've written this chapter to give you an idea how to put an action plan together. The action plan is to your goal what a blueprint is to the construction of a building. Without a proper action plan, your chances of succeeding in the accomplishment of your goal are reduced greatly. It does take both time and effort to develop an action plan but, the investment is well worth it.

·*Eleven*·
Proper Perspectives

Things aren't always as they seem. Two people can look at the same thing from different perspectives and the result might be two opposing perceptions. Our perspectives are determined by a number of factors, some of which include:

1) Who we are (our experiences, values, and understanding)
2) Our current situations (circumstances can cloud perception)
3) Our attitudes (we often see only what we want to see)
4) Influences (others use their perspectives to influence ours)
5) Our goals (single-mindedness often reduces perspective)
6) Tradition (helps to develop "pigeonhole" thinking)

The way you see things definitely affects the way you live and act. Just as you cannot consistently act in a manner that is inconsistent with the way you see yourself, neither can you act in the proper manner if your perspective is not proper.

Consider these three points concerning forming a perspective:

1) **What we see is probably what we'll get**. We tend to get what we expect to get. If we have improper perceptions, we'll probably get improper results.

2) **Sincerity is no substitute for accuracy**. Many a person has done that which he thought was right, only to find himself in serious trouble. Ensure that your perspective is based upon facts, not feelings.

3) **How we look determines what we see.** Do we look with open minds, willing to ask questions before we jump to conclusions? Or, do we accept that which we've always believed without even giving it a second thought?

If you adopt proper perspectives, you will find reaching your goals much easier. If, however, you fail to do so, you will suffer for it. Truth is that way. Apply it to your life and it will treat you well; ignore it and it will prove itself.

Nothin's Easy

Chapter seven was devoted to this first perspective. I considered it necessary to present it to you earlier, before the chapter on Obstacles and Roadblocks. It bears repeating here, however, in this important chapter on Proper Perspectives.

At Least Two Sides To Every Issue

Though we've heard it many times before, we often seem to forget that there are at least two sides to every issue. If there weren't, it wouldn't be an issue, now would it?

How often is it that we read or hear about something that makes perfectly good sense to us until we hear an opposing argument? It is especially embarrassing when we make wrong decisions because we viewed only one side of an issue. Eggs are good for breakfast but not on our faces.

After living in Orlando, Florida, for about nine months, I was determined to begin a campaign to lead the city in a boycott of the East-West Expressway which bisected the city. It was announced that the already high toll rates were about to be increased 50% to 100%, depending on the locations.

I had heard that the toll road had already received more than enough fees to pay for its cost in full and that the increase was only for the purpose of providing monies for future road construction. It seemed obvious to me that the proposed increases were uncalled for. I had discussed my idea of a one-month boycott with many people and had received only positive feedback. I felt certain that I could obtain the support of some radio stations and at least one newspaper. I was ready to go for it.

I decided to first make sure I had the facts right so I called the Expressway Authority — the organization in charge of the highway. After hours of discussing the matter with them, I became convinced that very few people, including me, really understood the situation. The highway wasn't already paid for and, in fact, wouldn't be until the year 2010. The proposed rate increases had actually been voted on in 1986, more than four years previously. In fact, in two previous public hearings, a combined total of only five citizens had shown up to voice their opinions concerning the vote!

I couldn't believe it, but I had come so close to devoting a great amount of time to the promotion of a boycott which I soon became convinced was wrong. In fact, by studying the other side of the issue, I decided to write a letter to the newspaper supporting the proposed increases and explaining to the average citizen the reasons for my support. I had been suffering from a wrong perception as to the true story about the history and future of this highway.

That wasn't the first time I had been shocked by looking at both sides of an issue. I had once listened to a debate held on the floor of the United States Congress over an issue on which I had already determined my position. I believed the issue was pretty much "black and white" and was shocked to see it wasn't so clear-cut! The other side had a number of good points which I had never even considered.

Thus, the proper perspective is to study all sides of an issue before choosing your position.

Pluses Have Minuses & Minuses Have Pluses

Living life is a lot like riding a roller coaster. As we do either, we experience many ups and downs. These are also referred to as "positive" and "negative" experiences, or "pluses" and "minuses." Having a proper perspective regarding these experiences will assist us greatly in realizing our potentials. There are pluses in every minus and minuses in every plus. While this may seem to be strange mathematics at first glance, it is extremely important that we adopt this perspective. To fail to do so is both to miss many blessings and to expose ourselves to many dangers. Let me explain.

First, we all have negative experiences. I call these minuses. They can range from having an argument with someone to the death of a close loved one. The negative experience might be one which causes great loss, or simply a major disappointment. These negative experiences are, in and of themselves, somewhat unpleasant. That is why we call them "negative." Obviously, it is from this word "negative" that I get the word "minus."

No experience is totally negative. Each has many positive aspects to it. In fact, I want to encourage you to see a negative as being filled with positives. These positives are found in the opportunities that the negative (minus) has brought you.

THE PLUSES IN MINUSES

```
+ EXPERIENCE   + EDUCATION   + CHARACTER BUILDING

+ SOME GAIN   + HUMILITY   + CREATES DESIRE
```

These are but a few of the pluses that can be found in our negative experiences.

Concerning the pluses (positive experiences), we must realize they too are filled with their opposites. While we usually accept the positive experiences in our lives with open arms, we are usually blind to the negatives contained within. All of us would probably be excited to find we had just won or inherited a million dollars. Wouldn't you?

Stop for just a moment, however, and think about the negatives that would also bring. Our "friends" would come out of their closets in droves anxious to renew their relationships. One of the problems many rich people have is the difficulty in knowing who their real friends are. We would also have to deal with the envy and jealousy of others. That can be pretty cruel. There is little doubt that we would be under constant internal pressure to make many major changes in our life-styles. While these might be quite enjoyable in the beginning, they can be quite painful in the end. Let me explain.

One has but to study the lives of past lottery winners to see this point clearly. A study I read many years ago revealed that the majority of these "winners" later looked back and regretted having won. Their lives had changed so drastically once they received the money. Often the changes included quitting their jobs, getting divorces, and moving into the high-priced fast lanes of life. Once the money ran out, they found themselves stranded in an unfamiliar world. What were their odds of winning another lottery?

Someone once said, "If you inherit a million dollars, you had better become a millionaire quickly or you will lose it all." What was meant by that, obviously, was that the millionaire who earned his million dollars has learned how to handle money — that is how he accumulated so much. He is not as apt to lose his money.

THE MINUSES IN PLUSES

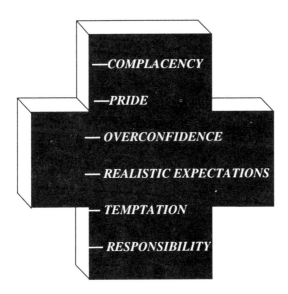

—COMPLACENCY

—PRIDE

— OVERCONFIDENCE

— REALISTIC EXPECTATIONS

— TEMPTATION

— RESPONSIBILITY

The minuses in the pluses are real. These, as with their counterparts, are often overlooked because they are not too obvious. The consequences of not being aware of their existence can be devastating.

The key for noticing the minuses in pluses and the pluses in minuses is, simply enough, to look for them. Most people never see them and therefore suffer as a result. Remember this proper perspective the next time you have a major plus or minus in your life.

A Year Is Only 365 Days!

Very few perspectives, if any, affect our decisions more than our perspectives on time. On the one hand we say life is too short and on the other hand, we think a year is a long time. Wrong decisions are often made because of a poor perspectives in this area.

Because of improper perspectives on time, some people:

- Decide to quit school because they can't wait
- Marry too quickly, before they really know each other
- Decide not to attend college — four years is a long time
- Never read a book because it takes too long
- Refuse to think about retirement — they're too young

Some think life is too short to spend time becoming educated and preparing for it. It is too short to watch what we eat and care for our bodies. It is too short to take the time to decide what we want to do in life. Isn't it because life is so short that we should be doing these things?

Often, one won't begin a project because it will take a year to complete. So what? How old will one be this time next year if he doesn't begin the project? Almost everyone I've ever known has agreed that the years seem to become shorter the older we get. Have you ever stopped to figure out why? I have. The answer is twofold. First, we increase our appreciation for the value of time, as we see the amount we have left becoming shorter and shorter. Next, the older we get, the more purposeful we become. Just as time seems to fly when we're having fun, it flies when we're doing things that are meaningful to us. For some reason, time always seems so distant as we look ahead to it, and so short as we look back on it. I'm amazed as I look back on some of my experiences and consider how quickly they passed.

Perhaps you'll agree as you look back on some of your experiences. As you do so, put things you are now considering in their proper perspective, as they relate to the time you have left to live.

The Value Of An Hour

What is an hour worth? That really depends, doesn't it? It depends on what is going to be accomplished in that hour, and what has to be traded for it.

This is actually a common question, one most people might answer too quickly. Many people go to work every day, expecting to be paid hourly wages which were determined the day they began working for their companies. That rates were determined, in each case, based on at least two factors:

1) The amount the employer was willing to pay. He determined that figure by considering:

- What the job was worth to him
- What he could afford to pay
- What he would have to pay to hire someone else
- What the employee needed to make (possibly)

2) The amount for which the employee was willing to work. He determined that after considering these factors:

- What he felt he could earn elsewhere
- What he really needed to earn
- How desperately he needed the amount offered
- The amount it cost him to go to work
- The value of what he must give up to go to work

It has always amazed me how cheaply some people will sell themselves. Some people work for minimum wage, or less (if they can find work), while others charge over $100 per hour and easily get it. Why is this true? A number of factors are involved, including:

- The amount someone else was willing to pay
- The uniqueness of his offering
- His ability to sell himself
- The competition factor (supply and demand)
- His level of expertise and credibility
- His reputation
- The value he places on his time

Based on all these factors, one can see there is no easy answer concerning the value of an hour. We could simply say that an hour, like anything else, is worth what a willing buyer can purchase it for from a willing seller. For what will you sell an hour?

Once you determine the answer to that, I'd encourage you to evaluate the things you do with your time compared to that figure. For example, if you're watching television, is the show you're watching worth that much per hour? I know you might say, "But I'm not working when I'm watching TV!" I know you're not, but you could be. Again, you might protest, "I couldn't be working because my job is only a 40 hour a week job." I still suggest that you could be working — maybe not for the same employer, but for yourself. In reality, that's who you work for anyway, isn't it?

Whenever I sell myself, I use these factors to determine my wage:

- What is the value of the problem I'm going to solve?
- How much do I want the job?
- What additional factors are involved?
- What are my competitors charging for similar services?
- Are there any extenuating circumstances?
- Is this a onetime job or will there be more work?
- What will it cost to do the job (my expenses)?
- Do I expect to enjoy the job?

- Have I worked for this company before?
- Have I done this kind of job before?
- What are their expectations of me?
- Should I consider an aggravation factor (traffic, etc.)?
- What can they afford? (I may charge less than regular fee.)
- If I refuse the job, what else will I do with my time?

This list may seem quite lengthy, but I assure you that I take most of these factors into consideration as I determine how much I will sell my time for. For example, I charge extra if a company wants me to begin work at 8:00 A.M. in the city. I call the extra fee an aggravation factor since I despise traffic jams. They can save money by allowing me to begin at 7:00 A.M. or 9:00 A.M.

Give Yourself An Edge on Your Competition

Did you realize that you could give yourself an extra 6 1/2 weeks per year by simply working an extra hour each day? Do you think you could accomplish more than your competition each year if you had an additional 6 1/2 weeks? Again, you might reply, "I don't have any competition; I'm just an employee!" That is where you'd be wrong — and would be operating from an improper perspective.

Each individual who enters the market place is in competition with every other person who would like to have his job. We're all competing in ways we've never even thought about. A potential customer or employer only has so many dollars to spend. Is he going to spend them hiring you (for your productivity), or will he spend them on somebody or something else? Ask all those who have been replaced by computers, or other equipment, if they were in competition.

The proper perspective I challenge us all to have is the perspective that we need to become the best we can, making the most of the time we have. We can determine the amount of time we'll work, then strive to be worth as much as we can during that time, within desired parameters. Those parameters include the type of work we'll do, where and when we'll do it, and with whom we'll do it with. How we do it will determine the value of our time.

Even if your employer limits you to 40 hours per week, you can still increase our hourly value to yourself by using the additional hour daily to gain a greater education in your chosen occupation. It only takes a little extra time or effort to become above average.

The Bottom Isn't Necessarily The End

It's tough to find ourselves in that downward slide, isn't it? If you never have been there, and you can only imagine, I'm sure you'll still agree. We work hard to climb that "ladder of success." While it may not always be fun on the way up, it seldom, if ever, is fun on the way down.

Few football games are ever played without each team having to punt the ball away at least a few times. No team likes to give up the ball, and that's understandable. The same is true with us in life. As a salesman, I recognize that people will act quicker to avoid a loss than to gain a benefit. Wise salespeople use this fact to their advantage by showing their prospects what they will lose if they fail to buy. This motivation to maintain the status quo is so powerful that we will do almost anything to keep from going backwards.

The emotions we feel in moving into a bigger, nicer house are multiplied many times (negatively) when we are forced to sell that house and move into a smaller, rented house or apartment. The same holds true when we lose our purchasing power. As pleasant as it is to go into a store and buy whatever we want, it is proportionally more unpleasant to search for the money to keep the utilities turned on.

Contrasted also to the very negative emotions of sliding toward the bottom is the "emotional high" one can get from finally arriving at the bottom. While this may sound strange to those of you who have never been there, those of us who have can tell you it's very exciting. "Why is that?" you ask. We can get excited by the realization that there is only one direction to go — UP! We know we are finally positioned to head in the right direction.

This logic may sound strange to many of you but I assure you that it is accurate, and it works. Often people look at the bottom as the end, meaning that their lives are totally ruined once they hit bottom. The bottom is not the end; in fact, it can be a new beginning!

It Is Impossible To Quit!

Have you ever thought about quitting? I don't just mean quitting your job, your role as a parent or spouse, or your responsibilities in some organization. I mean quitting it all!

Quitting it all means different things to different people. To some it might mean committing suicide. To others it might mean something like walking to the interstate and hitching a ride to California to begin a new life. Still to others, it might mean becoming a street person in the inner-city somewhere. Whatever it means, let me assure you that there is no such thing as quitting!

Let's begin by looking at the "worse case" scenario — suicide. This is an option I considered many times in my teenage years. What kept me from it, I don't really know. Perhaps it was a belief deep down that I might "make it" some day. It may have been the fact that I wasn't too sure if even that (committing suicide) would end my suffering. At any rate, I can still recall the loneliness, hopelessness, and despair I felt back then. If I could have quit, and truly ended it all, I think I would have.

Many positive events occurred in my life during my young adult years, the greatest of which was my becoming a Christian at age 22. Only twice since then did I ever again consider suicide. As I considered it then, I felt I had the answers that had been missing during my teenage years. As a young Christian, I knew what the Bible taught about life after death, that being absent from the body and present with the Lord was preferable (see 2 Corinthians 5:1-8 and Philippians 1:19-26).

The first time I considered suicide as a Christian was when I was still 22. I was going through some really tough trials and felt I was being persecuted without cause. I was extremely upset and had fallen into that "end it all" mood. My plan was to ram a huge concrete wall with my car at 100 m.p.h. As I approached the wall, having nearly reached the proper speed, I pictured, in my mind, myself standing before God. I pictured myself standing there attempting to answer the question from God, "What's the matter, wasn't my grace sufficient enough for you?" Answering that question seemed to pose a greater challenge than facing the trial I had been encountering.

The second, and last, time I considered suicide as a Christian was in 1979, when I was then 31 years old. My financial condition had deteriorated to a point where I couldn't afford to pay the utility bills, and I was behind on my rent. I must now laugh when I consider how insignificant that situation was compared to those financial hardships which were yet to come. At any rate, I was a proud man and had an extremely difficult time accepting the fact that I wasn't doing a good job of supporting my family. We were only 15 days late with our rent when the Sheriff delivered a summons to our door, giving me a few days to pay the rent or go to court. The very thought of going to court produced such shame and guilt in my mind that I really didn't know what to do.

It was then, because I had $300,000 worth of life insurance, that I considered suicide as a means of paying the bills. The policies were aged enough that they would be payable in the event of death by suicide. While I rationalized that suicide would be viewed by many as a coward's way out, I balanced that with the fact that the bills would get paid and my family would have the financial support they deserved. It was not an easy dilemma to work through. I'll always remember how the solution came.

One evening, when the family was out of town, I went for a long walk alone. I spent a couple of hours just talking to God about my dilemma. I've learned when I talk to God to also take the time to listen. I sensed that He was leading me into considering this situation as a solvable one, and that part of my problem was that I was looking at it with distorted perception. I was too close to the trees to see the forest.

I evaluated that I might be worth $300,000 dead, but I was worth much more than that alive. While I was disappointed in myself and discouraged, I still had tremendous earning potential and a bright future. I still had a friend in Jesus, a Savior who was more than capable of assisting me to become the person I could be. I became convinced that God was just as anxious as He had ever been to show Himself strong on my behalf. His strength could be made perfect in my weakness (see 2 Corinthians 12:9).

That night as I was preparing to go to sleep, I prayed, thanking God for the encouragement and asking Him to guide me. It was then that I thought about a number of items I had which could be sold to fulfill my financial obligations. I even knew whom I could sell them to. I knew the immediate problem was solved! I thanked the Lord and entered a peaceful sleep.

Although far greater financial problems were to come later, I never again resorted to considering suicide as a potential solution. I had learned two things. First, suicide is not the end since I'll live for eternity, and would have to stand before God in disgrace. (By the way, even the sin of suicide was paid for on the cross; it will not keep one who has believed in Jesus from entering heaven.) Second, I had learned that "there's always an answer!" No problem is too big for God. We simply need to be humble enough to accept His solution.

Another form of quitting is to walk away from it all. While it is true that one can quit a job or organization, resign from a position, or even quit trying to accomplish something, one can never really totally quit. We can never get away from ourselves, and the responsibilities that we know we have. We can hitchhike several thousand miles, change our names, and begin new lives as street people, but we'll still have to live with ourselves. We'll still have occasionally to look at ourselves in the mirror and acknowledge who we are. We'll still have to deal with problems. Even street people have problems. If you don't believe that, visit a shelter in a major city on a cold night and view those turned away due to insufficient space.

No, the truth is that quitting is not an option. The grass is not greener on the other side of the fence. Life without problems and challenges just doesn't exist. Perhaps a prison cell offers the closest thing to life without problems. Of course, most prisoners would probably want to debate that one. Think long and hard before you attempt to really quit. Recognize that it is far easier to hang in there and succeed than it is to quit. Then, with God's help, go on and succeed!

Wooden Nickels Don't Make Sense

This may sound cute but the meaning isn't so cute. Wooden nickels, as we all know, are a joke and have no redeeming value. All too often we who are well familiar with the phrase, "Don't take any wooden nickels" find ourselves not only accepting, but pursuing wooden nickels of another sort.

I'm referring to our endless pursuit of things that have little or no intrinsic value. Recently, I heard this interesting statement:

> *Why is it that people spend money they don't have to purchase things they don't want to impress people they don't like?*

This is a lot like accepting a wooden nickel, don't you think? Actually, time spent in pursuit of anything that is worth little or nothing to us is time poorly spent. Since time is the most valuable asset we have, we would be much wiser accepting a few real wooden nickels than wasting our time.

Consider The Value of It All

One of the most interesting, and initially puzzling, little books I've ever read was the Biblical book of Ecclesiastes. This book, inspired by God and written by Solomon, teaches us about "value" and "vanity." The book begins:

> *"Vanity of vanities," says the Preacher; "Vanity of vanities, all is vanity." What profit has a man from all his labor in which he toils under the sun?* **Ecclesiastes 1:2,3 (NKJV)**

As the book continues, we find that Solomon, considered one of the wisest men to ever live, had it all. He had accomplishments, wisdom, knowledge, magnificent wealth, power, position, the best of entertainment, and too many women. He said,

> *Whatever my eyes desired I did not keep from them. I did not withhold my heart from any pleasure, For my heart rejoiced in all my labor; and this was my reward from all my labor. Then I looked*

*on all the works that my hands had done and on the labor in which
I had toiled; and indeed all was vanity and grasping for the wind.
There was no profit under the sun.* **Ecclesiastes 2:10-11 (NKJV)**

Solomon finally realized, as he considered these things, that nothing this
world has to offer is really that valuable. He recognized that in order for
something to have value, it must be seen in its relationship to God and eternity.
Notice, he says:

*I have seen the God-given task with which the sons of men are to be
occupied. He has made everything beautiful in its time. Also He has
put eternity in their hearts, except that no one can find out the work
that God does from beginning to end. I know that there is nothing
better for them than to rejoice, and to do good in their lives, and also
that every man should eat and drink and enjoy the good of all his
labor — it is the gift of God. I know that whatever God does, it shall
be forever. Nothing can be added to it, and nothing taken from it.*
Ecclesiates 3:10 (NKJV)

He summarizes the book by saying:

*Remember now your Creator in the days of your youth, before the
difficult days come, and the years draw near when you say, "I have
no pleasure in them."* **Ecclesiastes 12:1 (NKJV)**

In essence, what Solomon is attempting to teach us is that we are vain, indeed,
to attempt to find fulfillment in this life while ignoring our Creator, God.
There is no lasting joy in a life lived apart from Him.

The next passage also sheds light on this important subject. Jesus gives us a
parable to teach us the value of considering God in our decisions. Since He
is the giver and sustainer of life, it doesn't make a whole lot of sense to ignore
Him. He can revoke it at any time. (By the way, that doesn't make God the bad
guy.)

*And He [Jesus] said to them, "Take heed and beware of covetousness,
for one's life does not consist in the abundance of the things he*

possesses." And He spoke a parable to them, saying: "The ground of a certain rich man yielded plentifully. And he thought within himself, saying, 'What shall I do, since I have no room to store my crops?' So he said, 'I will do this: I will pull down my barns and build greater, and there I will store all my crops and my goods. And I will say to my soul, "Soul, you have many goods laid up for many years; take your ease; eat, drink, and be merry."' But God said to him, 'You fool! This night your soul will be required of you; then whose will those things be which you have provided?' So is he who lays up treasure for himself, and is not rich toward God." **(NKJV) Luke 12:15-21 (NKJV)**

The following verses, also, lend some perspective on the emptiness of a life lived apart from God:

For what is a man profited if he gains the whole world, and loses his own soul? Or what will a man give in exchange for his soul? **Matthew 16:26 (NKJV)**

If in this life only we have hope in Christ, we are of all men most miserable. **1 Corinthians 15:19 (KJV)**

Some Rejection Is Inevitable

It is difficult to accept that some rejection is inevitable. We all have a desire to be liked and accepted by others. We can accept it when we are rejected for a good reason (e.g., we refuse to become involved with drugs, etc.). We have a more difficult time accepting rejection when it results from others' wrong perceptions.

The proper perspective I want to discuss here is the perspective we should have regarding the people who reject us. Rejection will occur, and occur often, for a number of different reasons. Here are a few of the reasons people reject us:

1) We have wronged or offended them. This is understandable. If we've

offended them, we should humble ourselves and make amends. It is foolish not to confess our sins.

2) They are jealous of us or of the things we have. This is often the case when others allow themselves to play the "comparison game." They decide that they don't compare too well in a particular category that seems important to them and they, therefore, become jealous.

3) They are simply prejudiced. Unfortunately, some people, for whatever reason, are prejudiced. They reject one because of his skin color, nationality, education or economic level, or some other illegitimate reason. It is they who have the problem!

4) They do not understand us. This is probably the rejection that hurts me the most. If people reject us for this reason, it may be due, in part, to our failure to explain ourselves adequately. Just as often, however, it is because they do not take the time to understand us, or are not open to understanding us. Just as a locked door doesn't swing, neither does a closed mind allow proper perception to enter.

5) They oppose things for which we stand. This can be as simple as having different political or religious perspectives, opposing value systems, or disagreement over any other issues for which we stand. They may reject us because of our positions, or because we have no positions.

6) They have inaccurate preconceptions. They judge us too quickly. If we are overweight, we must be fat slobs with no self-control. If we don't dress as nicely as they do, we can't be as good as they. If our grammar isn't up to their standards, we must not be very intelligent. If we are from some particular states or regions of the country, they automatically expect us to fit some molds that exist in their mind.

7) They view us through the lenses of their own lives. "Different" to some means "bad." We just don't measure up because we haven't experienced the same things they have. They are always one up on us. It may be that they've had to work harder for something than we did, or just the opposite. They tend to expect us to be just like they are. If we're not, they consider us worthy of rejection.

8) They have poor self-images. Strangely, these types of people reject us because they think we are like they are. If we are like they, and they feel worthless, they perceive we must also be worthless.

9) They feel guilty. Scripture teaches in St. John 3:19 that "men loved darkness rather than light because their deeds are evil." Since we Christians are the light of the world (Matthew 5:14-16), it only makes sense that they might feel uncomfortable around us. This can occur even when we are purposing to be gracious in our dealings with them and not to have condemning spirits.

10) They are lazy (rejection is easier than acceptance). Another reason we are rejected is that people are basically lazy. Responsibility comes with relationships and that can sometimes mean work and effort. It is often easier to reject someone rather than risk the effort that acceptance might bring.

The fact is that we will be rejected. For one reason or another, some people will want nothing to do with us. As it happens, we should keep two things in mind. First, we should not allow ourselves to become discouraged over rejection. Even Jesus was misunderstood and rejected, and He was God in the flesh! Second, we should focus on those who can appreciate and accept us. They deserve our attention. Keeping the issue of rejection in the proper perspective can mean a great deal to us as we go through life.

If It Is To Be – It's Up To Me!

It is painful to recall the number of times I have had the following maxim affirmed (the hard way): "If it is to be, it's up to me." This saying contains a lesson I'd like to be able to say I've learned, but instead only can say I'm learning.

God only knows how many times I wish this were not true! I find myself asking, "Why me? Why does it always have to be me?" From whom do I expect an answer? I don't know — from anyone who will listen, I guess. The point is this: Nobody is going to solve my problems for me. I can't depend on somebody else, or some miracle, to make life easier.

This is not reason enough to have a "pity party." It is actually a bright and glorious day when we finally adopt the perspective as our own, "If it is to be, it's up to me." Some of my greatest disappointments have come when I lost this perspective and trusted someone else to provide my solution.

Numerous circumstances make this perspective a good one, among them:

- Some will lie or misrepresent what they can do for us.
- Some will be mistaken.
- Some will mean well and lack the ability to fulfill their pledges.
- We let our guards down when we look to other for solutions.
- We pass up potential solutions thinking the problem is solved.
- We become passive and vulnerable when depending on others.

Consider the following example of a situation that confronted me on more than one occasion. When I owned my first computer store, I often left town for a week or more at a time. I always liked to stay in contact with my store, although sometimes my travels took me to a remote area of the world where this was not possible. Whenever I was able to make contact with the store, the story was always the same. Few sales ever occurred while I was gone. It was always the same story: "Things have been pretty slow." That is a sad refrain to a merchant who needs his store to generate gross sales in excess of $10,000 in his absence. On more than one occasion, I would have to make $10,000 or more within a day or two after returning, or the business would be in hot water. It always got done, but it was never easy.

I finally determined, "If it is to be, it's up to me," and I began to make those sales before I left. If I was going on vacation, I would go through my customer list, call the best customers, and say something like, "Ralph, get your checkbook out and come to the store. I'm having my semiannual Going Fishing Sale." Ralph, and the others would come, and I'd pad my ledger before I left. Then, and only then, could I fish in peace!

That, by the way, is not an indictment on my employees. They were great employees. They just didn't have the motivation that I did to solve my problems. They knew they'd receive paychecks on Friday, even if the company didn't bring in any money.

This perspective is also an important one to have when setting goals utilizing the Penalty Principle. If you're going to suffer by having to pay a penalty because a goal isn't successfully accomplished, it should be because you failed, not because someone else failed. Ultimately, however, it is your failure if you failed because you depended on someone who wasn't trustworthy.

Does this mean we should never trust others? No. It simply means that we should recognize their limitations and make the proper adjustments for them. We should also have a "Plan B," in the event that "Plan A" fails.

Cheaters Never Win!

I don't know about you, but I've often found it difficult to deal with my attitude when I've been cheated. Few things make me as angry as being lied to, stolen from, or cheated. Perhaps this is why I enjoy "Rambo-type" movies so well. They certainly appeal to the part of me that cries for revenge.

If it were not for God giving me a proper perspective in this area, I'm sure I would have gone off the deep end long ago. I'm the sort of person who usually does what he wants to do, so it has been very important that I maintain a proper perspective regarding this issue. I've often felt I could produce my own version of *Death Wish V*.

I've entitled this perspective "Cheaters Never Win!" because I'm convinced they don't — not in the long run. I've been cheated, lied to, and stolen from as much as anyone. It never gets easier to accept, especially when it comes from someone I've befriended and trusted. Few things hurt more.

In one two-year period, from 1988 to 1990, I was cheated by no less than six different people for amounts ranging from $1,500 to $10,000. In every case, except one, I considered these people to be trustworthy friends. The one exception, though not a friend, appeared trustworthy. I helped all of these people at times when I really couldn't afford to do so — and they knew that. Yet, in each case, for one reason or another, I ended up on the short end of the stick.

Perhaps you're thinking, and rightly so, that I must be an easy mark. I don't really understand it myself, as I consider myself a fair judge of character. My pitfall, I suspect, is that I really want to believe the best about people and do all I can to help them succeed. There are times when others don't fulfill their promises because they are unable to do so, and other times when they never intended to do so.

When we lose because of deceit, whether in a sporting event, business dealing, or some other arena, we have a choice to make: How are we going to react? As I've already stated, we can't always control our circumstances, but we are responsible to control our responses. That is certainly true here. Notice what God says regarding this matter.

> *If it is possible, as much as depends on you, live peaceably with all men. Beloved, do not avenge yourselves, but rather give place to wrath; for it is written, "Vengeance is Mine, I will repay," says the Lord. Therefore if your enemy hungers, feed him; If he thirsts, give him a drink; For in so doing you will heap coals of fire on his head. Do not be overcome by evil, but overcome evil with good.*
> **Romans 12:18-21 (NKJV)**

God is clearly telling us that we are to repay evil with good and leave the vengeance to Him. He promises to repay. If we seek vengeance ourselves, it is quite possible that we will be the ones in "hot water."

The following passage teaches us about proper conduct toward others — even those who mistreat us.

> *Servants, be submissive to your masters with all fear, not only to the good and gentle, but also to the harsh. For this is commendable, if because of conscience toward God one endures grief, suffering wrongfully. For what credit is it if, when you are beaten for your faults, you take it patiently? But when you do good and suffer for it, if you take it patiently, this is commendable before God. For to this you were called, because Christ also suffered for us, leaving us an example, that you should follow His steps: "Who committed no sin, nor was guile found in His mouth" who, when He was reviled,*

did not revile in return; when He suffered, He did not threaten, but committed Himself to Him who judges righteously.
I Peter 2:18-23 (NKJV)

Is God telling us that we are to follow Jesus' example regarding suffering? Obviously. We are to "take it patiently" (an act that is commendable before God) and commit ourselves to God, that His will might be done both in and through us. This is one of those passages that is "easy preaching — hard living." In fact, it is often "impossible" without the strength of God working in our lives. More about that later.

Whenever I mention to others anything about this perspective, I'm flooded with questions about, and examples of, those cheaters who do appear to win. Even as I write this, it certainly appears that there are many cheaters sitting in some pretty enviable positions. By the time you read this, however, I have no doubt that some of them will have fallen from those positions. See what God has to say about this situation.

> *Do not be deceived, God is not mocked; for whatever a man sows, that he will also reap.* **Galatians 6:7 (NKJV)**

The Psalmist asks the Lord,

> *Why do You stand afar off, O LORD? Why do You hide Yourself in times of trouble? The wicked in his pride persecutes the poor; Let them be caught in the plots which they have devised. For the wicked boasts of his heart's desire; he blesses the greedy and renounces the LORD. The wicked in his proud countenance does not seek God; God is in none of his thoughts. His ways are always prospering; Your judgments are far above, out of his sight; as for all his enemies, he sneers at them. He has said in his heart, "I shall not be moved; I shall never be in adversity." His mouth is full of cursing and deceit and oppression; under his tongue is trouble and iniquity. . . . He has said in his heart, "God has forgotten; He hides His face; He will never see it." Arise, O LORD! O God, lift up Your hand! Do not forget the humble. Why do the wicked renounce God? He has said in his heart, "You will not require an account." But You have*

seen it, for You observe trouble and grief, to repay it by your hand. The helpless commits himself to You; You are the helper of the fatherless. **Psalms 10:1-7; 11-14 (NKJV)**

God's answer to all those who think they can sin and get away with it, is found in **Numbers 32:23:**

But if you do not do so, then take note, you have sinned against the LORD; and be sure your sin will find you out. **(NKJV)**

The interesting thing about cheaters is that their sins usually catch up to them at times when they least want them to. It may be just before or just after great events in their lives. The higher they've climbed with their sin, the farther they have to fall. We've all had many opportunities to see this in both the sporting arena (Ben Johnson's fantastic 100 meter run) and in the political arena (take your pick). Consider the noted businessmen who have been convicted of insider trading; consider the immoral habits of respected ministers who were caught cheating. Perhaps, these are examples God is giving us today to help us realize the need to apply the following verse:

Do not let your heart envy sinners, but in the fear of the LORD continue all day long; for surely there is a hereafter, and your hope will not be cut off. **Proverbs 23:17,18 (NKJV)**

The truth is that cheaters may appear to win for a while. They may laugh and even mock you after they've cheated you. This may go on for weeks, months, or even years, but the day will come when the scales will be balanced. We can count on it! They will pay in at least three ways.

First, they pay in terms of reduction or loss of self-respect. They might not even recognize this themselves, but it will occur nonetheless. I once corrected a store clerk after she undercharged me more than twenty dollars. She became indignant when I insisted she recalculate my total. When she finally did so and found that I was correct, she asked, "Why didn't you just leave? You could have gotten away with it." I shared with her this concept that one never "gets away with it;" he has to live with himself the rest of his life.

Another way cheaters pay is by reaping the natural consequences of their actions. When a person "wins" by cheating, he increases the expectations of others concerning his future activity. He must not only repeat the performance in some cases, but must show improvement to meet those expectations.

Last, but not least, the cheater can expect a visit (sooner or later) from God. He is not blind that He cannot see. His wrath will be released at the proper time, to suit His purpose. It is extremely important that we, who have been cheated, maintain proper attitudes when this occurs. Notice the following passage:

> *Do not rejoice when your enemy falls, and do not let your heart be glad when he stumbles; lest the LORD see it, and it displease Him, and He turn away His wrath from him.* **Proverbs 24:17,18 (NKJV)**

God Owns It All

We all, at one time or another, get caught up in what I'll call the "it's mine" mentality. From the time we're little children and other kids attempt to take our toys to the day when, we're adults and people accidentally damage things of ours, we experience many frustrations in our feeble attempts to protect that which is ours.

Some take this mentality to the point where they get caught up in the "whoever dies with the most toys wins" game. We become very possessive people, and this possessive mentality causes us severe problems. The things we possess cause us great concern in our simply trying to protect them. We purchase security systems, special locks, service contracts, and insurance in our attempts to keep that which is ours.

This "it's mine" perspective is an incorrect one. The proper perspective is that God owns it. There are at least a couple of reasons that this is the case. First, He is the Creator, and as such, has first claim to everything. Second, He is the sustainer of the universe. It is by Him that all things are held together. Instead of allowing myself to get caught up in a materialistic rat race, I've adopted the

Biblical perspective of stewardship. A "steward," is "one who acts as an administrator, as of finances and property, for another." Take note of the following verses regarding this important perspective.

The earth is the LORD'S, and all its fullness, the world and those who dwell therein. For He has founded it upon the seas, and established it upon the waters. **Psalms 24:1,2 (NKJV)**

For every beast of the forest is Mine, and the cattle on a thousand hills. I know all the birds of the mountains, and the wild beasts of the field are Mine. If I were hungry, I would not tell you; for the world is Mine, and all its fullness. **Psalms 50:10-12 (NKJV)**

For none of us lives to himself, and no one dies to himself. For if we live, we live to the Lord; and if we die, we die to the Lord. Therefore, whether we live or die, we are the Lord's. **Romans 14:7,8 (NKJV)**

The Bible clearly teaches that Christians are stewards of that which belongs to God. He owns everything and entrusts us with many things, both for our provision and blessing. Often, Christians have the misconception that everything they can accumulate belongs to them and they are responsible only to give a portion of those things back to God. Many simply give 10% (an amount they feel comfortable giving) and spend the rest in whatever ways they desire.

What they actually do with this remaining 90% determines the peace they will experience. As they become "owners" of many things, they develop the emotional problems that come with ownership. Frustration becomes a way of life. Whenever something is damaged, stolen, or simply breaks down, their emotions suffer as well.

God's answer to this is that we should view Him in His rightful place as the owner. After all, He is the giver and it is He who promises to supply all of our needs. He is more than capable of meeting our needs; He is desirous of giving us exceedingly abundantly above that which we even ask or think! We simply need to trust Him for these things, while doing that which He leads us to do.

This perspective frees us from lives of frustration. When we assume the role of a steward, we also recognize the power of the true owner and realize that He is perfectly capable of providing protection which we cannot. We are still responsible to perform maintenance, act wisely in protecting valuables, and search His will concerning purchases and investments. It is He, however, who assumes the responsibility of seeing that "all things work together for good."

If someone breaks in and steals from us, or damages our property, and God allowed it, then we can trust Him to settle the issue. He is more concerned about building character in our lives, and seeing us have positive responses to negative situations than He is in making sure we never have problems. In fact, He uses problems regarding the possessions He has entrusted us with to build that character into our lives, and to test us. When we show ourselves faithful in the small tests, He then entrusts us with bigger tests.

Perhaps, for those of you who are new to this concept, I ought to share a personal illustration. I was first introduced to the practicality of this perspective in 1978. At that time I was experiencing a great deal of frustration with a situation over which I had very little control. I had purchased new tires at one store, and gone to another place for the alignment, to take advantage of a special half-price offer. Our money was very tight in those days.

Within a few weeks, after only 5,000 miles of driving, my two front tires were completely worn out. The steel belt was showing on each tire! I was 1,000 miles from home and needed to replace the tires. The tire manufacturer wouldn't replace the tires under warranty, due to the alignment problem, and I had to pay over $165 for two new front tires, plus another alignment. My car had never needed an alignment the entire time I'd had it, and now within a few weeks after having gotten an alignment, it was "off the charts."

When I returned to the shop that had performed the alignment, I was told that there was "no guarantee" on alignments and, therefore, I would receive no assistance in paying for my new tires. I was not a happy man. I immediately thought of picketing their store, calling the news department at my local television station, writing a letter to the editor of the newspaper, etc. I figured, they might not pay me the $150.00 or so I figured I had coming, but I could make them wish they had. About that time I was introduced to the concept that the tires really belonged to God, since I was only acting as His steward. I had long before accepted the concept that everything I had was really His (including me), but had never applied the concept in a situation like this.

It became obvious that I had done all I should do within normal boundaries, and that I should give God the opportunity to go to work. If He saw fit to collect the money for me, fine. If not, there was no doubt in my mind that He would still provide for all of my needs, including the new tires. I simply wrote the owner of the store that had done my alignment and informed him of my decision. I let him know that I felt I had been wrong in my attitude toward his store and had come to realize the tires which had been ruined as a result of his mechanic's poor workmanship were not mine anyway. Since I was a Christian and accepted God's ownership of everything I had, I now realized they were really His tires. I would not be bothering Him anymore. He could make the decision as to what to do before God. If He felt that his company was not liable, that would be fine with me. I would have no more ill feelings about it but would, instead, be at peace. A few days later I received his note and check for $150. I was both surprised and elated! I can honestly say, however, that I would have remained at peace had I not received the check.

I have experienced many situations since in which I've been cheated out of thousands of dollars. In some cases, God has seen fit to bring about a settlement; in others, He has not. In all cases I've experienced, and continue to experience, a peace of mind. The Bible expresses it this way:

> *Rejoice in the Lord always. Again I will say, rejoice! Let your gentleness be known to all men. The Lord is at hand. Be anxious for nothing, but in everything by prayer and supplication, with thanksgiving, let your requests be made known to God; and the peace of God, which surpasses all understanding, will guard your hearts and minds through Christ Jesus.* **Philippians 4:4-7 (NKJV)**

I'll close this section with a story I heard long ago. A billionaire died and someone was overheard asking another man the question, "Do you know how much money he left?" The reply was exact: "He left it all." That statement is true for all of us; we can't take it with us.

·Twelve·
Proper Principles

Rules, rules, rules, how can I follow so many rules? Have you ever felt that way? Life is full of do's and don'ts. There is an endless list of things we must do, or not do, in order to be accepted, be successful, or just make it. If you've felt that way, you're not alone. Most of us feel that way at some time in our lives.

I don't know about you but I can't even begin to remember all the rules I've been given. I've found it much easier to adopt some principles, which when adhered to, seem to get me where I'm wanting to go without violating the so-called rules. A principle is defined in *Webster's Dictionary* as "a fundamental truth, law, etc., upon which others are based."

I suggest you adopt similar principles for yourself. I'll share my list with you here, and explain each one so you can clearly see the application.

Principle 1: Never Do That Which Someone Else Can Do When It Keeps Me From Doing That Which Only I Can Do.

This may be the most valuable of all these principles. Life is too short to waste it and I'm wasting it every time I'm not properly delegating. I must admit that this principle is also probably the most difficult for me to apply. It is said to be "Easy Preachin', Hard Livin'."

You're reading this because you want to become better at setting and reaching goals in your life. As you've read, obviously you must first decide what you want before you can strive for it. It's impossible to strive for a goal you don't have.

When I attempt to apply this principle, I ask myself, "What are the activities that only I can do?" It's surprising how easy it is to answer that question. Now, I sometimes break it down like this:

- Activities that only I can do
- Activities that others could do but I want to do
- Activities that others could do but I should do
- Activities that I should have others do

First, begin a list of those things which must be done that only you can do. My list, at this time, includes the following:

- Write this book.
- Keep my body in shape with physical exercise.
- Feed my mind on a daily basis.
- Fulfill my roles as a husband and father.
- Eat proper meals.
- Sleep
- Personal and family decisions
- Church attendance

These are all things which I cannot easily delegate. They include some of my personal goals and responsibilities. Other responsibilities which I have that can be delegated include:

- Yard work
- Automobile maintenance
- House repairs
- Shopping
- Transportation needs of my children
- Accounting responsibilities

As you make your own lists, I think you'll be shocked at the number of things you now do which could be done by someone else. This information is only valuable if you do something with it. If you now have goals and responsibilities which aren't being fulfilled because you just don't have the time, then consider using this principle to justify buying yourself more time! Don't live, or die, leaving important things on your first list undone.

Delegation is a skill that can be extremely difficult to master, especially for some of us. I, for example, find it extremely difficult to accept less from someone else than I would have accepted from myself. I don't believe I'm a perfectionist but I do try to give my best at everything I attempt. When I delegate a task and see the person I've delegated it to doing something less than I've expected, I'll often become impatient and do it myself. It's a practice that has held me back from realizing my potential for years.

Principle 2: Make Certain That What I Am Doing Is Worth Giving My Life For Because That Is What I Am Giving To Do It.

Did you ever ask yourself what you would do if you knew you only had one year to live? Would you live your next year any differently? If so, how differently? Do you know that you have even a year left? Why not consider making some of those changes now?

When we often think about giving our lives for things, we usually are thinking in terms of "dying" for some great cause or purpose. Perhaps we say we would die to save our spouses or our children — maybe even friends. Perhaps we're even willing to die standing up to express our thoughts about particular issues. Often, witnesses to crimes have to make decision as to whether or not to risk their lives, and the lives of their families, by doing their part to see that justice is done. Yes, decisions like these are made by people every day but most of us find we're seldom, if ever, called upon to make those decisions.

In comparison, those decisions might be easy to make compared to those that this principle forces us to make. When I really think that I'm giving my life to do what I'm doing, that's a sobering thought. Is what I'm doing worth it? Is it worth it to me? Am I receiving a just reward? Is what I'm doing helping me to get where I want to go?

Years ago I came across the following material. It challenged me then as I suspect it might you now. I've never known, nor been able to determine, its author.

This is the beginning of a new day. God has given me this day to use as I will. I can waste it or use it for good. What I do today is important, because I'm exchanging a day of my life for it. When tomorrow comes, this day will be gone forever, leaving something I have traded for it. I want it to be gain, not loss — good, not evil — success, not failure — in order that I shall not regret the price I paid for it.

A day is a valuable thing and when I waste it, I've just thrown part of my life away. Now, it's important to realize that the application of this principle is a personal one. Another should not be allowed to decide for me what I'm to give my life for. It's my life! Only I can, and should, decide how I'm going to spend my day. It may be that I'll choose to spend eighteen hours working hard at the office, or I may choose to take the day off and go fishing. Whatever I decide, I'll pay for it with a day of my life.

Now what I reap from that day can be a different story. It's exciting to realize that there are no pat answers. Often I can be more valuable to myself taking the day off to relax and think than to keep toiling. When one is used to working ninety or more hours a week, like I often am, it's difficult to call "time out" and take time to "smell the roses," as they say. Every time I do, however, I gain a fresh perspective and become rejuvenated. I recognize that my time off was just as productive, and maybe more so, than if I'd continued working that day.

I might note that I'm sometimes criticized for working the hours I do. Some say my family must be suffering, that I'm neglecting them, or that I must not be enjoying life like I could. Those who criticize me are usually those who work forty hours each week and spend another forty hours curled up in front of television sets somewhere. They may actually spend more time with their families than I do mine, and then again they may not. While I've sat with my family watching television, I can't honestly call that a "family time." Think about it. It's difficult to discuss anything, or appreciate each other very much when a little box is sitting there demanding all our attention, isn't it?

Each of us must decide for himself what he will give his life for. In the end, we'll have no one to blame but ourselves if we feel we have wasted it. A day can only be seen as successful as it is viewed in light of ones overall purposes in life.

Principle 3: Be Careful About Making Decisions That Carry Irreversible Consequences.

It is easy to destroy in a few minutes that which has taken years to build. This is true with material things such as buildings, relationships of all kinds, and even life itself, or the quality of life.

I happen to be one who enjoys making fast decisions. In fact, I really hate having to take a lot of time to make a decision. I'm sure I'm like most people in that I don't really like making a decision unless it's an easy one.

An easy decision, for me, is one that is totally consistent with my goals and objectives. I can make a decision in a few seconds to spend several thousand dollars if I'm confident that the risk is minimal, and the contrasting potential for gain is great. The gain I'm expecting may, or may not, be financial. As long as I believe I understand the facts and am confident a deal is right, I'm quick to say "yes."

What I am careful about, however, is quickly making any decision which has the potential to cause me great pain or anguish over a long period of time. Perhaps I learned this the hard way by joining the U.S. Army. While I no longer regret having made that decision, I regretted it almost every day while I was "the Army's property." I found I'd made an irreversible decision and must live with it. I found that I had many false perceptions about what it would be like being a soldier, and hadn't even considered many of the issues at all. I'd lost my freedom and, in doing so, had learned to appreciate it.

Probably the biggest decision a person ever makes is to choose a lifetime partner. Most, when they marry, believe their marriage will last "till death do us part." They commit themselves to that end with their vows and soon find themselves regretting having done so. While some might think divorce prohibits this example from being a valid one, I disagree. Once married, the event is irreversible. A divorce may mean two people are no longer married but it doesn't change the fact that they were and will bear the scars from a marriage torn apart through divorce forever.

My using marriage as an illustration here isn't meant to imply that couples shouldn't get married. No, I believe that marriage is a God-given divine institution. I just don't believe it should be entered into lightly. It is very difficult for anyone, but especially someone only eighteen to twenty years old, to comprehend what it means to spend a lifetime with someone. I've been married well over twenty years and I'm only beginning to understand it.

There are many decisions which we can make that have the potential of having irreversible consequences. Those that come to mind first are those that are destructive in nature. These obviously include, but are not limited to, sins such as: lying, stealing, cheating, gossip and sexual immorality. While it's easy for us to believe that we can commit these sins and not suffer for it, that is just not the case. The Bible tells us our sins will find us out and that we cannot touch a fire without getting burned. Galatians 6:7 says, "Be not deceived, God is not mocked; whatsoever a man sows, that shall he also reap."

I'm known as an easygoing employer when it comes to firing a person. While I may expect 100% from all my employees, I'm usually gracious and forgiving when they fail or do things they shouldn't have. I've told some at times that I didn't know where the line was that they'd better not cross but I did know that they were close to it. I could feel it. It has been my way of giving them fair warning.

Principle 4: Always Have, Or Know How To Quickly Obtain A Plan "B" In The Event That Plan "A" Fails.

Things rarely go like we want them to the first time around. Usually a project will take longer to complete, cost more, and include far more obstacles than you expect. If you've done it before, or know others who have and you can benefit from their experience, you're more likely to have a good plan "A." Do you recall that little chapter you read on Obstacles and Roadblocks? Because those obstacles and roadblocks are real, it only makes good sense to have a backup plan. In the event that your original plan fails or falls short of your expectations, you have this backup plan "B" to bail you out. In reality, your backup plan is part of your overall plan. In putting this plan together, I often ask a lot of "What if?" questions. These are questions like:

- What if the cost exceeds your financial resources?
- What if the weather doesn't cooperate?
- What if a particular needed resource becomes unavailable?
- What if the need for this project changes before I complete it?
- What if I just can't do it the way I thought I could?

This may sound to some like negative thinking. One might ask how one could begin a project if these things are possibilities. While they are possibilities, we can face them. The reason we can do so is that we think we understand the probability factor, the odds that one or more of these things will occur. We're also confident that, if they do occur, we'll be able to come up with solutions. Creative people have little fear of such situations.

Principle 5: If I Must Make An Error In Judgement, Make It On The Side Of "Good" Or "Right" Rather Than On The Side Of "Bad" Or "Wrong."

I mention this principle because I use it often. There are many situations that confront me which make me wish I had the wisdom of Solomon. Perhaps you recall the situation he encountered where two women came to him, each arguing that a particular baby was hers. One said that the other's baby had died during the night and that mother had switched babies, leaving her with the dead baby. Of course, the other woman denied it and Solomon was left to decide which woman should get the baby. This sounds like the kind of thing we parents have to deal with concerning our children almost every day, doesn't it?

While Solomon had the proper response for those women, I don't always feel as wise. Oh, I know God promises me wisdom if I will but ask for it, and I do. Perhaps He has given me this principle to guide me in these matters. I first recognize that I don't know what to do but that I must make a decision to do something, even if it is nothing. I say this even though I know it sounds contradictory. Often, people think they can avoid making a decision by ignoring the issue. In reality, they've really made a decision to do nothing, which is okay in some situations. Making such a decision doesn't negate responsibility.

Once I recognize my responsibility to make a decision, even if it is to do nothing, I then attempt to determine my choices. Obviously, doing nothing is one of them. There may be several others. I attempt to visualize each choice from the perspective of each person that is involved. I ask myself, and them if I choose to do so, what they think about the choices. Once I've obtained all the information I think I can get regarding the matter, I consider the consequences of my decision. If I'm to make a mistake, I'm determined to do so on the side of grace and mercy, rather than on the side of destruction. Even this isn't always easy to know. This is especially true when it regards an employee I think I should let go. Will the damage caused by letting an employee go cause more problems than the damage caused by keeping him?

By the way, Solomon made the decision to announce he was going to cut the live baby in half with a sword and give half to each woman. The real mother then agreed to relinquish her rights in order to save the baby's life and Solomon awarded her the baby.

Principle 6: It Is Most Important That I React Properly To Negative Situations.

I believe that life is 20% what I make it and 80% how I take it. While I cannot control the circumstances (most of them anyway), I can most always control how I react to them. We might call this playing good "defense" in the game of life.

I'm a college basketball fan. Every year during the month of March, I must take time out to watch the NCAA Basketball Tournament. The tournament begins with 64 teams and crowns a champion in less than three weeks. It's an amazing sight to watch. While I always love to see my favorite team score, I know it's their defense that really puts them in position to win the game. In reality, even their offense is a part of their defense. The object is to keep the other team from scoring as many points as my team does. Time after time, the team that wins the tournament is the team that does the best job in keeping the other team from running its offense as it would like to. The 80's saw a couple of teams that consistently scored over 100 points per game against their opponents, (often over 130 points), but neither of those teams ever won the tournament.

I've determined to make this principle a key one in my life. Self-control, the ability to make sound decisions in the midst of critical situations, is something I strive for. The next chapter, on Self-control, will deal more fully with this issue.

Principle 7: Never Allow That Which I Cannot Do To Keep Me From Doing That Which I Can Do.

The world is full of people who stand and watch it go by. I've often said, "If life were easy, everybody would live it." By that I mean that I don't really think that most people live life; they simply exist. They sit around wishing that things were different.

Please believe me. I totally understand this attitude. I've often wanted to fall into it myself. Whether it's self-pity, or a huge dose of being awestruck by the tremendous potential of all that's available and going unrealized, I don't always know. What I do know is that it's plenty discouraging whenever I find myself envying someone else and asking myself, "Why couldn't that be me?"

There are some things in life I would really like to have done, but must face the fact that I didn't and will never do them. Almost every time I watch a college basketball game, I wish I could have been a good basketball player. No, not good, excellent! I would love to have been a starter on a team that won the national championship. I would love to have had the ability to make thousands of people happy by hitting game-winning three-point shots. That didn't happen, and will never happen. What did happen was that I was a substitute on a reserve high school team — one who didn't get to play very often. I loved the game, just didn't have the skill and experience the others did. Perhaps that is why I still play today whenever I get the chance. I'm still living my childhood, and expect to be doing so into my 50's.

I told that story to illustrate this point because I'm convinced that everyone reading these pages has many things they would like to do, or would like to have done, and can't or couldn't. Perhaps, you, like me, sit around feeling sad about that sometimes. The key to applying this principle is to get up and do what you can.

While it is true that I cannot become a star basketball player, it is true that I can become a star at making people happy in other ways, maybe even happier than if I had helped their favorite teams win championships. It is also true that I can play basketball games with others who have skills comparable to mine, and have a lot of fun doing it. It is true that there are a multitude of things that I can do that the basketball stars I've known could never do, and I should quit feeling sorry for myself and do them!

Whenever I allow that which I cannot do to keep me from doing that which I can do, I'm resigning myself to a boring and mundane life. I'm not living life, I'm just existing. I cannot enjoy life living that way and neither can you.

Consider this: The difference between ordinary and extraordinary is a little "extra." That's all it really takes to become extraordinary at something, a little extra. Most people just aren't willing to give a little extra. Are you?

Another application for this principle is for those times when one is tempted to drop a project or give up a goal just because he cannot do it himself. The key to solving that which we cannot do is to find someone who can do it. It should be accepted up front that not one of us can do it all. It is also true that none of us knows it all. Therefore, it only makes sense that we call upon the knowledge, skills, and resources of others to complete that which we cannot do.

The writing of this book is an example. I can type the words, putting my thoughts onto paper, but I don't have the necessary skills to design the cover, do the typesetting, draw the illustrations, nor print the book. Should I allow my inability to do these things to keep me from writing the book? No! Nor should I let the fact that I don't presently possess the $25,000 I expect the printing to cost, to hinder me from continuing to write. I'm confident that I'll either have the money to print it by the time I need it, or I'll have developed another plan. Actually, I already have plans "B", "C", and "D" in mind.

Principle 8: Always Have A Positive, Friendly And Helpful Attitude Towards Those I Meet.

It is real easy to become self-centered. At least it is for me. I can get to the point where I don't really care what others think of me. I don't live my life to please them; I live it to please me, and more importantly, I want to live it to please God. I do know that the Bible tells me that when my ways please God, He will make even my enemies to be at peace with me. It is for the reason of pleasing God that I need to be somewhat concerned as to how I come across to other people.

I'm told it takes 72 muscles to frown and only 14 to smile. While it may not be easy sometimes to smile, it's worth the effort. By keeping a proper perspective, I should always be able to smile. All I really have to do is count my blessings, naming them one by one, and I'll recognize how truly blessed I am by God. If I can't smile after that, then I don't deserve to be alive. The reason it is important that I smile is that most smiles are started by another smile. In other words, smiles reproduce themselves.

I'll never get a second chance to make a good first impression. If I want to make a good first impression, I can certainly begin by smiling. In relationships, there is something called "mirroring." Mirroring occurs when one person assumes, or mirrors, the exact attitude as the person he is talking to at the time. It's as if he were standing in front of a mirror. I can determine to help others feel good, and have a good first impression of me, by helping them smile, or I can choose to mirror their attitudes and we can be miserable together.

There is an old story I've heard a few times about an old man who used to peddle his goods alongside of a road just outside of a small village. Often travelers would stop at his stand to inquire about the village they were soon to enter.

One day he decided to test a theory he had been thinking about for some time. A man stopped to inquire about the village and asked about the friendliness of the people. The old man replied that the village consisted of the friendliest people the visitor could ever hope to meet. He would truly enjoy his stay. True to form, a few hours later the man passed by again beginning his return trip and said, "You were right! Those were the friendliest people I've ever met in my life." The old man just smiled and replied that he was glad the visitor had enjoyed his visit.

Just an hour or so later, another inquirer also asked about the type of people who lived in the village. The old man, attempting to test his theory, warned the visitor that he should be very careful if he dared visit the village at all. "That village is full of thieves and scoundrels," the man noted. "That's the very reason I sell my goods outside of town. I can't trust the people there for a minute. They would rob me blind!" With advice like that, the visitor approached the town cautiously. A few hours later, the visitor staggered up to the old man's stand and stammered, "You were certainly right about that bunch. They beat and robbed me. I'm fortunate to still be alive!" With that, the old man simply shook his head and said, "I knew it. It's just not safe in that village." He then silently chuckled to himself, thinking, "People really do act like mirrors. They simply give back that which is presented to them."

That fictional story is more true than we care to admit. People who have few or no friends don't expect anyone to like them. They expect to be rejected of all men, and they are. Everyone would do well to read Dale Carnegie's book, *How To Win Friends and Influence People* before they allow such an attitude to ruin their lives.

The Bible once again has the best advice I've ever read for finding friends. It says:

> *A man who has friends must himself be friendly, But there is a friend who sticks closer than a brother.* **Proverbs 18:24 (NKJV)**

The key, then, to having friends is to be one. In this world in which we live, where everyone has "Mefirstitis," people are dying for want of someone to first be friendly to them. We can be that person and, in doing so, accumulate more friends than we can count.

I've heard that people don't care how much we know until they know how much we care. I'm certain this is true. The nice part about taking the time to be friendly and helpful is that we reap far more than we sow. As in farming, a grain of corn can reap hundreds of grains, so can friendly and helpful acts. Even if this were not true, the self-satisfaction one receives from being friendly and helpful cannot be compared to very many things.

Principle 9: Anything Worth Doing Is Worth Doing Right.

How often have you heard this one? I've heard it often and I'm thankful I have. It's become a principle I believe we should all apply every day. The time saved by not having to do it over again will give me more time to do other things.

People who do things only halfheartedly lose out in a number of ways. First, they lose the self-satisfaction that can only come from knowing they did their best. Second, they lose the respect they would have received from others; and third, they lose the time it takes to do them over.

Whenever a project isn't done right the first time, resources are wasted. At the least, human resources are wasted. Often tangible materials are also wasted. Additional resources may not even be available to redo the job. Other projects may be put off because they were dependent upon the first project, or the time required to do the first project over ties up the human resources.

Principle 10: Focus On Maximizing Strengths & Minimizing Weaknesses.

This might seem too simplistic on the surface, but it's not. First, it isn't always true that a person even recognizes his own strengths and weaknesses, let alone those of the people around him. Second, how to manage so that the strengths are maximized and the weaknesses are minimized is a skill that must be learned. It doesn't come naturally.

There are tests available to help individuals recognize their own strengths. These tests are available through a number of sources. You can begin by looking at one of the bigger bookstores. If you know someone in the personnel department of a larger company, they might be able to direct you to a company that can sell you one or more. Obviously, it also makes good sense to inquire of friends and others around us to determine what they believe are our strengths. Often they see us better than we see ourselves.

Utilizing human resources properly is similar to utilizing other resources properly. While it is possible to heat a house with a furnace, it is also possible to heat it by using the kitchen oven and heat lamps in the light sockets. I'd only consider the second option if the first were no longer a possibility. I wouldn't take our sports car on a family vacation if the four-door sedan was running fine. I might, in a pinch, but I'd first attempt to get the sedan ready for the trip.

As an employer, it makes sense for me to know the strengths and weaknesses of my people, and to utilize them effectively. The only times I might not are when I want to help them improve their weaknesses by exercise, or in those times when I have no other choices.

Principle 11: I'll Always Tell The Truth So I Won't Have To Remember What I've Said.

This one has been a blessing to me thousands of times. As many conversations as I get into, and considering the number of speeches I give, I can't even begin to remember what I've said to whom. This used to cause me real problems when I was teaching several twelve-week sales courses simultaneously. I'd begin one each month so I'd be speaking to a different group three nights each week. Because I often use stories and examples to illustrate different points, I'd have real difficulty at times remembering if I'd already used a specific example with a particular group, possibly a few weeks earlier.

That was tough enough. Imagine how difficult it would be if I were not committed to this principle of telling the truth, but decided to stretch the truth a little. It's one thing to tell the same story to the same group twice, it's quite another to tell it with a different set of facts each time. I've found that telling the truth is not only the "best policy," as some say, but it's the only policy that makes sense.

It's hard to believe I even need to mention this principle. I've learned the hard way, however, that the truth is almost as scarce as a gift without an ulterior motive. Fortunately, somewhere along the way, I learned that telling the truth pays.

Perhaps, I learned the hard way. I learned the value of telling the truth by tasting the bitterness of telling a lie. When I was a child I was fairly creative in manufacturing lies as I felt they were needed. They came to my rescue many times, helping me to avoid punishment or ridicule for wrongdoing. The real problems I experienced in telling lies, however, seemed to counterbalance the perceived benefits. They were:

- The fear I felt, thinking I might be caught lying
- The pressure to produce a truly believable lie
- The need to remember accurately the details of my lie
- The guilt I felt in the pit of my stomach for having lied
- The loss of self-respect I suffered

There came a day in my life when I determined that lying just wasn't worth it anymore. It may have been before I became a Christian, I can't really recall. I do know that my having become a Christian has certainly strengthened my resolve to be truthful and given me the courage to carry out that resolve. The above negatives have been replaced by positives. They are:

- I no longer fear being caught in a lie. I hope people check.
- I find the truth is often unbelievable, but I don't care.
- I no longer need to remember what I've said.
- I have personal satisfaction in knowing I've been truthful.
- Not only do I respect myself, but others do also.

Probably the most important value I've gained from being truthful is that I've earned the trust of others. If a man lies, or is untruthful about one thing, others never know in which areas he is being truthful and which areas he is not. There comes a point in which everything is taken with a grain of salt. Many of my stories I share seem so unbelievable anyway that I can't afford to lie. If I'm ever caught lying, others would begin to doubt me when I'm relating truth. I can't risk that happening.

Think about this. If a person tells one lie, and it is exposed, how many times must he tell the truth again before he is believed? The answer is that some will always find him suspect. The only way for that man to ever be trusted again by some is for him to become trustworthy. The way to become trustworthy is to confess the sin of deceit to the person or persons he has been attempting to deceive, and ask for forgiveness. It is this procedure which will clean the slate.

Once, when I was teaching this principle to a group of prisoners in a jail, a man challenged me by saying, "I don't believe it's possible to be truthful and be successful in business." I asked him why he felt that way. He told me that he had been in business for many years and had felt compelled to lie many times, or lose business. Potential customers would ask him his cost for an item and he would feel compelled to lie, or risk having them try to get him to cut his prices. Another example he gave me was similar. He said he felt he needed to lie to his employees concerning his profit margins, or risk being pressured to give them raises.

Here was my reply:

"I've been in business for many years, and a Christian for several years longer than that. I determined to be truthful long before I began my first business and I can tell you honestly that I've never had to compromise that principle in order to be successful. In fact, I'm confident that one of the key reasons I've been so successful is that my customers, suppliers, and employees know of my integrity. They know I'd prefer to lose them than lie to them. Whenever they ask me questions I'd rather they hadn't asked, I handle them in one of two ways. They are:

1) I'll be happy to answer that, but first I want to tell you one thing. I've found that my best customers are mature enough not to care how much I've paid for something, but to decide for themselves if I'm offering them a really great deal, all things being considered. When I buy something, I'm the same way. I'll gladly pay $100 for something that only cost my supplier $5, if the $100 is a great price for me. I've made deals like that many times. With this in mind, my cost (before overhead and related expenses) was $____ .

2) Quite frankly, I'd prefer not to answer your question. It's not because I'm ashamed for you to know, but rather, because it's a question that deserves a very complex answer — one which I don't care to discuss in depth at this time. There are a great many factors which go into running a successful business, only one of which is the cost of an item. It could easily take hours to show you the whole picture, and I really don't want to do that. I don't want to do it for two reasons. First, I don't want to take the time. Second, I'm not interested in training my next competitor. The only real question you need an answer for is, "Is this a great deal for me?" I always attempt to make every deal I enter a "win-win" situation for both of us, and this is no exception.

I believe the prisoner was impressed. He said he had never before encountered anyone in business who was committed to honesty — that he knew about. My challenge to him was, and my challenge to you is, be committed to this principle. It will serve you well all the days of your life! Notice these Bible verses:

Let not mercy and truth forsake you; Bind them around your neck, write them on the tablet of your heart, and so find favor and high esteem in the sight of God and man. **Proverbs 3:3,4 (NKJV)**

Buy the truth, and do not sell it, also wisdom and instruction and understanding. **Proverbs 23:23 (NKJV)**

Therefore, putting away lying, each one speak truth with his neighbor, for we are members of one another. **Ephesians 4:25 (NKJV)**

I might add that being truthful is not simply a matter of telling the truth, or refraining from telling a lie. It includes that which is implied in what we say. If we subtly imply that which is not truthful, or the absolute truth, then we are not being truthful — in the true sense of the word. "Silence means acceptance," a concept believed by many, shows us that another way to be untruthful, or deceptive is to allow a lie to be believed simply because we do not speak up. No, honesty is not an easy thing.

Consider this. When a person lies, or exaggerates the truth, he usually does so to present himself to others in a different light than he really is. If his story is accepted, he must now live up to it. Since he knows the truth, he has a hard time accepting himself while knowing he is living a lie. If others catch him lying, they will doubt everything else he has told them. All credibility is lost. While it is true that even a liar tells the truth sometimes, it is just as true that it becomes impossible to know when a person is telling the truth and when he is speaking a lie. Trust becomes impossible.

This principle has also proven itself invaluable to me as a negotiating tool. I am known as a "wheeler-dealer" to many. I'm always making deals. While working in my computer store, I may have as many as twenty deals working at one time. Since I buy, sell and trade many different items, it's again impossible to remember a deal I offered a few days ago. Now, I usually write it down somewhere but finding the piece of paper I wrote it on could prove to be almost as difficult. Often, when I'm discussing a deal with a person a few days after my initial offer, I'll ask him what my offer was. I'll tell him I've got it written down somewhere but prefer just to ask him rather than take the time to look it up. I mention that while I don't necessarily remember what I said in our earlier meeting, I always remember what I didn't say. By the way, I expect him to remember our previous conversation because they probably only had one like it while I've had hundreds. By asking him what our deal was, I'm giving him a chance to be honest. It is true that I'll immediately recognize his answer as being true or false once he gives it. This is because, just as I know I wouldn't have told him a lie, I wouldn't have offered him a deal other than the one I did. It may seem strange, but it works.

Telling the truth does something else for me too. It makes me feel really good about myself. While I realize that many will doubt my integrity anyway, I can easily accept myself as I am. I've often realized how stupid it would be to exaggerate, as many of the events in my life are unbelievable enough as they are. Others may not always believe me but that's not my problem—it's theirs.

Principle 12: If I Can't Say Something Good About Someone, I Should Be Careful About Saying Anything At All.

I first heard this principle from a chaplain when I was in the Army. I've heard it a number of times since and think it has a lot of merit. I must admit, however, while I think it's a great principle, and one worthy of listing here, I don't think it's one that should never be violated. There are exceptions.

Before I get to the exceptions, I'll discuss the reason for the principle. The world is full of people who have such poor self-images that they constantly cut down others in attempts to make the others lower than themselves. In reality, they are trying to make themselves look better than the other people. They look for weak areas and exploit them. Doing so rarely works and often backfires. People walk away from an individual who does this, thinking, "If he says that about her, what will he say about me when I'm gone?" Nobody really wants to be around someone who is always cutting others down.

One also ought to be very careful about sharing negative information about another unless one knows it to be absolutely true and absolutely necessary to be shared. Much of the information that travels through the gossip vine is inaccurate, as is information which is obtained from sources such as newspapers and magazines. Having read something, or heard it second hand doesn't make it so. Even if the facts are correct, there may be additional information concerning the story which would shed a totally different light. It is our responsibility to know the whole story if we're going to tell it. We should also recognize that the fact we're telling the story will get back to the person who is the subject of the story.

I believe every person deserves the right to defend himself against false accusation. Before I accept a story I've heard as being true, I intend to call the subject and ask him about it. If I'm not willing to verify it, I'm not going to spread it. If it's being spread, and false, I want to do my part to help stop it. If it is true but there is absolutely no real reason why I ought to tell another (see exceptions below), then I'll still keep it to myself. Whenever someone tells me something like this, I'll ask, "Why are you telling me this?"

Now, for the exceptions. First, if the person I'm talking to is about to be in danger, either personally or financially, because of an affiliation and he is unaware of it, I'll share the negative information. I'll do this only if I'm absolutely sure the negative information is true, and I'm willing to acknowledge that I've said it. I'll give the person I'm talking to permission to use my name when confronting the subject with the question of the matter I'm raising.

Second, if the person is asking my advice in order to make a comparison, I'll share any information I know to be accurate and applicable. Again, I'll allow him to reveal the source. The reason it is important to give him permission to reveal the source is that every person has a right to face his accuser. I'd want that right, and therefore, want to give others that right.

Principle 13: I Should Never Be Too Aggressive But Always Be Aggressive Enough.

This is a great principle to learn, especially when you are making a sale. Your response might be that you are not in sales. Reality is, however, that everyone attempts to make sales — probably more often than he realizes.

Consider this. Whenever you are trying to get another person to adopt your point of view, or to reconsider his, you are selling. Whenever you are trying to impress someone, you are selling. You are also selling when you are giving instructions, making requests, and negotiating a purchase. Selling can be defined many ways, and one of those ways is "acting in a specific manner so as to bring about a favorable response from another person."

Good salesmen are made, not born. I have over 200 books in my library on selling and I'll not try to duplicate their efforts here. I do recommend that you research the psychology of selling until you understand why and how people make buying decisions. Different types of people desire to be sold in different manners, and it is up to us (as salespeople) to know what those manners are. Some like to make fast decisions, and some like to take their time. Some want all the facts, and others simply want the bottom line. Some make decisions logically, and others decide with their hearts. The Golden Rule in selling is to sell to others "the way they want to be sold."

This principle, "Never be too aggressive, but always be aggressive enough," has served me well for many years. I learned a long time ago that it is difficult to sell to someone whom I've already burned with my zealousness or enthusiasm. The heat can always be turned up as needed, but it is meaningless to try to save the sale by turning it down after the prospect has been burned. Salesmen who are too aggressive are called "pushy," "high pressure" and "money hungry." Salesmen who sell based on the principle of not being too aggressive are called "problem solvers," "buyers' helpers," and "consultants." As you might suspect, this latter group is respected much more than the former.

I worked as a commissioned salesman for a company for 3 years in the early 1980's. By the end of my first full year I had sold more in one year than anyone else had in one year in the company's 20-year history. We did a study after two years and found that my sales for the second year exceeded the next 10 salespeople combined. The amazing part of that story to me was that they were averaging a combined total of 140 appointments per week while I was averaging only 3! We were all selling to the corporate market and some of them had much larger cities than I did. I was in St. Louis, while they had New York, Chicago, and Philadelphia, to name a few. My sales percentage was approximately 90%. I always believe that a company worth calling on is a company worth selling.

One day my boss, the owner of the company, told me that he had almost made a big mistake by failing to hire me. After our first interview he had evaluated that I wasn't aggressive enough. Another person in his company, who had also interviewed me, had persuaded him to give me a chance. He was glad he had.

I told him I had been aggressive enough. The proof was in the fact that I was given the job. If he had wanted to see me get more aggressive, all he would have had to do was refuse to hire me. He hadn't given me a chance to prove my worth as a salesman. He had said "yes" too quickly!

Principle 14: I Will Never Allow Someone Else To Make Me Feel Inferior Without My Permission, And I Will Refuse To Give My Permission.

We live in a world where almost everyone believes that the way to get to the top is to step on enough other people. Those some people can't step on, they attempt to belittle through sarcasm, unfair comparisons, and lack of recognition.

Very few people are out to make us feel good about ourselves. They are much too concerned about making us feel good about them. The problem lies in the fact that we sometimes fall into the trap of playing the comparison game and end up as losers. We leave the game park with our heads hung low, feeling inferior.

While it is true that others are superior to us in many areas, it is also true that we may be superior to them in other areas. Few people have got us beat on all counts, and so what if they do? What we don't know is what kind of people they would be if they had been dealt the same cards as we were. Where would they be in life if they had been born into our families, with our sets of circumstances? God only knows!

The key here is to realize that being inferior in a particular area doesn't make one inferior as a person. Even if we determine that we are inferior in every measurable category, when compared to others, that doesn't determine the final score in the game of life. God keeps track of that scorebook. He teaches in His word that His "strength is made perfect in our weakness."

(2 Corinthians 12:9)

Where we are today is not as important as the direction we are headed, and where we will be tomorrow. I'd rather be on the bottom headed in the right direction than to be at the top headed in the wrong direction. Think about that.

Principle 15: I Should Never Sell Myself Short, Or Give Away The Store In Order To Make A Sale.

One of my purposes in writing this book has been to give you a vision of the person you can become. I've named my company Potential Unlimited to convey that idea as well. My point is this — you're probably worth much more than you think!

I once heard Earl Nightingale tell a story about the "Money Machine." He asked what we would insure a machine for that produced thousands of dollars each year, and was ours to keep for the rest of our life. The machine he was referring to was, of course, us. Many of us get to feeling low at times and don't think we're worth very much. Even at minimum wage, we're worth over $350,000 as income producing machines! An arm or leg can be worth more than $250,000 alone, according to some court settlements. Who would sell an eye for less than $100,000, or even $1,000,000?

Picture this one. In the year 1990, Patrick Ewing earned more than $4,000,000 as a professional basketball player. Wouldn't it have been a great deal if he had signed a lifetime contract, while still a high school student, for a guaranteed $100,000 per year? Of course not! That would mean he would have to live and work for 40 years to earn what he is now earning in only 1 year. While this illustration seems so obvious, and ridiculous, stories abound concerning the number of people who have made deals this bad, or worse.

Agents are always on the lookout for talent that can make them rich. There are good agents, and there are bad ones. The bad ones are those who protect all their own interests without even giving the talents a fair understanding of their options. They can make their deals sound so sweet by only focusing on a small portions of the whole picture.

Proverbs teaches that there is safety in a multitude of counsel. It only makes sense to seek and to receive counsel before one makes a deal that seems too good to be true. I've often remarked that I will gladly pay $1 million for an ink pen, if I can set the terms of payment. I learned long ago that almost everything is negotiable. Whenever I sign a lease for office space, I always give myself a "Two-Month Out" in case I need to move on short notice. With this clause intact, and all other terms acceptable, I don't mind signing a 100-year contract.

You should make sure that you are receiving value equal to the value you are giving. This is true, whether you are negotiating the terms of a contract or are agreeing to spend your time involved in a particular activity. Some of the questions which need to be considered are:

- What are the benefits of this situation?
- What are the drawbacks?
- What is the best thing that could happen?
- What is the worst thing that could happen?
- Are there any possible limitations or restrictions?
- What will happen if things improve more than expected?
- What will happen if expectations are not met?
- What are the penalties involved?
- How might inflation or a recession affect this situation?
- What are the terms of cancellation or nonfulfillment?

Remember: Think big! As you get more involved in setting goals, you are going to find yourself becoming more and more valuable. Everything about you will be subject to change. Your desires, interests, attitudes, and perspectives will all change to some degree, and you'll not want to be limited to decisions you made prior to the changes.

Here's an example. I'm writing this book, a project I consider to be the most important goal I've had thus far in my young life. It may actually be the most important thing I'll ever accomplish, depending on the effect it has on others' lives. I plan to publish it myself initially, and if I ever allow a publisher to do so, I'll retain enough rights to assure me the flexibility I desire for the future. I don't have grandiose expectations for this book, but I am keeping my options open just in case it helps others as much as I hope it will.

Principles 16 – 20:

These remaining principles are those which I cover in detail elsewhere in various chapters. I only list them here as additional examples of principles I've personally chosen to guide my life.

Principle 16: Always evaluate where I am in relationship to where I desire to be, and have a plan as to how I will get there.

Principle 17: Always attempt to learn from the mistakes of others instead of having to make them myself.

Principle 18: Always look at each failure and mistake I do make as a positive learning experience for which I have paid tuition.

Principle 19: Never accept defeat without first doing my research and evaluating my options.

Principle 20: Never allow the circumstances in my life to determine my attitude. Allow my attitude to determine my circumstances.

·Thirteen·
Self-Control
(Making Yourself Do It)

You have done well already in that you've read this far in the book. As one of my former bosses used to say, "Good on you!" You're about to accomplish something that over 50 percent of all adults never do — read an entire book after getting out of school. Those who do read average only 1.6 books per year.

In reading this far you've exhibited a quality that will be very necessary as you attempt to become the person you want to be. That quality is self-discipline. I define self-discipline as "one's ability to make himself do that which is necessary to complete a task or accomplish a goal." Self-discipline involves training oneself in the art of self-control.

There are many aspects to consider when attempting to improve our self-control. First, we ought to ask ourselves why it is that we don't always exhibit self-control. Why do we lose our battle to get out of bed an hour early to exercise? Why, after determining that we are going to do whatever is necessary to lose weight, do we find ourselves eating more sweets than ever before? If we are not controlling ourselves, who or what is? As a productive exercise, reflect on this last question for a few minutes; then jot down your conclusions.

As I contemplated my answer, my thoughts immediately turned to the Bible. God is not only the divine author of this book; He is also our Creator. Because He created us and is concerned with each of us, He has provided us with answers to many of life's questions in the Bible. Man is a very complex being and his design demands a Creator. To ignore the Creator, and His instructions in this most important matter, is to err indeed.

In discussing the topic of self-control, I desire to give the best information available concerning the ways and means of getting what we really want out of life. I realize that there are thousands of books available in libraries and bookstores that tell us how to pick ourselves up by our bootstraps. However, inasmuch as these books rely solely on an individual's own strength and ignore the God who made them, the information they contain ultimately falls far short.

The information falls short for two reasons: it fails to recognize the real source of our problems and it provides inadequate solutions.

First, these books often deal only with the symptoms while ignoring the root source of our problems. It's like taking an aspirin to relieve the pain of a headache instead of working to eliminate the cause of the headache. Perhaps one has a headache because one is under extreme stress. While stress may be the cause of the headache, it is not the real source. To find that, one must find the reason for the stress. The stress might be caused by one factor, (bitterness, financial difficulties, guilt, job overload, fear, etc.) or a combination of several factors.

The root cause of our lack of self-control is that we are born with a sinful nature. We've inherited it from Adam. Left on our own, without God's influence, we will not become better, but more depraved.

The second reason most self-help books fall far short is that they provide us with inadequate solutions. Often, their solutions are only partial or temporary. While they may prove worthwhile in helping us deal with small problems in our lives, they are only tools; they do not provide us with a total solution.

For example, I could help you win the battle of getting up an hour early to exercise by implementing one or more principles I've already mentioned. We could apply the "Penalty Principle" and agree that you'd pay me $500 for each time you fail to rise on time. Perhaps we could hire a Marine Drill Sergeant to help you up each morning, in the manner to which he is accustomed. Or, we could design a bed that automatically raises on one end two minutes after the alarm sounds off, dumping you into a pool of ice water if you are still in bed. Utilizing the "Reward Principle," you could promise yourself something special such as a new sports car or a fabulous vacation, to be received after six months of faithful adherence to this new activity. You could place a body builder's picture on your bathroom wall to help you visualize and constantly remind you of the physical conditioning you plan to attain. Yes, there are many ideas and principles that can prove useful in helping us to win some of the inner battles we frequently face.

Not all of our battles, however, are so easy to win. Let's say you're married and have a very real objective to remain faithful to your spouse. Your marriage has become somewhat mundane and boring, and the arguments have increased over the past few months. Your spouse doesn't seem to appreciate or care about you very much anymore, and you've become attracted to someone else with whom you are in contact on a regular basis. This new person seems also to enjoy our company, and you find yourself longing to be together more often. You realize you are treading in treacherous waters, and thus, the internal battle begins. You can actually get to the point where you are in love with two people and become quite confused as to what to do. Most people who get involved in adulterous affairs didn't plan to do so. They say, "It just happened!" What really happened is that they lost the internal battle when they failed to recognize and apply Biblical principles to their situations. The Apostle Paul addresses this very problem:

> *For what I am doing, I do not understand. For what I will to do, that I do not practice; but what I hate, that I do. If, then, I do what I will not to do, I agree with the law that it is good. Now then, it is no longer I who do it, but sin that dwells in me. For I know that in me (that is, in my flesh) nothing good dwells; for to will is present with me, but how to perform what is good I do not find. For the good that I will to do, I do not do; but the evil I will not to do, that I practice. Now if I do what I will not to do, it is no longer I who do it, but sin that dwells in me. I find then a law, that evil is present with me, the one who wills to do good. For I delight in the law of God according to the inward man. But I see another law in my members, warring against the law of my mind, and bringing me into captivity to the law of sin which is in my members. O wretched man that I am! Who will deliver me from this body of death? I thank God —through Jesus Christ our Lord! So then, with the mind I myself serve the law of God, but with the flesh the law of sin.* **Romans 7:15-25 (NKJV)**

Don't feel bad if you have to read that passage more than once or twice to understand its full meaning. Most of us who have been Christians for many years still have to read this one through more than once, and very few can say they understand it fully. We do recognize that Paul is describing an experience to which we can often relate. I'll summarize it for you.

Man is a three-dimensional being. He consists of body, soul, and spirit. It is the body which houses the soul and spirit. The term "flesh" in the passage above refers to that which is within man that makes him want to sin. It includes both the body (physical flesh) and the heart (seat of emotions). What Paul was saying was that his will was not strong enough, in and of itself, to control his flesh, which was already being controlled by the law of sin. His will was desirous of doing that which was consistent with God's law, but he was still experiencing an inner battle with the sin that was always present.

Without God, man's prospects aren't too good. Consider these verses:

> *As it is written: "There is none righteous, no, not one; There is none who understands; There is none who seeks after God. They have all gone out of the way; They have together become unprofitable; There is none who does good, no, not one. Their throat is an open tomb; With their tongues they have practiced deceit; The poison of asps is under their lips; Whose mouth is full of cursing and bitterness. Their feet are swift to shed blood; Destruction and misery are in their ways; And the way of peace they have not known. There is no fear of God before their eyes."* **Romans 3:10-18 (NKJV)**

> *The heart is deceitful above all things, and desperately wicked; Who can know it? I, the LORD, search the heart, I test the mind, even to give every man according to his ways, and according to the fruit of his doings.* **Jeremiah 17:9-10 (NKJV)**

(This passage certainly throws water on those who suggest we should just follow the dictates of our hearts. One song even has asked, "How can it be wrong when it feels so right?" The answer is simple. Our hearts will attempt to trick us, for they want their own way. Please note, however, what we can expect when we follow the dictates of our hearts.)

There is a way which seems right to a man, but its end is the way of death. **Proverbs 14:12 (NKJV)**

But we are all like an unclean thing, and all our righteousnesses are like filthy rags; We all fade as a leaf, and our iniquities, like the wind, have taken us away. **Isaiah 64:6 (NKJV)**

(That last passage describes our goodness as it compares to the righteousness of a Holy God. The result of the evaluation is that "our righteousnesses are like filthy rags.")

This I say then, Walk in the Spirit, and ye shall not fulfil the lust of the flesh. For the flesh lusteth against the Spirit, and the Spirit against the flesh: and these are contrary the one to the other: so that ye cannot do the things that ye would. But if ye be led of the Spirit, ye are not under the law.

Now the works of the flesh are manifest, which are these; adultery, fornication, uncleanness, lasciviousness, idolatry, witchcraft, hatred, variance, emulations, wrath, strife, seditions, heresies, envyings, murders, drunkenness, revellings, and such like: of the which I tell you before, as I have also told you in time past, that they which do such things shall not inherit the kingdom of God.

But the fruit of the Spirit is love, joy, peace, long-suffering, gentleness, goodness, faith, meekness, temperance: against such there is no law. And they that are Christ's have crucified the flesh with the affections and lusts. If we live in the Spirit, let us also walk in the Spirit. Let us not be desirous of vain glory, provoking one another, envying one another. **Galatians 5:16-26 (KJV)**

(The key to gaining control over the flesh, as Paul describes it, is to yield control to the Spirit of God which indwells every believer. In this next passage he tells us that righteousness cannot come by keeping the law — only by allowing the Son of God, Jesus Christ, to live in us by faith.)

I am crucified with Christ: nevertheless I live; yet not I, but Christ liveth in me: and the life which I now live in the flesh I live by the faith of the Son of God, who loved me, and gave himself for me. I do not frustrate the grace of God: for if righteousness come by the law, then Christ is dead in vain. **Galatians 2:20,21 (KJV)**

If we could have lived righteous lives, Christ would not have had to give His life on the cross. It was not within our power to do so. Only He has the power over sin, and we can experience it by allowing Him to live in and through us. To the degree that we yield to Him, to that degree we will experience victory.

Consider these next two passages. They shed additional insight into this conflict. The conflict occurs, in part, when we desire, or lust after, things which are not consistent with what God desires for us. He knows what is best for us, and even desires to give it to us in accordance with His will, as revealed in His word, the Bible. The world is actually Satan's domain, and it is his goal to woo us away from God's will through his many devices and temptations.

Do not love the world or the things in the world. If anyone loves the world, the love of the Father is not in him. For all that is in the world — the lust of the flesh, the lust of the eyes, and the pride of life — is not of the Father but is of the world. **I John 2:15,16 (NKJV)**

Where do wars and fights come from among you? Do they not come from your desires for pleasure that war in your members? You lust and do not have. You murder and covet and cannot obtain. You fight and war. Yet you do not have because you do not ask. You ask and do not receive, because you ask amiss, that you may spend it on your pleasures. Adulterers and adulteresses! Do you not know that friendship with the world is enmity with God? Whoever therefore wants to be a friend of the world makes himself an enemy of God. Or do you think that the Scripture says in vain, "The Spirit who dwells in us yearns jealously"? But He gives more grace. Therefore He says: "God resists the proud, but gives grace to the humble." Therefore submit to God. Resist the devil and he will flee from you. **James 4:1-7 (NKJV)**

I recognize that some readers may be blown away by now. You probably didn't begin this chapter expecting anything quite so heavy. The fact is that I could "sugar coat" it and perhaps leave some of you feeling more comfortable — for now. I'm convinced, however, that if you've read this far, you're mature enough to handle the truth, not some sugarcoated version of it. My primary goal is to give you the information and tools you need to get the most out of life. I'll switch gears after quoting this next passage.

> *Finally, my brethren, be strong in the Lord and in the power of his might. Put on the whole armor of God, that you may be able to stand against the wiles of the devil. For we do not wrestle against flesh and blood, but against principalities, against powers, against the rulers of the darkness of this age, against spiritual hosts of wickedness in the heavenly places. Therefore take up the whole armor of God, that you may be able to withstand in the evil day, and having done all, to stand. Stand therefore, having girded your waist with truth, having put on the breastplate of righteousness, and having shod your feet with the preparation of the gospel of peace; above all, taking the shield of faith with which you will be able to quench all the fiery darts of the wicked one. And take the helmet of salvation, and the sword of the Spirit, which is the word of God; praying always with all prayer and supplication in the Spirit, being watchful to this end with all perseverance and supplication for all the saints.* **Ephesians 6:10-18 (NKJV)**

As a Christian and student of the Bible for over 23 years now, it is often difficult for me to comprehend the thought processes of those who have never been exposed to this material. I can only faintly recall my thinking from my early adult years. I believe it was a mixture of bewilderment, curiosity, fear, and frustration. I didn't know where to even begin in my search for answers to my many questions. Fortunately, for me, my search for truth included an education found within the pages of the Bible. As you can see, I became convinced it does contain real answers which are practical for today!

Perhaps you've determined by now that this issue of gaining self-control through self-discipline is not an easy chore. If so, you're correct! It is, however, worth the effort. Life is too short and too valuable to waste. It is, as

I've stated throughout this book, much more exciting when you live it with a purpose rather than as a wandering generality.

Let me use an illustration I once heard about possessions. Often we desire certain material possessions. We set a goal and, after much work and effort, we save enough to make the purchases. It isn't too long in this game called "accumulation" that we open our eyes to that fact that we don't own our possessions — they own us! If we're not careful, we find ourselves spending much of our free time repairing and maintaining those possessions we purchased to enjoy.

In this same way, we were given bodies by God to house our souls and spirits. Our bodies provide us with many advantages, and can be real blessings if we take care of them. We have the responsibility to properly care for our bodies (eat, sleep, exercise), and to maintain control over them. Our bodies can become terrible masters if we allow them that liberty. In the scripture quoted previously, John talked about the "lust of the flesh." It is this lust of the flesh that strongly encourages us to sin against ourselves.

This encouragement (some would call it a demand) may come in the form of a desire to eat too much (or eat something not good for us), become involved in sexual immorality, relax when we should be working, or yield to some addictive habit it has developed. Is it any wonder that James refers to this situation as a "war" in our members? Yes, there is a real battle going on and we, like Paul, must often admit, "For the good that I will to do, I do not do; but the evil I will not to do, that I practice."

The Apostle Paul encourages us to live our lives as if we are running a disciplined, confident race:

> *Do you not know that those who run in a race all run, but one receives the prize? Run in such a way that you may obtain it. And everyone who competes for the prize is temperate in all things. Now they do it to obtain a perishable crown, but we for an imperishable crown. Therefore I run thus: not with uncertainty. Thus I fight: not as one who beats the air. But I discipline my body and bring it into subjection, lest, when I have preached to others, I myself should become disqualified.* **I Corinthians 9:24-27 (NKJV)**

Notice that Paul says, "I discipline my body and bring it into subjection." He says that he runs with a purpose, his direction clearly determined. He didn't waste time shadowboxing but entered into a real battle to bring his body under control. We must do the same.

Our bodies, if left to their own desires, will not help us to achieve the goals we've set — especially if they are goals which require extraordinary effort. If great achievements were easy, everybody would be realizing them, and they wouldn't be considered "great" anymore.

The next question to be answered is, how does one bring his body "into subjection?" In other words, how do we gain self-control? The answer is: through self-discipline. We train our bodies to do that which is best for us. Because of the sin that dwells in us (something we inherited from Adam), we will never achieve total control or dominance over our bodies. Sin will often, like a dragon, rear its ugly head. It simply waits for us to drop our guard. Have you ever noticed how a good habit, like exercise, is quickly abandoned if you don't continually focus on doing it?

I suggest that there are ten disciplines we can apply to our lives in order to obtain self-control. These are:

1) Remove or eliminate those things which tempt us to do what is in opposition, or contrary, to our stated goals.
2) Replace bad or negative habits with good or positive habits.
3) Associate with and learn from others who challenge and encourage us.
4) Maintain healthy attitudes by feeding our minds on a daily basis.
5) Be accountable to those who will be faithful in holding us accountable.
6) Establish "base acceptable bottoms."
7) Use "Memory Joggers" as prompts.
8) Make daily "To Do" lists.
9) Learn to say "no."
10) Trust God for the strength to do what we ought.

Now, let's look at each of these guidelines in some detail.

Remove or Eliminate Those Things Which Tempt Us To Do That Which Is Contrary To, Or In Opposition to, Our Stated Goals

Our own physical natures (or "flesh") can impede us from achieving our stated goals. Paul gives us some insight into controlling our flesh in the book of Romans, where he says:

> *But put ye on the Lord Jesus Christ, and make not provision for the flesh, to fulfill the lusts thereof.* **Romans 13:14 (KJV)**

One way to control your flesh is to fail to make provisions to fulfill its lusts. If you have a drinking problem, don't hang around the bar and don't stock your cabinets with liquor. If you're trying to lose weight, stay out of the candy store. If you can't seem to get out of bed early enough, become accountable to someone else to do so. Do whatever you have to do to establish control over those desires which hinder you in the attainment of your goals.

Removing stumbling blocks is not always an easy thing to do. We fight internal battles all the way to victory; the flesh does not give up. It may cause us to feel childish, or encourage us to rationalize why we should accept particular situations which will later make compromise easy. If our flesh has a favorite phrase, surely it must be among these: "Go ahead; just this once," "You can handle it," "You'll still make it," and "Nobody else will know." I've known people who carried packs of cigarettes around with them while attempting to quit, just to prove to themselves that they had power over the habit. Few have remained "smoke-free" very long. I've known girls who, in spite of their desire to marry as virgins, thought they could go "parking" on lover's lanes — they became pregnant! Others who decided to quit gambling couldn't just stand and watch friendly poker games — they lost all they had. The truth is that "if you play with fire, sooner or later you'll get burned." Make no provision for the flesh to fulfill the lusts thereof!

Replace Bad or Negative Habits With Good or Positive Habits

Improper habits are an obstacle to goal achievement. We previously discussed the following bad or negative habits:

- Poor sleeping
- Poor eating
- Poor personal hygiene
- Sloppy dress and grooming
- Lazy work
- Inadequate study
- Excessive entertainment
- Immorality
- Vices
- Poor communication

When exchanging a bad habit for a good one, it is important that you understand the "Principle of Displacement." This principle states that the easiest way to eliminate a bad habit is to displace it by establishing another, more desirable habit in its place. Establish good eating and sleeping habits and the bad ones will be displaced. The same is true with all the other categories listed above.

Since a very large percentages of our lives are governed by habits, it only makes sense that we take the time to determine that those habits are positive ones. It may take great effort to establish a habit, but once in place, it will serve you well, requiring only a fraction of the effort to maintain it. Many attest that it only takes 23 days to establish a habit. Whether it takes 23 days or three months, the important thing is that once you form that habit, you can enjoy the benefits from having done so for the rest of your life.

I recall watching Peter Vidmar being interviewed after the U.S. Men's Gymnastic team won the gold medal in the 1984 Olympics. He was asked if he ever got nervous before an activity. If so, what did he do about it? He replied that he simply focused on the very first move (grabbing the bar correctly) and once that was completed, his body would take over from there and do as it had been trained to do — execute the routine. That was his answer to maintaining self-control in the face of great pressure.

Yes, one of the easiest ways to gain self-control is to develop good habits through self-discipline. We can literally train ourselves to do what we ought.

Associate With and Learn From Others Who Will Challenge and Encourage Us

Whenever I move into a new area, one of my first priorities is to develop relationships with sharp men who will both challenge and encourage me with their life-styles. Many years ago I was told that I'd always be the same except for two things: the ideas I allow to enter my head and the people I encounter. I've found this to be true.

In 1989, I moved to Orlando, Florida. Because I had sold a business and therefore had enough cash to carry me for a few months, I decided to use those months to meet new people and develop relationships. I had moved from the St. Louis area where I had developed some great relationships in my almost 10 years there. I wasn't sure what to expect in Florida.

We purposed, as a family, to meet and get to know as many neighbors and church families as we possibly could, as quickly as we could. For several months, we invited an average of two families per week over for dinner: the results were fantastic! Within eight months, I felt like I'd lived in Orlando for several years. I'd already developed a base of exciting new friends that were challenging me. We had left a great neighborhood in Missouri and moved into one just as great. We left several families we really loved in our church and quickly met and developed relationships with even more people in our new church. I soon realized I'd been doubly blessed. I still had my friends in Missouri and had significantly increased the number of positive people in my life just by making the move.

This, of course, would never have happened had we not disciplined ourselves to make it happen. At one point we had entertained over 30 families in our home while having been invited to someone else's home only once. While this may seem unusual, it really isn't. Only a few people take the initative to be hospitable by inviting families which they don't already know. We have had families over for dinner who said it was their first such experience. I've known people who talked about getting together for years before they finally got around to it!

By the way, I don't mind this situation. First, because I understand it. Second, because I still gain a great deal from the relationships which are built by this discipline. I'm strengthened, challenged, encouraged, and greatly blessed by the lives of those I'm given the opportunity to know better. All of these benefits motivate me to become even more disciplined, and thereby give me greater self-control. Three Bible verses that have guided my thinking regarding this matter are:

> *As iron sharpens iron, so a man sharpens the countenance of his friend.* **Proverbs 27:17 (NKJV)**

> *He who walks with wise men will be wise, but the companion of fools will be destroyed.* **Proverbs 13:20 (NKJV)**

> *Make no friendship with an angry man, and with a furious man do not go, lest you learn his ways and set a snare for your soul.* **Proverbs 22:24 (NKJV)**

It is extremely important to constantly learn from others, especially those who have excelled in the areas in which we are striving. In this respect, we can benefit from the lessons of both the living and the dead. Remember, "Only a fool learns from his own mistakes when he could have learned from someone else's mistakes."

Probably no investment you ever will make will be any greater than the investment you can make in your future when you take the time to learn from others. At the least, make use of the vast resources available at your public library. Always realize that one good idea might easily be worth millions of dollars — if you discover it and use it!

Maintain Healthy Attitudes By Feeding Our Minds on a Daily Basis

Once your desire has become a goal with a defined action plan to achieve it, you might expect the fulfillment of that desire to be "a piece of cake." Right? Not so fast!

You're well on your way, all right, but you still can be easily sidetracked. The best laid plans of men have often become null and void when the men who laid them decided they no longer wanted to "pay the price."

Our emotions and our frames of mind are funny things. One day we can want things so badly that we would almost offer our lives in exchange for them, and the next day, we won't even get out of bed for it. In order for dreams to come true, we must wake up and begin the day! The reality is, however, that often we yield our bodies to the emotions and temptations of the moment. We yield to our attitudes, our states of mind. If they're positive — great! If, however, we don't really "feel" like making the effort to put forth the work required, we often don't.

Probably nothing has a greater effect on our daily walks than our attitudes. Our attitudes determine how we respond to conflicts and problems which frequently occur in our lives. Circumstances, like the weather, are constantly changing. We cannot afford the luxury of allowing our attitudes to be determined by our circumstances. Our attitudes must remain fixed far above the levels of our circumstances.

Consider God's perspective on this important subject:

> *Set your mind on things above, not on things on the earth.* **Colossians 3:2 (NKJV)**

> *You will keep him in perfect peace, whose mind is stayed on You, because he trusts in You.* **Isaiah 26:3 (NKJV)**

Rejoice in the Lord always. Again I will say, rejoice! Let your gentleness be known to all men. The Lord is at hand. Be anxious for nothing, but in everything by prayer and supplication, with thanksgiving, let your requests be made known unto God; and the peace of God, which passes all understanding, will guard your hearts and minds through Christ Jesus. Finally, brethren, whatever things are true, whatever things are noble, whatever things are just, whatever things are pure, whatever things are lovely, whatever things are of good report, if there is any virtue and if there is anything praiseworthy — meditate on these things. The things which you learned and received and heard and saw in me, these do, and the God of peace will be with you. **Philippians 4:4-9 (NKJV)**

He who heeds the word wisely will find good, and whoever trusts in the LORD, happy is he. **Proverbs 16:20 (NKJV)**

These verses make it very clear that the right attitude, a peaceful, thankful, happy attitude, can come from focusing on and trusting in the Lord. He is far above all circumstances. There is nothing too hard for the Lord.

Some call our attitudes the "wanna" that is a must for us to do our best. It is seldom that any of us give our best anyway — let alone when we don't "wanna." I can easily run two miles when I "wanna," but I can barely run at all when I lack that "wanna."
Until now, you've been writing your dreams on paper and working on action plans (blueprints) to show you how to make them happen. It has become somewhat easy to want these dreams to come true, hasn't it? Goal setting is based upon figuring out what you want in life.

The day you begin walking through your plan, is the day "the rubber meets the road," so to speak. Reality hits you square in the face. I faced reality when I decided to conquer my fear of jumping from an airplane.

I had feared the feeling of falling for long enough. I often envisioned myself being in a situation where I would need to jump from a burning building or a crippled airplane, and didn't like the thought that I might "freeze" and be afraid to jump. I've learned that attacking my fears, meeting them head on, gives me great joy — once I've done it, that is. Thus, I determined to make the jump on my 40th birthday. I figured a person ought to make an exclamation point on his 40th, and this would be mine.

Some say one goes "over the hill" when he reaches 40 years of age. While that may be true, it is also true that one picks up speed when going downhill. We've all heard the saying that "life begins at forty." Deciding to jump from an airplane gave me mixed feelings. Sure, I felt some fear, and yet joy, as I looked forward to being on the "other side" of the jump.

Writing my desire to jump in my "Goal Book" was the first step. Setting a date to fulfill that desire was the second. I called an airport and received the name of a jump school. All that was required was for me to attend a four-hour class and pay $95.00. That seemed like a small price to pay to conquer my fear. I made the plans and invited my wife to attend.

The lessons went fine, and the time to enter the airplane soon arrived. Before I knew it, the time also arrived for me to step out of the plane and onto the jump step. I was instructed to grab the wing braces and "walk" my hands out several feet until I was leaning as far out as I could lean. My next move was to remove my feet from the step and hang onto the wing brace, facing the front of the plane.

Saundra later asked me if I found it difficult to hang onto the wing traveling through the sky at over 100 miles per hour. I answered, "Not at all! Hanging on was easy; the hard part was letting go!" Not until I stepped out of the plane did the full impact of what I was about to do hit me. It hit me right "in the face," so to speak. Not only did I notice we were up 3,000 feet, but the wind was very real!

I did as I had been instructed to do: I leaned out and stepped off. I then looked at the instructor and received the "thumbs up" signal letting me know I could go ahead and jump. I had been instructed to look up to the bottom side of the wing and fix my eyes on an eight-inch, red dot painted there. Once seeing it, I was to shout "dot" and let go, falling away from the plane, my arms and legs extended from my body, forming an "X." I looked for the dot; I saw the dot; I yelled "dot." I waited and nothing happened! My hands had failed to hear me. I didn't have the courage to look at the instructor again, so I returned my gaze to the big red dot. Once again I yelled "dot," even louder than before.

Still nothing happened! I began to rationalize. I said something like: "Gene, you're traveling at 100 miles per hour away from the spot where you were supposed to jump. You're not going back in that plane; you came here to jump, so let go!" I think I may have even quoted Philippians 4:13 to myself, which says: "I can do all things through Christ which strengthens me." At any rate, I finally jumped and lived through it. I don't know that I'm anxious to do it again, but I'm awfully glad I did it once!

I'm convinced the thing that most helped me to fulfill that goal was my ability to see myself on the other side of the jump. I knew the odds were very slim that I'd die making the jump. I was more afraid of the feeling I'd experience before my chute opened. I was driven by my intense desire to have that experience behind me. I visualized myself as being able to look back on the experience and feel good about it, as I'm doing now. It was worthwhile!

You can tell that I had the "wanna." I'm not sure, however, that the desire to make the jump was enough to help me through the experience. To assure myself of success, I did one more thing — something that is vital for us if we are ever going to realize our really tough goals: I became accountable!

Be Accountable To Those Who Will Be Faithful In Holding Us Accountable

Accountability means having to answer to others for our actions. As children we were accountable to our parents. As students, we were accountable to our teachers. And as employees, we are accountable to our employers. When I really want to do something requiring courage or great effort, I become accountable. I may be accountable to one or two people, or I might be accountable to a very large number of people.

When I decided to become accountable to others in my goal to parachute from an airplane, I told almost everyone I came in contact with in the two weeks preceding the jump. I announced it at work to my customers and employees, and at my church to all my friends. I wouldn't have been able to face them if I hadn't jumped. Through becoming accountable, I actually made the cost of "not jumping" greater than the cost of jumping. The cost of jumping was "courage," whereas the cost of not jumping would have been great embarrassment.

I don't think it is necessary to become accountable to someone else for every single goal. Only you can decide for which of your goals you need to become accountable. If you are able to walk through your action plan without wavering, it is obvious you don't need to be accountable. If, however, you are continually procrastinating, or falling behind, you should become accountable immediately!

I'm often asked about the proper frequency of meeting with an accountability partner. (These meetings, by the way, can occur via telephone, letter, or in person.) My answer is simple: as often as is necessary. If just knowing that you'll be held accountable at the end of your deadline keeps you on track, then that's great! If, however, you need the boost to get going every day, then be accountable on a daily basis, at least in the beginning. The frequency necessary depends totally on you, and your degree of self-discipline.

Perhaps you're wondering to whom you should become accountable. In determining the right person, you might consider someone who:
- Cares about you
- Has demonstrated success in the same area
- Will also benefit as, or when, you succeed
- Will be encouraged by your success
- Will be faithful to hold you accountable
- Will not easily accept your failure
- Is willing to share in the required activity

Establish *"Base Acceptable Bottoms"*

There are at least two different levels at which we operate much of the time. The first might be referred to as "our best," or a 100% effort. (Some talk about giving 110%, but let's face it, 100% is all there is.) The other level might be classified as the "acceptable level." This is the least we'll accept of ourselves, if we're going to do anything at all.

Another level, although not a mode of operation, is the lazy or "do-nothing" mode. It becomes extremely difficult to accomplish very much that's worthwhile while we're in this mode. Thus, it behooves us to make sure we're always operating at one of the other two levels.

I was challenged many years ago by an instructor of a sales course who taught those attending his classes to establish what he called a "Base Acceptable Bottom" for every important activity. He defined this base acceptable bottom as "the least amount of work that we will accept from ourselves before quitting." If we are calling on potential customers, we might set our base acceptable bottom (or "base") at 10. Or, we might make the base the least amount of time that we would spend performing the particular activity. Yet another approach using this principle would be to determine the least success we would find acceptable before quitting.

The point is this: If we have established "bases," we will generally be more consistent and accomplish more over the long haul than if we just work when we feel like it. We will find it much easier getting started when we know all we have to do is to meet our bases.
Two amazing things happen when you work under this principle. First, the base's productivity adds up very quickly. The principle of a thing being "a cinch by the inch" becomes reality. Second, you often find additional energy and motivation waiting for you at the finish line of the base. There is an old adage that really applies here: "Go as far as your headlights will allow you to see, and when you get there you will always be able to see farther."

Here's a personal example. Several years ago when my son, Joel, was about eight years old, we often went running together. We set a base acceptable bottom to run a chosen lap consisting of various streets in our neighborhood. Usually, we ran one to two miles. One day, after running about one-and-a-half miles, we passed in front of our house. Joel started complaining that he couldn't run any farther. He said he was "totally exhausted" and couldn't make it to the end of our run, another half mile away. He was holding his side and saying "No way, Dad!" I continued to encourage him to at least make it to the next corner, about 200 yards away. (I was establishing a new "base" in his mind.) He agreed and we continued running. When we arrived, I turned the corner and said, "Come on, let's at least make it to the bottom of this hill. Running downhill is easy."

As we continued running, I got this bright idea. I slowed down to allow him to pull even with me. As he did, I said, "Joel, you get in front and you lead the way. Quit whenever you need to quit." I figured I'd pulled him toward my base as far as I could and he needed to establish his own. To my surprise, he not only kept running when he got to the bottom of the hill, but he even picked up the pace. It became obvious to me that he was going to run all the way to my original base acceptable bottom! I was excited, to say the least.

When we arrived at the corner, having a full two miles behind us, I fully expected him to stop and we'd rejoice together at his having made it. I couldn't believe my eyes when he turned the corner and kept running! After a few steps, I couldn't help it; my curiosity was getting the best of me and I had to ask, "Joel, how far are you going to run?" He replied, "To the bank and back home." That was a full additional mile which included one big hill! I said, as an encouragement, "Do you know that if you do that you will have run three full miles, farther than you've ever run before?" He just kept running — and at an even faster pace! He made it. Old Dad was tired; I realized that soon it would be I who would have to work hard to keep up.

I have since used the base-acceptable-bottom principle countless times to help me accomplish much more than I otherwise would have. In fact, a day seldom passes when I don't use it. I usually begin my day by asking myself, "What is the least I will accept from myself today before I'll allow myself to quit tonight?" It's not that I'm trying to see how little I can do but I want to make sure that I at least accomplish something worthwhile. I know I'll almost always do more.

Whenever I exercise, I make use of this principle on every exercise. I set a minimum objective, then strive to see how far past it I can go. I always know that I can quit anytime I want — after I've reached my base acceptable bottom.

Use "Memory Joggers" As Prompts

I was first introduced to the idea of "memory joggers" about 20 years ago when I heard a story about a little girl who wanted to discipline herself to begin each day with prayer. Each night, upon retiring, she would remove her shoes and place them far under the bed. Then, as she would kneel to retrieve them each morning, she would be reminded to remain in that kneeling position and take time to pray. The "shoes under the bed" technique worked as well as a billboard along the highway. It reminded her to stop and do a particular task.

I heard of another person who used this discipline to make sure he fed his mind on a daily basis. He knew he wouldn't forget to feed his stomach, so he committed himself to always feed his mind first. He placed a large note on the refrigerator which said, "Have you fed your mind yet?" It worked. Often, the reason we fail to establish particular habits or disciplines in our lives is that we forget. If it's not foremost on our minds, we will do what we've always done. And remember, if we do what we've always done, we'll get what we've always gotten!

There are various ways you can install memory joggers. You can make motivational notes to place in strategic places to grab your attention. You can carry an unusual item in your pocket so that each time you reach into that pocket you'll be reminded of something in particular. I once wrote a list of my most important annual goals on a six-inch piece of two-by-four and kept it on my desk as a paperweight. People often saw it and remarked about it, which served two purposes: I was reminded of the goals regularly and became more accountable to accomplish them.

Another example of a memory jogger we've dealt with for years is the sorry-sounding buzzers that auto manufacturers place in our cars to remind us to fasten our seat belts. Most cars now have buzzers and dash lights. Some cars were built that wouldn't even allow us to start the engines unless we first fastened our seat belts. Now, because it's the law in most states, signs are also placed along the highways to give us "friendly reminders."

Be creative when you develop memory joggers to help you gain more self-control. Use lights, buzzers, signs, plaques, unusual situations, and anything you can think of to get your attention. Otherwise, chances are, you'll continue to march through the day as you always do, ignoring the disciplines you really want to establish. A pastor I know has a "Do It Now!" sign to remind him of his tendency to procrastinate. He says it helps him a lot.

Make Daily "To Do" Lists

Few tools, if any, can help you obtain self-control more than making a daily "to do" list. I use a tool called a *Planner Pad*—a notebook I purchase annually to record everything I must do, or want to do. (There are many different time-management planners on the market.) I literally plan and organize my life in that notebook, and carry it almost everywhere I go. It took me a few years to find the notebook that worked the best for me. Study the different ones available before choosing one for yourself. Like me, you may decide to experiment with different ones before settling on the one that's right for you. The important thing is that you use one!

The key is to have a daily plan. Remember, "most people don't plan to fail; they fail to plan." Having self-control is simply a matter of being able to do what you really want to do. These ten disciplines will collectively give you that control.

Learn to Say "No"

People hate to make decisions — that's a fact of life. They hate to say "yes" and they hate to say "no." This is why so many salespeople often hear the phrase, "I'll think about it."

Good salespeople learn how to get around this. Instead of forcing a prospective buyer to make a decision and say "yes" or "no," they simply make decisions with which the prospect will agree. It is much easier for a salesman to get a prospect to agree with a decision than to make one for himself. While this may sound like a moot point, it's often the difference between a highly successful salesman and a mediocre one.

In order for us to develop habits of self-control, we must develop the discipline of saying "no" when we should. We need to learn to say "no" to anything that is incompatible with our goals and objectives.

Many things make it difficult to say "no." Let's consider some of the reasons it can be so difficult:

- We want to be seen as "nice" people.
- We want to be "agreeable" people.
- We don't want to disappoint others.
- We like to help and encourage others when we can.
- We don't want others to think less of us.
- We cannot think of good reasons for saying "no."
- We are receiving pressure from others to say "yes."
- The thing we are being asked to say "yes" to is a good thing.
- We are concerned that others will misunderstand our "no."

Years ago I learned an important lesson regarding this issue. I had developed a friendship with Jack, a man who lived in a nursing home. When I entered the home and walked down the halls to his room to visit him, I would pass many lonely people who were begging for help. One person wanted to be moved to another place in the building while another wanted something else to eat. Another needed to go to a bathroom, and someone else just wanted someone to talk to. Sometimes I would stop and attempt to meet their needs, and other times I needed to hurry to check Jack out of the home to attend a meeting somewhere.

It dawned on me once, when I was trying to figure out why so few people visit others in nursing homes, that it was because they didn't know how to say "no" to these people. At times my friend Jack asked for something that I was either unable to provide, or just didn't want to provide. I would explain to him, as I've explained to my children many times since, that I needed to reserve the right to say "no"; otherwise I wouldn't allow myself ever to be put in a position to say "yes."

In fact, I've instructed my children to refrain from asking me anything unless they're willing to accept a "no" as the answer. I'm happy to say "yes" when I can, but they need to recognize that the answer will sometimes be "no."

The key to developing the discipline of saying "no" is knowledge. We must know where we are in relationship to where we want to be. We must also know how the activity under consideration will affect our objectives. It is important always to keep in mind that, while the activity might be a "good" thing, good is the enemy of best.

If we spend our lives doing good things and are thereby prevented from having the time to do those things we consider "best," we are the big losers. While it's true we always run the risk of offending someone when we must say "no" to remain consistent with our stated objectives, it's also true that we'll feel better about ourselves. People who always do what everyone else wants, and never become assertive enough to say "no" to others' requests, often spend their "golden" years feeling cheated. It is they, however, who are to blame. They never learned to say "no!"

Saying "no" is also important when it comes to avoiding temptation. Tempting situations are any situations that are not consistent with the principles we've established to govern our lives. They are usually related to the "lusts of the flesh" and they may come about because we've made provision for them. The key thing to remember when assailed by the lusts of the flesh is — get out of there! Speed is extremely important. The longer we deliberate over the issues, the greater the odds are we will make the wrong decisions. Our emotions are often very subtle and deceptive when battling our minds in hopes of bringing about compromise. It is in these cases that a quick "no" is the proper answer.

Trust God For The Strength To Do What We Ought

Trusting God for the strength to do what we ought is quite possibly the most important area of self-discipline. If you've never personally experienced God's supernatural strength at work in your life, an amazing treat awaits you.

Few experiences can match this one!

While I realize that some of you readers might think I'm talking about some mystical occurrence, I assure you I'm not. The Christian is not someone who simply believes in a God that lives way "out there" somewhere. True Christianity is not a religion; it is a relationship. When a person places his faith in the Lord Jesus Christ, the Holy Spirit of God indwells that person and gives him a new birth. A new relationship has begun!

Sad to say, but many Christians seem to stop there. They seldom, if ever, take advantage of this unique relationship. God promises never to leave or to forsake us (Hebrews 13:5), to make His strength perfect in our weakness (2 Corinthians 12:9), and to liberally give us wisdom (James 1:5).

The following three passages are copied from three of the Apostle Paul's epistles (letters) in the New Testament. Note what Paul says about God's power working in us:

For this reason I bow my knees to the Father of our Lord Jesus Christ, from whom the whole family in heaven and earth is named, that He would grant you, according to the riches of His glory, to be strengthened with might through His Spirit in the inner man, that Christ may dwell in your hearts through faith; that you, being rooted and grounded in love, may be able to comprehend with all the saints what is the width and length and depth and height — to know the love of Christ which passes knowledge; that you may be filled with all the fullness of God. Now to Him who is able to do exceedingly abundantly above all that we ask or think, according to the power that works in us, to Him be glory in the church by Christ Jesus throughout all ages, world without end. Amen.
Ephesians 3:14-21 (NKJV)

I know how to be abased, and I know how to abound. Everywhere and in all things I have learned both to be full and to be hungry, both to abound and to suffer need. I can do all things through Christ who strengthens me. **Philippians 4:12,13 (NKJV)**

For this reason we also, since the day we heard it, do not cease to pray for you, and to ask that you may be filled with the knowledge of His will in all wisdom and spiritual understanding; that you may have a walk worthy of the Lord, fully pleasing Him, being fruitful in every good work and increasing in the knowledge of God; strengthened with all might, according to His glorious power, for all patience and longsuffering with joy; giving thanks to the Father who has qualified us to be partakers of the inheritance of the saints in the light. He has delivered us from the power of darkness and translated us into the kingdom of the Son of His love, in whom we have redemption through His blood, the forgiveness of sins. **Colossians 1:9-14 (NKJV)**

I'll tell you about the first time I personally experienced the power of God, over 23 years ago. I assure you there have been many dramatic events since, but none that were more valuable. I say that because this was a real "eye opener" for me and set the stage for all experiences to come later, including those still in my future.

I'd been a Christian just a few weeks when I determined to clean up my act, so to speak. Psalm 119:9 teaches me that the way to clean up my act (cleanse my way) is to take heed according to God's Word. An area of my life I decided to attack and gain control over was my language, specifically my foul mouth. I'd picked up some pretty sorry words while in Vietnam and on construction jobs after returning home. I used them freely in almost every sentence I spoke on the job.

I became convinced that God probably wasn't too pleased with this cursing, and my lack of self-control in this area wasn't a very good Christian witness. I diligently attempted to stop for about three weeks. It was then that I realized I was getting nowhere fast. I barely had slowed down and had only really managed to eliminate taking the Lord's name in vain. The vulgarity was continuing to flow freely from my mouth, as it was from the rest of the guys.

They, however, were not trying to stop. I was.

Then one morning I read **Philippians 4:13**, "I can do all things through Christ which strengthens me" (**KJV**), and I recognized that could be my answer! Since I was a new Christian, and still had a lot of doubts and questions, I determined that I would put the word of God to a test. Either the Bible was true, or it wasn't, and I should find out. God was promising me the strength to "do all things." I understood that "all things" referred to all things that are consistent with His will but that was fine with me. I knew that obtaining self-control over my language was consistent with His will. Thus, I decided to "take heed according to His word" (**Psalms 119:9**) and trust God for the strength to quit.

Within three days my cursing was gone! I say gone, but what I really mean is that it was cleaned up. I have actually counted some four or five times I've slipped with a curse word in the 23 years since. That, to me, was pretty remarkable!

Here's how I applied the verse. Beginning that first morning with the first curse word I caught myself saying, I said something like this: "Lord, please forgive me and give me the strength to quit. You say in your Word that I can do all things through Christ who strengthens me. I'm trusting you to help me." I had a large vocabulary of curse words and, perhaps, it took three days to get through it all — I don't know. All I do remember is that I knew the problem was gone by the end of the third day. I simply prayed, and have repeated the prayer a few times since, "Thank you, Lord!"

A few weeks later, my eyes were opened even wider. I had developed control over my language to the point where I could, after hitting my finger or thumb accidentally with a hammer, say to myself: "Gee, Gene, I wish you wouldn't do that." Then, one day I added after those words, "Gene, you're really getting good; you never even thought of a curse word that time!" Immediately, after saying or thinking those words, I banged my thumb with the hammer again! I've got to admit — I thought of a curse word that time! I didn't say it, but I

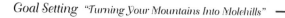
threw the hammer as far as I could across the field nearby. I was angry, to say the least.

It was then that this scripture came to mind:

> *Wherefore let him that thinketh he standeth take heed lest he fall.*
> **1 Corinthians 10:12 (KJV)**

God seemed to be saying to me, "Gene, just who are you giving the credit to for this victory? Are you bragging on yourself?" Needless to say, I stood corrected and apologized to the Lord. It had been His victory, not mine. I walked across the field, picked up my hammer, kissed my blue thumb, and went back to work.

I've had many opportunities to make use of God's strength since. I often have to call on Him to give me the strength, courage, or fortitude to humble myself — either to apologize for something I've done, or failed to do, or to possibly accept criticism or counsel. I especially need His strength to see me through some of the trials I encounter and to overcome the temptation to "go my own way." I'm far from being perfect (and always will be) but I have been able to see growth and believe I've attained a level of maturity that I used to only dream about. I thank God that yesterday's mountains are today's molehills!

There is no feeling in this world to compare with the feeling you get when you know without a doubt that God is working in, and through, you. This is true whether you are standing against a multitude with only God on your side, speaking on His behalf to someone He has guided you to, giving sacrificially to meet someone's need, or trusting Him to meet some major need in your life.

If you strive for self-control in your life using these ten disciplines, you'll be able to say with me, "I'm still not the person I will be, but I'm also no longer the person I once was!" Amen.

·*Fourteen*·
Decisions... Decisions...
Decisions...

Don't you sometimes wish that someone else would make the decisions and you could just relax? While you may wish that for awhile, you'd get tired of it pretty quickly if you really didn't have the opportunity to make decisions for yourself. With the need and freedom to make a decision comes the responsibility to choose between the options.

Often, the choice may simply be a "Yes" or a "No." At times it may be "Multiple Choice," making you decide between several options. And then, there are times when, as in a test, you're given an "Essay Question." You must decide how you'll answer it, and you're given no options. Life is full of opportunities to make decisions — in fact, there is seldom a day that we're not presented with numerous opportunities to do just that. Some we make without giving them a second thought and others, we put off until another day.

The truth is that most of us hate to make decisions. A good salesman learns quickly to use this fact to his advantage. He doesn't attempt to get his prospects to say "Yes." He simply makes the decision for them and makes them have to say "No" in order to stop the sale from taking place. Of course, the really good salesman does this very tactfully and doesn't close until he is sure the prospect is ready. Often he will use an *Alternate-of-Choice* close, having the prospect choose between two colors or sizes. When the prospect selects the color he wants, he has just told the salesman he wants the product.

The good salesman doesn't make the poor customer have to decide "Yes" to a stupid question like, "Are you going to buy tonight?" He assumes the sale, thereby protecting the prospect from the pain of having to decide "Yes." He has made a decision with which the prospect can agree. Agreeing with a decision is easier than making one, although in reality they are one and the same.

If the salesman attempts to manipulate the prospect into purchasing his product before the person is ready, the salesman will be seen as pushy and won't be appreciated. It is because of tactics like this that most states have adopted a three-day law, allowing the prospect to change his mind after signing the contract. Only when the customer truly has been offended or feels ripped off will he cancel, however, because that, too, would require the making of a decision.

Goal Setting Requires Making Decisions

When you have decided to become a *goal-setter*, you've made a decision to live your life on purpose. You've decided to personally determine the direction you will go in life, rather than be pushed around by the tide of circumstances and other people's desires. That doesn't mean that you won't consider both circumstances and other people's desires when determining your direction; it just means that you will decide that which you will do — not they.

In setting your goals, you'll do as I've suggested and always keep a long list or "Life Menu" showing everything you think you might like to do during the rest of your life. Each year, you will look at the menu and select those items which you have decided it is time to do. You begin putting your action plan together (your blueprint) in which, after determining the resources you'll need and the obstacles you'll face, you set the deadlines. Once your action plan meets all the requirements, as set forth in an earlier chapter, you're ready to accomplish your goal.

The Key In Decision-Making

The key in making decisions is to attempt to make "wise" decisions. Remember the teaching of Proverbs 16:20a, "He that handles a matter wisely shall find good." It is extremely important when making decisions to remember that good is the enemy of best. Often, the choosing of a good thing eliminates the possibility of having the best. Sometimes, the choosing of a good thing only delays having the best. At any rate, it makes good sense to carefully consider the issues involved in the decisions we make.

This, the making of wise decisions, is often easier said than done. Let's face it — almost everyone thinks he is choosing that which is wise when he makes a decision, and nobody wants to choose unwisely. Look at the admonition of scripture concerning the seeking and finding of wisdom.

Wisdom is the principal thing; therefore get wisdom: and with all thy getting get understanding. Exalt her, and she shall promote thee: she shall bring thee to honour, when thou dost embrace her. **Proverbs 4:7,8 (KJV)**

For wisdom is better than rubies; and all the things that may be desired are not to be compared to it. I love them that love me; and those that seek me early shall find me. **Proverbs 8:11,17 (KJV)**

If any of you lack wisdom, let him ask of God, that giveth to all men liberally, and upbraideth not; and it shall be given him. But let him ask in faith, nothing wavering. For he that wavereth is like a wave of the sea driven with the wind and tossed. For let not that man think that he shall receive any thing of the Lord. **James 1:5-7 (KJV)**

Our Decisions Determine Our Choices

It is interesting to note that many decisions we make in life determine other decisions. Some of the more obvious ones are:

- We decide to marry someone.
- We choose an occupation.
- We choose to live in a particular place.
- We choose our friends.
- We decide which groups or organizations to join.

Each of these decisions determines to a large degree many of our future actions. They eliminate many questions, decisions, and options. Once we've made certain decisions, we don't ask some of the questions or face the decisions we otherwise would.

As an example, because I married my wife I no longer experience the fear of rejection concerning asking a girl for a date. I no longer have to wrestle with the issue of dating and choosing a lifetime partner at all. When I decided to marry, I was also making a decision to allow her life to become a part of mine. Her relatives became mine, as did mine hers. Her tastes (likes and dislikes), fears, dreams, and limitations also became a part of me. I no longer had to decide if I would accept a particular aspect of her life as my own, on an individual basis. I had made all those decisions by making the one. The others were automatic.

My occupation itself takes me in a particular direction. I'm no longer subjected to certain dangers and concerns of other occupations. I'm now committed to learning certain things that I wouldn't need to if I were in a different occupation.

When I decided to live in the Midwest, I automatically became subject to having to deal with snow in my driveway, the potential of tornadoes, extreme weather variations during the course of a year, no ocean nearby, and friendly good-natured people.

Our friends actually influence us much more than we realize. The saying, "Birds of a feather flock together" is very true. We become what we think about most of the time, and what we think about is often determined by what our friends are thinking about. It is easy to find ourselves doing things we would never have considered before, just because our friends are doing them and have encouraged us to join them. This doesn't have to be bad; they may be a good activities. It does, however, behoove us to consider carefully who we allow to become our friends. Make a decision to join a street gang and you've probably made a decision to steal, and maybe even to kill. Decide to join a local Kiwanis Club and you've made a decision to donate a portion of your time to fulfilling community needs.

To Limit – Or Not To Limit – The Choices

I'll use the illustration of the restaurant menu again. No matter how hungry you are, you cannot possibly eat everything on the menu. Therefore, you must make a decision, and in deciding realize that you are making a decision as to what you will not eat as well. Let's face it, one of the reason smorgasbords are so popular with many of us is that we don't have as difficult a time making our choices — we can select a little of each of many items.

I suspect that too often we are guilty of having the restaurant mentality when it comes to making decisions in life. We think we can only select one item and must, by doing so, eliminate the rest. The only decision I can think of where this kind of thinking is absolutely necessary is regarding marriage. God instituted marriage to be a lifetime decision. The other major decisions we make in life are usually not as rigid. Even though someone spends eight or more years studying to be a doctor, he can, if he chooses, still change his mind and enter a totally different occupation. (It is true, however, that in most cases his income potential will prohibit his doing this.) We can decide to enter particular fields of work for the sole purpose of developing ourselves in particular areas. After a while, we can choose to leave these fields of endeavor and use the skills and knowledge gained to assist us in other areas.

I understand the thinking that many have regarding this matter of "jumping around," so to speak. They feel that they gain much more landing in one place and staying there for the rest of their lives. In the case of jobs, they build both seniority and retirement benefits — the benefits which they feel they will lose if they make the decision to change. I cannot count the number of people whom I've known with this philosophy that lost their jobs after fifteen or more years and were devastated. They thought they were playing it safe and they still lost.

It is important to remember that goal setting is not meant to become our master, but is simply to be a tool to be used by us as we wish. In the same way, this issue of making decisions is to be seen as only a tool. As we are better able to work on an automobile with the proper tools, so are we better apt to direct our life with the proper tools. Two of these are goal setting and decision-making.

We should remember that among our choices when making decisions are the following:

1) No.
2) Yes.

3) Wait until later.

> I need more information.
> I need time to consider the options.
> I need additional resources.

4) Additional options.

When Is A Decision Not Enough?

Have you ever made a decision to do something and then failed to follow through? Of course you have. Many times! Our lives are full of things we intended to do but never got around to doing. Some of the reasons we've failed to follow through on decisions are as follows:

- We lost our focus and forgot about it.
- We lost interest and no longer desired to do it.
- We decided the cost was too great and it wasn't worth doing at that cost.
- We couldn't gather the resources to do it.
- We tried and failed.

While there may be other reasons, I suspect most of them would fall into one of the above categories.

We've all watched a TV western where a woman was faced with the opportunity to shoot a bad man who was threatening her in some way, but she couldn't bring herself to shoot. She wanted to but just couldn't pull the trigger. Or, we've watched a show where a bad guy was down, but not out, and the good guy walked away only to regret not having finished the bad guy off. Our question might be, why couldn't or didn't they pull the trigger? The answer is really simple — the movie script wasn't written that way. Actually, all kidding aside, the answer really is simple. The victims' value system wouldn't allow them to pull the trigger. Their minds were in a defensive mode and the value they placed on a human life, even the life of the perpetrator, was greater than their desire to protect or defend themselves by killing the person. They believed that there must be another solution and, thus, they failed to shoot. They failed to do that which they had decided they would do.

I recently had an experience that caused me to think about this issue in greater detail than I have in the past. I decided to take my 17-year old daughter to go bungy jumping — something that she said she wanted to do. Deep down, I had also wanted to do it for some time. My motivation, however, had been somewhat different from hers. She was looking for the thrill, but I was looking for another way to meet one of my greatest fears head on and tackle it — the fear of the feeling of falling. Every time I've seen someone on TV do it, I've cringed. I'm reminded of the many nightmares I've had throughout my life in which I fell from the roof or ledge of a tall building. I never enjoy that feeling — it's no thrill for me.

Now, I can say I don't have any fear of the bungy breaking, although I know it sometimes happens. One person was killed and another injured during bungy jumps just the weekend before our jumps. Cars wreck and planes crash too, but I don't fear riding in either one of them. My fear is just that feeling I get when I'm falling. I wish I could enjoy it but I don't. As I mentioned in the last chapter, I parachuted from an airplane when I turned 40 years old in hopes of conquering this fear. While I managed to go through with it, I still didn't feel I'd conquered the fear — only confronted it. I hoped this bungy jump would help conquer it once and for all.

When we arrived at the site at 7 P.M., I can say that I was glad to see them putting the crane down, beginning to close up for the night. I felt somewhat relieved. That quickly vanished, however, when the manager said they would start it up again for us. I paid for the jumps, then allowed them to properly outfit us with our harnesses. My attitude was, if others can do it, so can I. I had absolutely no trouble stepping into the metal box or cage so they could lift me 130 feet above the ground. There were no air bags or nets below, just a blue plastic tarp to show me where I'd be landing. I was instructed that all I had to do was stand at the edge, outstretch my arms to the sky, and fall forward, sort of like Superman would do it. I was told it was easier if I looked at the horizon instead of the ground. I, however, wanted to meet my fear head on and experience a full victory, so I focused on the ground. In fact, I was still standing there focusing on the ground some five minutes later, long after the crowd below had given me much encouragement, including a couple of loud countdowns.

I couldn't jump on their countdowns, I had to go on my own schedule. I talked to myself a lot during those five minutes. I gave myself every pep talk I knew. I attempted to quote the Bible verse, "I can do all things through Christ who strengthens me" but what came out was John 3:16, "For God so loved the world that He gave His only begotten son, ..." I knew I was in trouble then, when I couldn't even quote the right verse. I tried rocking back and forth, hoping I'd be able to use the momentum to just push myself out of the cage. I tried stomping like a bull, getting ready for the charge. I just couldn't seem to let go. I analyzed how I'd explain it if I changed my mind and refused to jump, attempted to picture the humiliating ride back down amidst the crowd. What would I say to my daughter? My wife was also there. She was dead set against us doing this, but realized she couldn't stop us. She had told me she would never forgive me if anything happened to Kim. Even though she was against my doing it, I was sure it would be an embarrassment to her if I failed to jump. I couldn't get a peace about jumping and I couldn't get a peace about being lowered to the ground a failure.

Let me say, I finally did jump. How? I don't know. I think what finally happened was that the level of embarrassment finally exceeded the fear of the feeling of falling and my mind just pushed my body out of the cage. I've never before heard the noise that came out of my mouth as I began falling. Those on the ground couldn't hear it but I sure could. It was one I hope I don't hear too many more times in my life.

I've told the story because it illustrates a point that deserves repeating. People act quicker to avoid losses than they do to gain benefits. We will do more to avoid pain than we will to gain pleasure. I couldn't jump to gain the benefit of having met and tackled my fear head on; I could only jump when the pain of embarrassment exceeded the pain of my fear. The loss I needed to avoid was a loss of my self-esteem. How could I face my daughter, my wife, and even myself if I didn't go through with the jump? I didn't really care about what everyone else on the ground thought, as they didn't even know me. I was concerned about the fact that my employees would also find out soon thereafter, as well as my friends. To add to this, my actions were being videotaped so my daughter would have a record of our jumps to show her friends. I wouldn't be able just to forget it tomorrow, or possibly ever live it down.

I asked myself why that I find it much easier to ride a big roller coaster when I know I'm going to experience the same feeling. The answer seemed simple enough. In order to make myself ride a roller coaster, all I have to do is sit down in a semi-comfortable seat in a little car. Someone straps me in and all I have to do is hold on for the ride. If they took me to the top and waited for me to throw a switch so we could charge down the slope at a high rate of speed, it would be more difficult. I'd have to make additional decisions and take additional actions. As it is, all I must do is sit there. Bungy jumping would be much easier if I just stood in the cage and when we got to the top, a trap door would automatically open and dispose of its cargo. In other words, the truly difficult decision could be eliminated by becoming subservient to a seemingly minor decision.

A good illustration of this point is another experience I recently gave myself. While in Zimbabwe, Africa, on a fishing trip I visited Victoria Falls. Just below the falls begins what is billed to be the most challenging one-day commercialized white water rafting trip in the world. The rapids are class five and six (five being the highest class which is passable). I cannot swim, or even tread water, and have almost drowned twice. If I were placed at the mouth of a class five rapids and had to make a decision to say "Go," I'd probably never do it. I found it easy, however, to step into a rubber boat which was sitting in calm shallow water away from any sight of the rapids around the bend. Sure, I knew what was to come but I also knew that I would only have one decision to make once we encountered the rapids — to hold on! That decision would be an easy one. I did hold on through fifteen rapids. Even though I was thrown out of the boat I still held on to the rope and lived to write these words.

Thus, in answer to the question, "When is a decision not enough?", it is not enough when it does not contain the additional elements necessary to allow you to fulfill that which you have decided to do. It is not enough when it stands by itself — without the plan to see it through. It is not enough if, when after you obtain all the information you need to understand everything which will be required to fulfill it, you decide that you either cannot follow through, or you no longer have the desire to do so.

There is nothing wrong with changing our minds regarding decisions we've made — if we do it for the right reasons. The only people we really need to please in this world are God, and ourselves. Others may be disappointed but if we can live with the decisions we make, holding our heads high with our self-images still intact, they'll just have to learn to deal with it.

The Pain Of Going Backward

It is important to realize how much the PAIN of regressing, or going backward, determines the decisions we make in life. None of us particularly likes to lose, or go backward. If you have nice cars, you don't want to have to go back to driving old junkers. If you live in a big nice house, we don't want to lose it and go back to a smaller house. If you are making $50,000 per year, you don't want to accept a job making only $28,000. I've seen people go a whole year without any income while looking for a job that would provide them with their former income. They never got it and had to settle for something similar to that which they could have had the week after they had lost their previous job.

Often, because people refuse to accept negative situations as a fact of life, they hold on as long as they can, thereby reducing or possibly eliminating altogether any chances they have for full recovery. When they finally collapse, they crash and burn. If they could simply have made wise decisions along the way, they might have prevented total collapse.

It is for this reason that we ought to be careful before making decisions that could overextend us. Once our economic situations worsen, for example, our emotions are affected negatively as we cling to that which we have, not wanting to go backwards. We make decisions to "give up" certain benefits ever so slowly, and waiting to do so often magnifies and intensifies the negative situation. It becomes very difficult to decide which cuts to make. It is only when we attempt to set aside our emotions and make intelligent decisions which are consistent with our priorities that we can have real hope for recovery.

Making a decision to go backwards isn't so painful when we realize that it is often necessary in life to do just that. I've never seen a football game in which both teams didn't have to punt at least once, thus losing the ball altogether.

Chuck Swindoll wrote a book I highly recommend that everyone read entitled, *Three Steps Forward, Two Steps Backward.*

I've experienced this pain of going backwards a number of times. I'm sure I'm stronger because of having done so. I realize that the present doesn't equal the future, nor does the past. Where I am today, and even the direction I'm headed doesn't, by itself, determine where I will be in the future. If I lose it all, I'll be a blessed man when I hit bottom because I'll be in a position where the only way to go will be up. Then, with my increased knowledge and experiences, I'll be able to get where I want to go more quickly.

The Role Of One's Personality In Decision-Making

Certainly, a person's personality style plays a role in determining his approach to these decisions. If we use the terms, *Driver, Socializer, Thinker,* and *Relator* to describe the four basic personality types, we'll see that they each make decisions differently, based on their comfort levels and priorities. It is actually fairly easy to predict, given a set of circumstances, the criteria each of these personality styles will use to reach a decision. I mention it here only to encourage you, the reader, to obtain additional reading material concerning these styles. The more you understand the differences in people, the greater your potential for success will be.

In a nutshell, *Drivers and Socializers* are fast-paced individuals who are also risk-takers. *Drivers* are task-oriented and usually make their decisions based upon that which they believe will best achieve the tasks being tackled, while *Socializers* are more relationship-oriented and give a greater weight to how their decisions will be viewed by and affect others. *Thinkers and Relators*, on the other hand, are slower-paced people who become uncomfortable when rushed to make quick decisions. *Thinkers* are task-oriented individuals who want to carefully analyze everything before making their decisions. *Relators* are relationship-oriented and are extremely security-minded. They will seldom make decisions in which they know they'll upset someone else.

Questions To Help Me
Make Wise Decisions

There are some questions we can ask ourselves that can help us make our decisions easier. Some of them are:

1. Is it morally right? What, if anything, is wrong with it? Does it violate any principle I've chosen to guide my life?

If it's not right, don't do it! That's a good rule to follow at all times. It is never right to do wrong in order to do right. Many people are in prison today because they thought differently. Perhaps there is not a law against it but you know it isn't the best thing for you. You know you will probably live to regret it. If this is the case, don't do it!

2. Is it consistent with my life purpose and my written life goals?

Life is short, and if I'm going to make the most of it I must be extremely careful not to get sidetracked too often. It is, therefore, important that I evaluate every decision with the question, "Will it move me closer to where I want to be?"

3. What are the risks? What is the worst thing that can happen? Can I accept the worst? Who is it that stands to lose?

Risk is a funny thing. Someone once said that we should not be afraid to go out on a limb for that is where the fruit is. While that sounds right, we should remember that there are ways to pick fruit without going out on the limb. Risk is not always good and it is not always bad. It's true that most highly successful people have taken great numbers of risks to get where they are. It's also true, however, that their risks were usually calculated risks, ones they felt stood a high probability of succeeding.

Whenever we ask the question, "what is the worst thing that can happen?', we need to attempt to determine both the extent of the potential damage, who it is that will suffer, and what the potential for partial or full recovery might be.

We need to be realistic with our answers. Talk to others who have tried and failed. What did they do wrong? If they would do it again, how would they do it differently?

While it is extremely difficult, if not impossible, we should attempt to become unemotional when making these decisions. Emotion, left unchecked, can cause us to literally give our lives for unworthy causes in a moment. This can be done because of a combination of things: (1) We underestimate the risks, (2) We don't consider the alternatives, (3) We overestimate the importance of taking the risks, and (4) We are not emotionally healthy when making the decisions.

4. What is the potential for gain? Does the potential for gain make taking the risk worthwhile?

Gain is an amazing thing. We all like to gain. Millions of dollars are spent every week on state lotteries by individuals hoping to receive great gain for little investments. One can simply walk through a casino in Las Vegas and see the same thing. I once knew a young man, about 22 years of age, who made more than $400,000 in one year as a stock broker and lost it all gambling! Can you believe it? His mother later explained to me that they had learned that chronic gamblers don't gamble to win, they gamble for the thrill they get by risking it all. When they win, they must do it again and again until they finally lose. Only then will they be happy. Happy? Think about that one.

Actually, I think the reason a gambler has great difficulty quitting while he is ahead is that he has an intense desire to win all he can. The only way to know just how much he can win is to keep going until he loses it all. While I don't gamble (except with the decisions I make in my business), I do occasionally play Las Vegas games on my computer. I might quit one evening ahead but I've found that I'll eventually lose it all. The only question is how long it will take. I used to have one merciful game that would inform me I'd broken the bank and the game was over. If it hadn't, I'm sure I would have eventually lost it all in that game too. In real life, it is impossible to "win it all" gambling. Yes, gain is an amazing thing. We all like to gain. We spend a lot of our time dreaming and thinking about gain. There's nothing wrong with that. The danger, however, occurs when our desire for gain becomes so strong that we become unwise concerning the risks we are willing to take in order to gain.

I tend to think if the potential and probability for gain is at least double or triple the potential and probability of loss, I should find a way to do it. An example of this concept is:

> I have the opportunity to purchase an item for $1,000 which I believe is easily worth and can be sold for $1,600. As a worse case scenario, I believe I can sell it quickly to someone else for $800 in a distress situation. Thus, the potential for gain is triple ($600) the potential for loss ($200). The probability for gain instead of loss also seems greater.

5. Is this a decision that I believe would be good to make for others, whom I love? Would I want my own children to do it?

This question becomes important because it gives me the opportunity to step back and look at the decision I'm contemplating more objectively.

We've all heard of the parent who says to his children, "Don't do as I do, do as I say." We consider this somewhat hypocritical, and it is. We should be good examples to our children. Therefore, if it wouldn't be a good decision for them to make if they found themselves in our situation, how can it be good for us?

6. Are there any other ways to accomplish the same objectives? How do they compare? Why is this way better than those?

What are the creative alternatives? Let's face it; most of us get caught up with the attitude, "I want it!" and we really don't care about even looking into the alternatives. In fact, we often avoid finding out about the alternatives because we fear that they might make good sense and cause us to change our minds. In reality, though, we shouldn't think this way. The reason is simple. We are still in control and we can still select the choices that we want, after looking at all the alternatives. We can't really expect to realize our potential if we adopt the attitude, "Don't confuse me with the facts, my mind is already made up." How often can we look back on decisions we've made with regret, wishing we had known then what we now know? There are too many such decisions to count, right? Actually, we probably can't even think of most of them now — not because they don't exist but because the mind has a tendency to forget pain.

A great brainstorming exercise, as mentioned earlier, is to get a number of people together and compile a list of 25 different possible solutions to a problem. While some solutions may be utterly ridiculous, you'll be quite impressed with the potential of others that you would never have thought of without this exercise.

7. What do my counselors say? Have I only asked those whom I know would agree? Have I asked and received counsel from others who have faced the same dilemma as I am now facing?

Proverbs teaches us,

> *Where no counsel is, the people fall: but in the multitude of counsellors there is safety.* **Proverbs 11:14 (KJV)**

The walk through life is a long journey and the path is full of many pitfalls, some like the holes that are dug in order to trap lions. Remember, "Only a fool learns from his own mistakes when he could have learned from someone else's mistakes."

Without counsel, we can lack proper perspective, especially when emotion is given the rule over logic. We might make decisions too quickly, or take too much time and miss opportunities. It's easy to make decisions with only self-interest in view, not considering the whole picture. There could be conflicts with other objectives within our organizations of which we are not even aware.

All too often, I've made decisions based upon my emotions, without really giving the proper merit to logic. While I may have had counsel advising me to the contrary, I still did what I wanted to do in the first place. Often, I've regretted doing so. At times, however, my desire to make it work, in spite of the contrary counsel I'd received, gave me the momentum to insure that the decision was a positive one. Therefore, I don't always follow the advice of my counsel, but I do attempt to receive it.

The person who thinks he has all the answers when he doesn't even have all the questions is headed for disaster. The old saying, "Fools dash in where angels fear to tread" can apply here. It makes all the sense in the world to seek counsel, especially regarding decisions which can, in and of themselves, change your future.

Study The Pros And Cons

Many years ago, during the mid-70s, I was taught a method of decision-making which I was told was a favorite of Ben Franklin's. I was told that when Ben had a hard time making a decision, he just let the decision make the decision.

The way he did this, supposedly, was to draw a vertical line down the middle of a sheet of paper. On one side he wrote the word "Pro" and on the other, "Con." He would then list under each all the things that applied. Whichever list seemed to carry the more weight, that side won the decision.

Notice, I did not say that the side with the most items listed won. We might be able to list ten reasons for doing something (pros) while listing only two reasons for not doing it (cons), but the cons would win because they carried more weight. It might be that one of the cons is that the risk is life-threatening. That fact could carry more weight than all the pros (advantages) put together.

Consider Use Of The Matrix

This next method is one I used to assist me in making the most difficult decision of my life to date. I used what is referred to as a matrix.
In 1990 we were living in Orlando, Florida. We had sold our business in Missouri the year before and moved there in what I thought would be the last move of our lives. (Big joke — we're about to move the third time since then.) We purchased a house that was to become our dream house. My wife

decorated each room just as she wanted and we even had a nice screened-in pool built with a waterfall. We even had 11 large solar panels installed on the roof to keep our pool warm year round. Our giant living room with fireplace had three sliding glass doors which disappeared behind a wall to open our living room into the patio area — a 600 sq. ft. area which was under a roof adjoining the pool area. For us, it was a truly magnificent place to relax.

I had taken at least six months off (no work) to adjust to Florida. Those who know me well can't imagine me taking two weeks off, let alone six months. All I did during that six months was relax, build relationships, play basketball and teach a few groups my Goal seminar. I really enjoyed myself. After living there almost a year, I was in the process of beginning a new business when Saundra informed me that she wanted us to move back to Missouri. She said that she had been hesitating telling me for several months that she wanted us to move back. (The primary reason we had moved to Florida was that she had wanted us to for many years.)

It came as a real shock to me. I had been concerned that I might not like living in Orlando but I hadn't even thought about the possibility that she might not enjoy it. After discussing it for a couple of days, we decided to table the discussion for a couple of weeks, during which time we were scheduled to be separated by a thousand miles. This gave us time to pray for wisdom, and to seek our own desires without any pressure from each other.

When we were reunited two weeks later, we found that both of us were 99.9% sure we knew the right answer. She had determined we should move back to Missouri and I was certain we should stay right where we were. "We have invested too much over the previous year," I insisted. Our roots were growing well and we were in a great position to begin a new business. Besides that, we were out of money and couldn't afford another move. I figured it had cost us approximately $250,000 to move to Florida. (This took into consideration not only the actual cost of the move and relocation, but also the difference in my income for the next two years.) She understood but insisted that she still really wanted to move. I was dumbfounded!

As we discussed the pros and cons of living in each city, we realized it was quite difficult for us to properly weigh each issue. It was then I designed the following matrix to assist us in making our decision.

You will notice that we decided there were 12 different issues which concerned each of us regarding this decision. Some were more important than others so I decided to give those which seemed equally least important a multiplication factor of 1.0. All issues which we considered more important received higher multiplication factors, ranging from 1.2 to 2.0. These would be the factors by which the respective values would be multiplied.

CATEGORY	X	FLORIDA	MISSOURI
SCHOOL	2.0	6.0/ **12.0**	6.0/ **12.0**
CHURCH	1.8	9.0/ **16.2**	5.0/ **9.0**
NEIGHBORHOOD	1.5	7.0/ **10.5**	7.0/ **10.5**
FRIENDS	1.2	7.0/ **8.4**	7.0/ **8.4**
FAMILY	1.0	3.0/ **3.0**	6.0/ **6.0**
BUSINESS OPPORTUNITY	1.5	6.0/ **9.0**	8.0/ **12.0**
MORALITY OF COMMUNITY & CITY	1.8	4.0/ **7.2**	6.0/ **10.8**
FRIENDLINESS OF PEOPLE	1.0	3.0/ **3.0**	5.0/ **5.0**
PROGRESSIVE ATTITUDE	1.5	5.0/ **7.5**	7.0/ **10.5**
TRAFFIC	1.0	5.0/ **5.0**	5.0/ **5.0**
HOUSE	1.2	8.0/ **9.6**	6.0/ **7.2**
WEATHER	1.0	9.0/ **9.0**	6.0/ **6.0**
TOTALS		*99.9*	*102.4*
DIFFERENCE			*+2.5*

Notice the biggest value difference in the "church" category. Having a good church for our family to attend is very important, so we gave it a multiplication factor of 1.8. We were so impressed with the church we were attending, we evaluated it as a 9.0 on a one-to-ten scale, ten being most excellent. If the decision had been made on that decision alone, we would have stayed in Florida.

Interestingly enough, the total scores were almost identical. Saundra and I had completed the matrix together and we were in agreement with all the figures we used. (In other situations, we might each have to make our own matrix using a different set of values and evaluations.) The bottom line was this: we decided that the scores were too close to allow the matrix to make the decision for us. Even though the matrix was not to be the deciding factor this time, it had greatly assisted us in clarifying our thinking regarding the issues.

The Emotional Graph

To make this most difficult decision, I decided to use one more method, a method I'll call "the emotional graph." I drew two lines and placed numbers between them as you see below:

ILLUSTRATION OF EMOTIONAL GRAPH

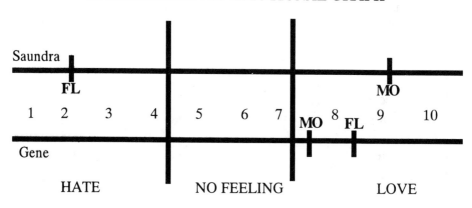

When we used this graph, I think I understood for the first time how badly she really wanted to move back to Missouri. I said, "If I felt the way you do, there's no doubt in my mind that we would move back. Therefore, we'll move." It was settled.

This is not to say that all, or even most, decisions should be made emotionally. Obviously, if our emotions are not consistent with the other things we've chosen to guide our life (for example — our morals), then they must take a back seat. Here, however, there was no such limiting factor. Within two months, the Ryder trucks were loaded and we were on our way back to Missouri. Two months after that we had a Grand Opening at our new computer store. We've never regretted having made the decision to return to Missouri; nor have we ever regretted the fantastic year of vacation in Florida. We'll always cherish the friendships we were blessed with during that year. Some of them will remain the rest of our lives.

Summary

In summary, few things affect our lives as much as the decisions we make. Our decisions ultimately determine our levels of success and/or failure. It is impossible to set goals without making decisions. It is also impossible to realize the fulfillment of a goal without making many more decisions.

It behooves each of us to consider the issues in this chapter as we make those decisions. Recognize, however, you cannot be right all of the time. The person who doesn't make mistakes doesn't do very much else either.

The next chapter, "No Time To Spare" should prove quite valuable as you attempt to determine how to schedule your life from this point on. The person who plans to accomplish much, should make the most of the little time he is given.

·*Fifteen*·
No Time To Spare

The clock of life is wound but once,
And no man has the power
To say just when the hands will stop;
At late, or early hour.

Now is the only time we own
To do His precious will,
Do not wait until tomorrow;
For the clock may then be still.

Selected

What a challenge to write on the subject of time! The importance of time cannot be overstated. I am not a master when it comes to making the most of time and I get excited at the very thought of improving my use of it.

If we would live life to its fullest, maximize our chances for realizing our potential and finish our days without that awful feeling of regret, we must take the time to focus on our use of time itself. Truly no resource on earth is more important than time. Volumes could be filled with the dying statements of the wealthy, powerful, and talented who would have given everything for another hour. This is understandable because they definitely couldn't take it with them. Time is so precious because it is the very stuff that makes up life. Think about it — the murderer is really a thief who steals time from his victims. Since this is true, isn't it a form of suicide to "kill" or waste our own time?

Managing Time Is Impossible!

Eventually, everyone who talks about self-improvement talks about time management. I am no exception. Yet, when we think about it, we realize that managing time is impossible. Time marches on at the same pace, regardless of what we want to do about it. At times we would like to speed it up, and at times we would like to make it go slower. What we want really doesn't matter, does it? Today will still include 24 hours — just like yesterday and all the days before it.

Voltaire, the noted French infidel and one of the most prolific and talented writers of his time, wrote the following in his book *Zadig, a Mystery of Fate.*

> *The grand Magi puts the following question to Zadig. "What, of all things in the world, is longest and shortest, the swiftest and the slowest, the most divisible and the most extended, the most neglected and the most regretted, without which nothing can be done, which devours all that is little, and enlivens all that is great?"*
>
> *Here is Zadig's answer:*
>
> *Time. Nothing is longer, since it is the measure of eternity. Nothing is shorter, since it is insufficient for the accomplishment of your projects. Nothing is more slow to him that expects; nothing more rapid to him that enjoys. In greatness it extends to infinity, in smallness it is infinitely divisible. All men neglect it; all regret the loss of it; nothing can be done without it. It consigns to oblivion whatever is unworthy of being transmitted to posterity, and immortalizes such actions as are truly great. Time is man's most precious asset.*

That writing, I think, is a masterpiece. I debated whether I should reprint it, as its author devoted his life to wasting time. Voltaire once boasted, "In twenty years Christianity will be no more. My single hand shall destroy the edifice it took twelve apostles to rear." Shortly after his death, the very house in which he printed his literature became the depot for the Geneva Bible

Society. The nurse who attended Voltaire said: "For all the wealth in Europe I would not see another infidel die." While his physician, Torchim, waited beside his deathbed, Voltaire cried out most desperately: "I am abandoned by God and man! I will give you half of what I am worth if you will give me six months' life. Then I shall go to hell; and you will go with me. . . ." Someone once said,

Great thoughts are not responsible for those who repeat them.

Now, back to time management. Voltaire's question and answer regarding time demonstrates the inability of man to manage time. You might ask, "What can he do then?" The answer is simple. He can manage himself in relationship to time. That, precisely, is the reason this is a book on goal setting, and not on Time Management. Time carries with it no guarantee that it will serve us. Time is only made available.

How Do You Measure Time?

Before you dismiss this question as having an obvious answer, think about it. Is time simply to be measured by the clock, or might there be other ways worthy of our consideration? Isn't it possible that we also could measure time in terms of accomplishment? For example, regarding travel, we used to measure distance between cities by miles. We might say the distance between St. Louis and Indianapolis is 260 miles. Now, smart businessmen think of that distance in terms of the time it takes to get there. One can drive there in five hours, or one can fly by plane in an hour. Housewives used to measure the amount of laundry they had to wash by the days it would take to do it. Now, they measure in terms of washer loads. Once, a purchase was measured in terms of "a week's pay." Now it's measured in terms of dollars.

The time it takes to do a given task can vary, depending on several factors. One of those factors is energy. In fact, energy was a major deciding factor in each example just mentioned. The time necessary for each task was shortened by using one or more forms of energy more efficiently or effectively. I have a friend who farms over 5000 acres of land. Several years ago he experienced a very wet spring and rushed to plant his crop. In one 24-hour period, he and his brother planted 1000 acres of corn (using two planters). This was only made possible through a better use of energy. In some parts of the world it is still difficult for a hundred men to plant that much in several days. Thus, the time it takes to perform a particular task can be shortened tremendously by a better use of energy.

Time is money. Time is valuable because with it a man can earn money. If a man earns $10.00 per hour, then an hour on the job is worth $10.00 to him. I once heard a man ask, "If time is money, why is it easier to get another person to give you his time than his money?" Still it's true, that time can be equated to the money that can be earned during a period of it.

I once helped a friend mix and pour concrete for the basement of a house he was building. We spent about twelve hours on a portion of it and finally decided to quit around midnight. I then asked him how much he saved by our pouring it ourselves, and he replied, "About fifty dollars." I couldn't believe it! I had just worked like a dog (whatever that means) to save him $50.00! I told him if he ever needed my help again, just to let me know the circumstances and I'd give him the $50.00. I was happy to help, but my time was worth more than $50.00 to me that day. I thought I was saving him at least a couple of hundred dollars.

Consider this: Suppose someone gave you one billion dollars in dollar bills on the condition that you count each one. Do you know how long it would take you? Even liberal estimates say it would take you sixty years, counting eight hours a day and 365 days per year. In other words, it would take a lifetime to count that money. Now, to go back to my illustration, a proper utilization of energy could reduce this to a matter of hours.

Ideas, also, measure time. A task can take a year or a day to do, depending on the ideas and methods applied. A New York Times analyst estimated the cash value of Thomas Edison's brain to be no less than twenty-five billion dollars! He based his estimate on the business interests that were largely due to Edison's inventions. The only thing that can make one man's brain worth that much is the value of the ideas produced by it. A simple answer to, "How do you measure time?" would be:

Time is measured by what you can do with it.

I found more than fifteen definitions of "time" in Webster's dictionary. I suggest you look them up yourself. His first definition was, "the period between two events or during which something exists, happens, etc." For our purposes now, we are referring to a lifetime, the period between the moment of one's birth and death. We don't know exactly how long that will be, but we can decide what we will accomplish during that time. Whether a person lives to be 40, 70, or even 100 doesn't matter as much as what he does with the time he has. The goal-setter will make the most of his time.

Do You Save, Spend, Waste, Buy, Or, Invest Time?

If you had a bank that credited your checking account each morning with $86,400, carried no balance from day to day, allowed you to keep no cash in your account, and finally every evening canceled whatever part of the amount you didn't use during the day, what would you do? Draw out every cent — of course! Well, you have such a bank and its name is "Time." Every morning it credits you with 86,400 seconds. Every night it rules off — as lost — whatever of this you didn't invest to good purposes. It carries no balances. It allows no balances. It allows no overdrafts. Each day the bank named "Time" opens a new account with you. Each night it burns the records of the day. If you fail to use the day's deposits, the loss is yours. -Robert G. Lee

We've all heard about saving time, spending time wisely, and wasting time. Seldom do we hear of "investing time," and yet, this is the thing we must do to increase its value! We also can "buy" time, and we can even "make" time! What we can do with time is amazing, if we will but use our heads regarding it. Let's look at each of these in detail.

Can Time Be Saved?

That depends on the meaning of "saving" time. If we mean, can we decide to call "time-out" and relax for awhile, then resume where we left off, with nothing changed? — the answer is no! Change is constant and waits for no man. Does that mean that we should never rest, never take vacations, never take the time to enjoy life? Of course not! Now, if by saving time, we mean that we alter or eliminate something in our schedule to make more time for something else, then we can do that. In fact, the world is full of "time saving" devices. Saving time is a way of making time for activities for which we would otherwise have no time. We can do this through wise planning, taking short cuts, using efficient procedures, or even eliminating some activities altogether. We save time when we make it available for other uses.

Why does one even need to save time? Why not just wipe the slate clean, and begin to fill in only what we want to do? It sure sounds good, and it would be practical . . .

- If we didn't already have the habits we do
- If we didn't have possessions that "break down" often
- If we weren't continually interrupted by others
- If all of our time was really our own

Since these things are not so, then we need to concentrate on ways to save time. During a given day, most of us are wasting, or throwing away, at least two hours. Two hours per day amount to six and a half weeks per year. What could you do with an extra six weeks each year?

Once we have concentrated on saving time, we need to be prepared to spend it properly. An Indian student was riding in a car with one of our modern speed demons. The driver saw a train coming and said: "Unless we beat that train to the crossing, we will have to wait five minutes." He stepped on the gas, and barely made it, with only seconds to spare. When they were safely across, the Indian asked quietly: "Now what are you going to do with the five minutes?"

Working hard to save time, only to squander it somewhere else, doesn't make sense. Goal setting will help you know what to do with the time you save.

How Can We Spend Time Wisely?

Your life is like a book. The title page is your name; the preface your introduction to the world. The pages are a daily record of your efforts, trials, pleasures, discouragements, and achievements. Day by day you inscribe your thoughts and acts in your book of life. Hour by hour, you make the record that must stand for all time. Once the word "finish" must be written, let it then be said of your book that it is a record of noble purpose, generous service, and work well done. -Grenville Kleiser

I learned early in life to choose carefully those things for which I would spend my money, as there was never much to go around. My family was very poor, and we two boys never had the luxury of an allowance. Saving a few dollars might take me several months, and when the time came to spend them, I was very selective. I can remember being so poor that my parents would "borrow" my money to purchase something for us to eat. I hated those times because I knew I usually never would see the money again. Once, I either lost my money, or had it stolen — I was devastated! Before long I realized that, if I didn't spend it quickly, I probably wouldn't get to spend it at all.

That is the way it is with the 24 hours I'm given in a day. I can choose either to spend them wisely, or they will be taken away — never again to return. Among the saddest words in the English language are, "What might have been?" Allowing this to happen doesn't make sense. If we can envision the value of even a few minutes, then we'll be on our way to spending time wisely.

An 80-year old man kept a detailed record of what he had done during each hour of every day. He then figured out how he used his time during the entire period of his long life. He spent 26 years in sleep, 21 years working, 228 days shaving, and 140 days paying bills. He also spent over 26 days scolding his children, and two days yelling at his dogs. He spent only 26 hours laughing.

We can look at spending time like we look at spending dollars. I'm one of those who does not have more money than he can easily spend. I could spend easily at least a million dollars more per year than I now do. Therefore, when

I attempt to decide what I will spend my money on, I make three lists, as follows:

MUST BUY	SHOULD BUY	NICE THINGS TO BUY
1)	1)	1)
2)	2)	2)
3)	3)	3)
4)	4)	4)
5)	5)	5)

I make the list as long as I need to in order to get everything on it. I make sure I place items in the order of their priority. I would like to buy many things — more than I can afford. By making a list, I put those things I'm tempted to purchase in proper perspective. This doesn't mean I always will purchase a "Must Buy" before a "Nice To Buy," nor does it mean I always purchase a number one priority before a number eight priority. There can be exceptions. It does mean, however, that when I do something, I know what I am doing and why I am doing it. I also am fully aware of the possible consequences. This kind of listing can work for prioritizing and scheduling how I will spend my time.

MUST DO	SHOULD DO	NICE THINGS TO DO
1)	1)	1)
2)	2)	2)
3)	3)	3)
4)	4)	4)
5)	5)	5)

Breaking your planned activities down like this will force you to acknowledge which activities are really important to you, and which ones aren't. We might say that spending more time with our children is very important. If we don't put it on the "Must Do" list, then we admit that it isn't as important as everything else on that list. Or, if it makes it on the list and still doesn't get checked off, then we are lying to ourselves. It is a case of "What I do speaks so loud you cannot hear what I say."

Let's calculate just how much discretionary time you have to spend. We have some of our time already spoken for, based upon decisions we have made and needs that cannot be ignored. A typical employee's schedule might look like the following:

TYPICAL	ACTIVITY	YOUR SCHEDULE
56 hours	Sleep	___hours
48 hours	Labor	___hours
12 hours	Meals	___hours
4 hours	Hygiene	___hours
120 hours	TOTAL	___hours

There are 168 hours in each week, so subtract your total from 168.

```
      168
-
_____
=          TOTAL DISCRETIONARY HOURS
```

As you can see, our typical employee has 48 discretionary hours that he can, and will, spend as he pleases. If he chooses to spend three hours each day in front of a television, then he is down to only 27. Let's say that he spends three hours each week working on the yard, or around the house, two hours talking on the telephone, five hours running errands, and three hours reading the paper. He's now down to only 14 hours. If he goes to church, even three times a week (including travel), he might use another eight hours. Now he's down to only six hours remaining to be used as he pleases. Six hours isn't much, but by spending it wisely, he can accomplish a great deal. How do you spend your discretionary hours?

Figure it below:

TIME	ACTIVITY
___hours	_____
___hours	_____
___hours	_____
___hours	_____
___hours	_____
___hours	_____
___hours	_____
___hours	_____
___hours	_____
___hours	_____

Note: Be sure your schedule does not exceed your allotted time. It's all you have!

What About Wasted Time?

Webster defines "waste" as, "to use up or spend without need, profit, etc.; squander" or "to fail to take advantage of." Thus, when I speak of wasted time, I am speaking of time spent in a way that yielded, or has the possibility of yielding, very little in return.

We have no choice whether or not we will spend time. Yet, we do have the choice of how we will spend it. I've heard the following poem quoted often:

MY WAGE

I BARGAINED with Life for a penny,
And Life would pay no more,
However I begged at evening
When I counted my scanty store;

For Life is a just employer,
He gives you what you ask,
But once you have set the wages,
Why, you must bear the task.

I worked for a menial's hire,
Only to learn, dismayed,
That any wage I had asked of Life,
Life would have paid.

Jessie B. Rittenhouse

We seldom get more than what we bargain for, and we often receive less. Therefore, we must decide beforehand what we wish to accomplish in any given time period. We will not do more, and we may do less. Any person who must look back on a wasted life and ask, "Where did it all go?" should realize that it slipped away a day at a time.

Procrastination has been called the "thief of time." Some define it as "putting off until tomorrow what you could do today." I personally don't care for that definition as I believe it is appropriate to put many things off until tomorrow that I could do today. The best definition I've ever heard came from a friend, Dr. Larry Baker, who teaches Time Management seminars all over the country. He defines procrastination as, "Doing low-priority actions or tasks rather than higher-priority ones." Both he and Dr. Merrill Douglass produced *The Time Management Profile* for Performax Systems. This excellent profile is one I highly recommend. The following excerpt is taken from that profile.

What Causes Procrastination?

It is all very well to admit that procrastination is a bad thing. If, however, we are to do anything effective toward its cure we must know something of what causes it. One main cause of procrastination is habit. You develop the habit of procrastinating. When you have done anything for a long time, it's easier to continue as you are than to make the effort to change. Take eating habits, for instance. Weight Watchers International reports that it will take at least 38 days of consistent behavioral change before people form new eating patterns. Much of the way we approach things, even the way we think, we base on habit. This is the cause of procrastination. To overcome it will undoubtedly require changing some habits.

Many of our procrastination habits are hidden from us. What kind of habits? Here are a few of the common ones:

1. We do things that are quick before doing things that take more time.
2. We do easy things before we tackle difficult ones.
3. We do things we enjoy before doing things we don't like.
4. We do things we know how to do, before tackling things we don't understand so well.
5. We wait until the deadline is on top of us before we get moving.
6. We tackle first those things that are politically expedient and that advance our personal objectives.

The truth is that we tend to postpone doing things that seem at the time to be unpleasant, distasteful or difficult. When we have something like that to do, we putter around with little things, trying to keep busy so that we have an excuse that will ease our consciences. Dreading and postponing a task may be more tiring than doing it, and apprehension over delayed unpleasantness may so preoccupy us that other things cannot be done effectively. Perhaps now you'll see why I believe procrastination is a major reason for wasted time. Wasted time isn't time that's not spent, for all time is spent at the rate of 24 hours per day, every day of the year. Procrastination is time spent on a low-priority action instead of a higher-priority one. If you were to spend $24.00 for a piece of bubble gum, you probably would feel you had wasted the money — especially when you found out how much more you could have received for the same $24.00! That is the way it is with wasted time. You spent it, but you just didn't receive anything of equal value in return.

I might pause to raise another question. Who is guilty of wasting time? The answer is — we all are! I know of nobody who gets the most out of every minute. Of course, wasted time for one person may not be wasted for another. Only the person himself can decide and even he may sometimes have difficulty in doing so. I'll discuss later how to recognize wasted time.

There are several excellent books on the subject of Time Management, and frankly, I recommend you read several of them. Time is such a valuable resource that it's easily worth the time and effort it takes to learn how to maximize it. One book I highly recommend is *The Time Trap*, by R. Alec Mackenzie. His material on "Time Wasters" and their possible causes and solutions is easily worth the price of the book. Most of us believe the biggest time wasters are the faults of other people and their interruptions. He points out that he has found, through much study, that the real villain is not the "other guy." He writes:

> *Isn't it human nature after all to look to others and conditions outside ourselves as the causes of our misfortunes? It takes a painful reassessment, a willingness to be self-critical, to see how much of our ineffectiveness we cause ourselves. When there is assurance that one can admit error with impunity, the real reasons appear. As the cartoon character Pogo said: "We has met the enemy and they is us."*

What Alec Mackenzie has done is to put the blame for wasting time right where it should be — on our own shoulders! Successful people willingly accept responsibility for their failures and shortcomings. Failures, on the other hand, always blame someone or something else. They constantly use the "if only" routine for explaining why they fail. If we are going to quit wasting time, or at least reduce our wasted time to a minimum, then we are going to have to do it. No one will do it for us, for no one can!

The major reason for wasted time is lack of planning and commitment. Of course, that is why you're reading this book, to improve yourself in this area. It is impossible to know how best to spend, or invest, your time if you have no idea what kind of return you want for it. Thus, we have the need for goal setting. When you know what you wish to accomplish over the long haul, it becomes infinitely easier to decide what you need to do in the short term. Four Laws warrant our consideration during this discussion on wasting time:

1) Parkinson's Law
2) Parkinson's Second Law
3) The Law of Diminishing Returns
4) Pareto's Principle

Let's now look at them in detail to see how they might be affecting our use of time or more specifically our waste of time.

Parkinson's Law

This law states that work expands to fill the time allotted for its completion. Thus, if we estimate, or expect, a project to take too much time, we will tend to use that much time. We tend to get what we expect to get in life, and we tend to accomplish only that which we expect to accomplish in life.

Parkinson's Second Law

Parkinson's Second Law states that we tend to devote time and effort to tasks in inverse relation to their importance. In other words, we spend the greatest amount of our time and energy on the projects that deserve the least. Thus, we waste our time by spending it on activities that do not return the greatest profit.

The Law of Diminishing Returns

This law states that there is a point beyond which we reduce our effectiveness. This reduction of effectiveness is usually in proportion to the span of time wherein we have gone beyond our peak. In other words, we might do far more in two 8 hour days than we would in one 20 hour day. If so, we would have wasted at least four hours!

The Pareto Principle
(Sometimes called the 80/20 Rule)

This principle, named after Vilfredo Pareto, states that the significant items in a given group normally are a small portion of the total items in the group. Stated another way, 80% of the productivity might come from only 20% of the activity. In sales, 80% of the sales volume probably comes from only 20% of the clients. I have dramatically increased my income each year by carefully studying my activity and results from the previous year. I might not always come up with 80/20 figures, but I do look for, and find, figures that prove the validity of this principle. The first year I decided to check this principle against my records, I found that about 30% of my income had come from 10% of my activity. Though it wasn't 80/20, I decided to make some changes quickly. The next year, I increased my income by almost $20,000!

You Can Buy Time At Bargain Prices!

Had you ever thought about this? While it is true there are only 24 hours in any given day, you can literally buy as much as you can afford!

Actually, you're already buying time and may not even know it. I never realized it until I read the following by Robert R. Updegraff in his book, *All The Time You Need.*

> *Closely watching myself and my fellow humans use our allotted 24 hours-a-day over the past 15 years, I hold to the conviction that we have not really grasped the nature of time. We have never taken the clock apart to see how it ticks. To do this we must begin to challenge our familiar ideas of time. For example, an ancient Chinese proverb reads, "An inch of gold will not buy an inch of time." This may have been true of life in ancient China. It is not true of life in*

the Twentieth Century. Today time is a most purchasable commodity. We all buy time, in one form or another each day. By giving conscious thought to the matter, and watching our opportunities, we could buy a great deal more time than we do.

Robert R. Updegraff's book, published in 1958 by Prentice-Hall, Inc., is excellent! I found it somewhat amusing to read some of the examples he used to show how we buy time. He spoke of a new "Miracle Machine" that duplicated a letter in a couple of minutes. This saved the secretary from having to type another copy. We now take copy machines for granted, don't we? He helped me to see that I'm really "buying time" whenever I mail a letter, place a phone call, fly somewhere, purchase a copy of a condensed book, or purchase a ready-made meal. I'm buying time when I purchase a book that shows me how to do things more easily and/or more quickly. I'm certainly buying time whenever I hire someone to work for me, whether it's a boy to mow my yard or a secretary to take care of my filing and paperwork. I was buying time when I purchased the computer on which I am typing this book. I'm buying time whenever I'm employing an expert or specialist. It might, otherwise, take me a couple of years just to learn what he can do for me in two days. I'm buying time when I purchase and listen to audio cassettes. I can listen to them while driving down the road. So, I save myself the time it would take to read the book on the same subject by the same person. Yes, there are literally thousands of ways to "buy" time. We must make the decision on when it is wise to buy time, and when it is not.

Of course, it only makes sense to buy time if we're going to use it. It is wise to apply a principle I have already mentioned in Chapter 12. That principle is: Never do that which someone else can do when it keeps you from doing that which only you can do. In applying that principle, I first must know what it is that only I can do, that at that time I'm not able to do. I must then decide to do it when I've purchased the time I need. Buying time and then wasting it is very foolish. Anytime we hire people to work for us, purchase a piece of equipment, or use some service, we're making investments in time. We should always determine to obtain good returns on our investments!

Mr. Updegraff closes his chapter on buying time with the following exhortation to us all:

Most of us, whether we keep house, manage a business, or engage in an art or profession, could profitably go shopping for time. It is on sale in department stores, office equipment establishments, home furnishing stores, variety stores, hardware stores, and supermarkets. If we would train ourselves to look around us whenever we are in any kind of store, to see if there is some device, product, or piece of equipment, old or new, that would over a somewhat short period, save more than its cost in time, we probably would be surprised at the many forms in which this most precious of commodities is found. Not to take advantage of them is to live and work in inexcusable inefficiency.

In the field of services, too, there are many individuals and organizations ready to sell us time. They can do things for us that we are presently devoting a needless amount of our all-too-limited time and energy. If for a week or two we were to analyze everything we do and ask ourselves whether we might buy, from some person or some service organization, a part or all the time we are devoting to this segment of our work, we probably would be astonished at the time-buying opportunities we are overlooking.

Let's take an example that might apply to many. We might have two jobs that need to be done around the house. I need to have my yard mowed and cleaned up, and my car needs a new alternator. If I know how to do both, but only have time to do one, which should it be? I can hire a boy to mow my yard for $5.00 per hour, or I can hire a mechanic for $30.00 per hour. Either job would take me about the same amount of time. The choice, as far as I am concerned is an obvious one.

Now, let's add another dimension to this picture. I believe I am worth at least $50 per hour to myself, when I'm working in my business. Is it then wise for me to do the $30.00 per hour job? Here, I probably would go ahead and do it because of the additional time it would take me to deliver my auto to a shop and either wait for it or have to return for it later. The hassle would not be worth it. There is a way to solve that problem. I now have a mechanic who will come to my house and fix it for me. Anytime I can buy time for $30 per hour and sell it for $50 per hour (with all other things being somewhat equal), I would be wise to do it. So would you.

Investing Time — A Wise Move!

I have discussed saving time, spending time, wasting time, buying time, and now we are ready to look at investing time. Each of these categories deserves our attention, but none more than this one.

This is the one category that often gets overlooked, especially as we get older. We are investing time any time we are spending time to improve or secure the future for ourselves or our loved ones. Gaining an education is just one way of investing time. The high school student has been told often enough that he would be wise to invest at least four years in the college and curriculum of his choice. He is told that the improved income opportunities will justify having invested that time. This is usually true. It is sad that most don't realize this is also very true after college. Investing time to improve one's mind always will reap large dividends.

We invest time when we take time to get organized. We would be shocked to find out how much time and money we waste or lose because we did not invest the time necessary to become organized. Five or ten minutes here and there can soon add up to days and weeks! Also lost are many opportunities hidden under the pile.

Another way of investing time is to use it to earn money that can be used to buy time, either immediately or in the future. If you can earn enough money to have the extra that you need to purchase time, you can pursue those things which most interest you.

Taking the time to perform maintenance on equipment can be a wise investment. Many an hour has been lost because an automobile became stranded due to neglect. "A stitch in time saves nine." I don't sew, but I understand the significance of that saying.

Last, but certainly not least, we invest time when we take time to care for ourselves. Physical health is important in determining just how much time we will have in the "long run." A few minutes a day to this end can add years to your life on the other end.

Summary

In summary, I have discussed the subject of managing yourself in relation to time from many angles. I would like to challenge you to consider this chapter as only the beginning in your quest for knowledge on how you might make the most of your time. Another book you might want to read is, *How to Get Control Of Your Time And Your Life* by Alan Lakein. This may be the most popular book on the subject. Lakein suggests you ask yourself always, "What is the best use of my time right now?" He suggests that we make a habit of asking that question until we figure out the answer, and act upon it.

I suggest that you can only know what is the most important thing to do now when you know what you want to accomplish in the long run. Once you have the big picture, breaking it down into the smaller parts is much easier.

In closing this section on time, I would like to add some thoughts from the Bible. One cannot read the Bible without noticing God's concern with how we review and use time. Read the following passages:

> *To everything there is a season, A time for every purpose under heaven: A time to be born, And a time to die; A time to plant, And a time to pluck what is planted; A time to kill, And a time to heal; A time to break down, And a time to build up; A time to weep, And a time to laugh; A time to mourn, And a time to dance; A time to cast away stones, And a time to gather stones; A time to embrace, And a time to refrain from embracing; A time to gain, And a time to lose; A time to keep, And a time to throw away; A time to tear, And a time to sew; A time to keep silence, And a time to speak; A time to love, And a time to hate; A time of war, And a time of peace.*
> **Ecclesiastes 3:1-8 (NKJV)**

REMEMBER now your Creator in the days of your youth, Before the difficult days come, And the years draw near when you say, "I have no pleasure in them." **Ecclesiastes 12:1 (NKJV)**

See then that you walk circumspectly, not as fools but as wise, redeeming the time, because the days are evil. Therefore do not be unwise, but understand what the will of the Lord is. **Ephesians 5:15-17 (NKJV)**

Come now, you who say, "Today or tomorrow we will go to such and such a city, spend a year there, buy and sell, and make a profit"; whereas you do not know what will happen tomorrow. For what is your life? It is even a vapor that appears for a little time and then vanishes away. Instead you ought to say, "If the Lord wills, we shall live and do this or that." But now you boast in your arrogance. All such boasting is evil. **James 4:13-16 (NKJV)**

Do not boast about tomorrow, For you do not know what a day may bring forth. **Proverbs 27:1 (NKJV)**

..."Take heed and beware of covetousness, for one's life does not consist in the abundance of the things he possesses." **Luke 12:15 (NKJV)**

There is time enough to do everything we need to do — and certainly everything God has for us to do. We need, however, to be wise stewards of that time. God is not only concerned about time, but also that we have a quality life while living it. Why not take some time to read how to have an "abundant life?" While you're at it, be sure you get the answer to "eternal life" as well. That is a "time" which money cannot buy — it's the gift of God.

·*Sixteen*·
Problems Goal Setters Experience

The purpose of this chapter is to assist you, who are new at setting goals, with the problems you are about to encounter. The problems I'll be dealing with almost all exist within your own mind. They are, therefore, very real and must be dealt with.

The problems I'll be addressing are:

- What do I do if I've set too many major goals?
- What should I do when I realize my goal is unrealistic?
- What should I do when my action plan is inadequate?
- What should I do when I realize I no longer desire my goal?
- How can I keep from feeling so guilty and defeated when I fail?
- How do I determine which goals are most important?
- How can I make myself get started?
- What should I do when others won't cooperate?
- How can I keep from feeling so frustrated?
- Why are the goals that are less important easier?

MOST IMPORTANT!!!

This may be the most important paragraph you'll read in this chapter. Goal setting is a tool to help you do that which you really want to do. It is nothing more, and nothing less. Treat it the same way you would any other tool — use it as it will best serve you! You are the master and it is your servant — not the other way around.

Keep this in mind and the questions you are about to consider will become much easier to answer. In fact, you won't really need my answers for many of these questions.

What Do I Do If I've Set Too Many Major Goals?

This is a common mistake for new goal setters. The excitement of it all carries us away when we're just beginning and we want to conquer the world. We get clear visions of the people we can become and we want to become those people overnight.

If setting too many major goals is what you've done, don't worry — be happy. Just kidding. Actually, you should be happy that you have a vision. Now just temper it somewhat. You can still accomplish everything you want to; it may just take longer than you were hoping. Don Hutson once told me that "people don't have unrealistic goals; they just have unrealistic time frames." That may very well be true.

Evaluate your goals and consider them carefully. Figure out which ones are the most important to you. Prioritize them. Once you've done this, begin with number one. If you believe you can also tackle number two simultaneously, do so. Once these are accomplished, begin number three, and so forth. You get the picture.

I'm not meaning to imply that you can only work on one or two goals at a time. While it may be true that you can only handle one major goal at a time, I suspect that you can tackle several minor goals simultaneously. Don't sell yourself short. Try it. If it's too much, fall back. Tackle a load with which you are comfortable.

It is a lot like carrying buckets of water. You can often carry two buckets easier than you can carry one. While you may not be able to carry two full buckets, you can certainly carry two buckets that are only half full. If you have large pockets, you can also carry many other items at the same time. Place everything in a wagon, and you'll be amazed at how much you can carry.

You'll have some major goals that will be easy to work toward simultaneously, and some that won't. For example, if you have the following major goals, they might be very compatible.

MENTAL — Read one book each month
SPIRITUAL — Attend church every Sunday
PHYSICAL — Lose 10 pounds monthly until I reach my goal weight
FAMILY — Have a family-time three times weekly
SOCIAL — Invite one family to dinner weekly
FINANCIAL — Increase my income this year by $12,000
CAREER — Begin my own company

You could choose a book each month that will help you obtain information concerning your other goals. It might be a book on proper diet, exercise techniques, family projects, income opportunities, or on small-business management. You could easily combine family times with exercise. Your new business could be that which fulfills the additional $12,000 you wish to earn. You need to eat dinner anyway, so inviting a family over should be easy to fit into your schedule. Make a family commitment that you'll all rise early enough on Sunday mornings to attend church.

Notice that these goals are not conflicting goals. They may conflict with current entertainment habits but they don't necessarily, by definition, conflict with one another. The financial, career, and possibly the mental goals all work together quite well. The physical can work well together with the family goal, as long as the family goal isn't centered around eating.

The key here is to choose goals in each category that will easily work well together. As an example, it's easier to change your eating habits when you are also instituting an exercise program into your schedule.

What Should I Do When I Realize My Goal Is Unrealistic?

The answer to this is to figure out why it is unrealistic. The answer may be one or more of the following reasons:

- Poor Attitudes and Poor Thinking
- Poor Habits
- Poor Influences
- Poor Information
- Poor Resources
- Poor Plans
- Poor Situations

You should recognize this list. It is the list that appears in the Obstacles & Roadblocks chapter. An unrealistic goal can usually be traced to an inadequate Action Plan. Any action plan that does not deal properly with the potential obstacles is inadequate.

Therefore, the real answer to this dilemma is to return to the drawing board. You may have initially prepared your plan the best you could, based on the information and knowledge you possessed. Now that you've experienced a degree of failure, you've gained additional insight and can improve your plan.

There are solutions to each of the obstacles. Sometimes, however, because the solutions may not be feasible, or they may cause the goal to become no longer worthwhile, the goal will need to be postponed or canceled. Only you can decide. Should you decide to scratch a goal, based on your new information and experience, then do so — and without feeling guilty about it.

Remember the personal illustration I mentioned in chapter ten about how I tripled my income overnight by developing a better plan? I transformed my unrealistic goal into a realistic one by spending only one night working on the action plan.

I heard recently that a president of a large corporation was credited with saying, "Every hour we spend in planning reduces our execution time by four hours." That is powerful. Sure, you couldn't carry that to the nth degree; there are only twenty-four hours in a day. But you can discipline yourself to quit feeling negative and begin planning a solution.

Too often, we become so discouraged by focusing upon what we cannot do that we tend to overlook the obvious — that which we can do! We can continue to do the things which we know will produce while searching for ideas that will enable us to improve to where we want to be. A hitchhiker who walks in the direction he is headed will often arrive hours before he would have by standing still.

What Should I Do When My Action Plan Is Inadequate?

The easy answer is, of course, improve it until it's adequate. You might be tempted to reply, "Easier said than done," and you'd be right. Building a proper action plan does require work, but it is worth it.

The first thing you need to do is figure out why your plan is inadequate. Is it because you lack the information and experience to know just what is required? If so, and information is available somewhere, get it. If the information is not available anywhere, gather what you can and develop theories from there. Approach the task based upon what you know and learn more as you go.

I'll refer back to my example of losing the 52 pounds in 89 days, which I described in detail in chapter 10. I didn't know exactly what I would have to do in order to successfully attain my goal. I did know, however, that I could analyze my situation weekly and make adjustments as necessary. I actually weighed every morning and every night. I began to learn a lot about how my body responded to various foods and exercises. I knew it would be very important to have that information available as I came down the stretch.

It is often wise to test your theories before allowing too many details in your action plan to hang on them. I prepared a plan once for a project that I thought would make me rich overnight, so to speak. I had grandiose plans to hire at least 100 college students for the summer and have them selling a product door-to-door. Everything looked great — on paper! It was when I attempted to sell the product in that manner myself that I realized the blueprint had a flaw in it. I had to revise my projections downward to the point where these college students would be working like crazy to earn about $2 per hour, if that much. If I couldn't easily sell it, how could I expect these inexperienced students to do so? Needless to say, I had to scrap my original plan. Fortunately, I only lost a few thousand dollars on that deal — instead of the several thousand I could have lost.

Whatever you do, don't get too discouraged when you find your plan won't work. This is a learning process, not a firing squad. Having been stopped in your tracks by an inadequate plan is not the end of the world. You can still make revisions, or begin all over again. You're calling the shots. Do what you want to do.

What Should I Do When I Realize I No Longer Desire My Goal?

Quit. Now that was easy, wasn't it? Just because you wrote it down on a piece of paper doesn't mean you have to follow through on it. Now, when I say, "Quit," that doesn't mean that you just drop everything and walk away. You still want to be intelligent about it. You may be able to receive your investment back, as well as some profit, if you handle this "quitting" correctly.

If you have no investment, and if there are no penalties or repercussions to be suffered, then go ahead and quit. Your time is too valuable to waste it doing something in which you no longer have an interest.

How Can I Keep From Feeling So Guilty And Defeated When I Fail?

You can begin by realizing that only those who attempt a thing can fail. You tried and, in doing so, have become one of a select group. Very few people ever attempt anything of value, so pat yourself on the back for, at least, attempting.

Next, realize that you have gained. No failure is a complete loss, if you learned from the failure. It is obvious you learned at least one thing — what won't work. Attempt to determine why you failed and make necessary corrections based on the knowledge you now possess.

There is absolutely no reason to feel guilty over failure, unless you didn't even attempt to succeed. Even if you didn't attempt, try to determine why you didn't attempt and build from there. There are always reasons and if you'll look closely enough you'll find them.

Last, but not least, don't consider yourself defeated unless you are throwing in the towel. One loss does not make a loser. Many a war has been won after losing many battles.

How Do I Determine Which Goals Are Most Important?

Ask yourself this question: What is the one major thing I want to do before I die? If that already was accomplished, what would be the one major thing I would desire? Keep asking that question and you will go a long way toward determining your priorities.

As I've discussed in other chapters, good is the enemy of best and the urgent usually has a way of replacing the important. It is extremely important that you don't allow this to happen to you. Once you've determined your priorities, go for them!

How Can I Make Myself Get Started?

If you have had a difficult time getting started, but you still want to, become accountable to another person. You can always use the Penalty Principle to get you started. Call me and I'll promise to hold you accountable, or execute the penalty.

I find that people who can't seem to get started usually don't have good action plans. Even those who think they do, are still missing some important ingredients.

What Should I Do When Others Won't Cooperate?

It really depends on who the "others" are. If you can replace them, do so. If the relationship is such that a replacement is not in order (family, employment situation, school), then figure out some creative alternatives.

How Can I Keep From Feeling So Frustrated?

Don't make unrealistic demands on yourself. Set goals that meet the ten requirements of properly set goals, and become accountable to others to do that which you've committed yourself to do, according to your action plan.

Why Are The Less Important Goals Easier?

I'm not so sure they are. The importance of a goal is determined by its relationship to your life purpose and priorities. The more closely it is related to those two, the greater is its importance.

As an example, let's say one of my goals is to find out approximately how many spiders there are in the state of Missouri, where I live. I don't really need to know this information for any particular reason except that I'm curious. In other words, it is quite possibly my least important goal. Do you think it will be my easiest?

On the other hand, let's look at one **important** goal of mine — that of assisting my children in choosing a college. Fulfilling this goal is relatively easy compared to my previous example.

Another important goal could be to purchase new glasses or contact lens in order to improve your eyesight. Obviously, few things are as important as being able to see well, and yet this is not a very difficult goal to achieve for most of us.

The size of a goal also has very little to do with determining how easy its fulfillment will be. One man might find it easier to earn $100,000 while another man has great difficulty in earning only $20,000. It might be considered easy for a construction company to build a house, while at the same time they might find it difficult to keep their truck running properly.

•*Seventeen*•
The Final Challenge

I've titled this chapter The Final Challenge only because it's my last opportunity to challenge you through the pages of this book. Your challenges — those you face on a regular basis — will continue the rest of your life. In the introduction, I challenged you to complete this book within three weeks. I did so because I knew that you might otherwise set it aside and never complete it. However long it has taken you, hopefully it wasn't as long as it took me to write and publish it.

Many times in my life I've begun writing, or preparing to write, a book on a topic that I considered extremely important. Usually, however, my research has led me to numerous good books that already said what I wanted to say and I didn't feel my writing would provide enough additional information to warrant the effort. I've written over 100 pages on a couple of subjects, only to allow the pages to wither away in a file somewhere for this very reason. This book was different. While I have over 1,000 books in my own library on the subject of self-improvement, none do what I've attempted to do in these pages.

I'm somewhat disappointed that the book is so long. I know that some will not read it because of that fact. I've been advised by some to divide it into two volumes, making it easier for some to tackle. While I gave that advice serious consideration, I decided against it because I wanted to make certain that those of you who did read it would get everything — without having to purchase, and set a goal to read, another book. Only God truly knows if I made the right decision.

Reading this book wasn't an easy task. I know that. I'm proud of you for sticking with it and finally completing it. Now, having paid the price of spending those 17 hours or so reading my book, you owe it to yourself to accept my final challenge. That challenge is this. Put the information you've just encountered to the test for the next 90 days — three months! Select at least one mountain you would like to see cut down to the size of a molehill over the next 90 days and determine to make it happen. Set it as a goal, develop your action plan, become accountable to others, and simply march through your plan!

Make it a goal that will mean something to you for the rest of your life. Surely there are some mountains out there that have been standing in your way for a long time. Surely, you have some mountains in front of you that you've wanted to conquer for many years.

One of my favorite quotations in the entire Bible is one in which Caleb said to Joshua after having waited for 40 years for his opportunity — "Give me this mountain!" He had desperately wanted to tackle the giants in the promised land some 40 years before but had been outvoted because of the lack of faith of his comrades. He knew that there are no giants and no mountain that can stand up to a man who has God as his partner. Your mountains are not too big to tackle — if you are willing to tackle them with the principles you've just read about.

I've written this book to help you — not to entertain you. It will help you, however, only if you apply it to your life. Nothing in life gives me more pleasure than to know I've helped another human being to grow closer to realizing his or her potential. I'd like to think that the chances of us becoming friends has increased because of the common bond we'll share by having applied the principles contained herein.

In closing, I'll share with you one final drawing which depicts what I believe is a balanced view of success. A friend, Debbie Woodall, drew it after I gave her a brief sketch of the concept I wanted to show — that of first building a foundation (who you are) and then allowing the pillars (what you do) to determine ultimate success. Notice how each leg is important and without them, a balanced and stable success cannot be achieved.

I'd love to hear from you. You can write me at P.O. Box 1073, St. Charles, MO 63302, or call me at (314) 949-6900. While I cannot foresee just how long into the future that information will be correct, it will hopefully, at least, put you on the right track toward locating me.

I don't do as much public speaking as I used to due to my involvement in my computer and copier business (I was speaking as many as 50 hours or more per week a few years ago), but I am still available for bookings for dinner engagements, business meetings, and one-day seminars. My fees are quite reasonable and all my presentations are sold with a 100% satisfaction guarantee.

Today is the first day of the rest of your life. It is for that reason that I do not say "The End" but instead will end this book with:

THE BEGINNING

Epilog

The purpose of this epilog is to share some personal information about myself. It is my desire to be completely honest with everyone, including — of course — those of you who have taken the time to read this book. I don't want to deceive anyone.

At this time, the Summer of 1993, I'm experiencing turmoil on a number of fronts. While I don't believe these problems should prevent me from publishing this book, or be allowed to destroy my credibility, I do believe I should make you aware of them — lest, upon your learning about them, you might decide to disregard everything you've read in these pages. The truths I've presented herein are no less important or valuable for you.

First, the major event which has occurred in my life this year is that my wife has filed for and received a divorce. We had been married for 22.5 years and she reached a level of dissatisfaction which, she believes, forced her to seek a different life. There has never been any immorality or physical abuse involved in our marriage. I have not lived a double standard, teaching one thing and living another. While I can say that I have never done anything intentionally to hurt her, there is no doubt that she has felt pain a number of times as a result of our marriage. I won't attempt to list her complaints here —I will only say that she has many valid ones.

I still love her and believe I always will. I've failed to show her over the years just how much I do, at least, consistently enough for her to feel wanted and cherished — as she deserved. Our kids are essentially raised, being ages 17 and 18 (if kids are ever really raised). Somehow, I believe I may always see them as still being raised, many years from now. While Saundra feels our differences are irreconcilable, and she may be right, I am still convinced that they are reconcilable. It is my heart's desire and "goal" to reconcile this relationship. Even though the divorce is final, I still believe we may one day reunite. At this point, there are no other parties involved.

She has often felt that she was just one of my goals, and that once we were married and my goal had been accomplished, I placed her on a shelf. While that was not my intention, I understand and accept her feelings. I've spent a very large percentage of my life helping others, sometimes to the detriment of my own family. I've brought people into our lives who have taken advantage of us and left us fighting for survival. Lest I appear to be casting the blame on others, let me say I accept full responsibility.

Perhaps you can tell by what you've read in this book, I don't have a great need for security. Unfortunately, for our relationship, my wife did. I guess I never really have realized just how much. While I don't feel really comfortable unless every available asset is being used to its potential, she would certainly feel much better if some of those assets were more liquid, in the case of an emergency, for example. I've always believed I can handle whatever emergencies might arise. We wouldn't even have had health insurance were it not for her insistence. I have carried a large amount of life insurance to cover the event that I'm not here to personally deal with such emergencies.

At any rate, my marriage is now history. I've failed to be the husband I should have been. I've been insensitive and failed to understand just how lonely my wife was. Oh, she has told me many times but, as I must say, I didn't really understand the word "lonely" until she left. I had not known loneliness since the day we married. Since then, my life was always full. While I've done many things alone, I've always seen a "we" or "us," not a "me" or "I." I never have even thought that this day might come. You could say I've been thoughtless.

The second major turmoil in my life this year has been that my 17-year old son, Joel, decided to leave home so that he could "do whatever he wants" without my supervision or rules. I love him dearly, and I hope that he someday realizes the depth of my love. Oh, I've told him thousands of times, and have attempted to prove it. My love, however, has forbade him from doing some things, or becoming involved in some activities which I believed would destroy him (things like smoking, drinking, taking drugs, immorality, pornography, lying, stealing, heavy-metal music, etc.). While I recognize that my prohibiting some of these things has only served to strengthen his resolve to try them, I have not considered it wise to compromise and allow them.

He has come home on a couple of occasions only to decide within a few hours, and after being fed, that my "rules" are just too hard to accept. Of course, many of his friends (most of whom do those things just mentioned) agree. They believe life would just be too boring without being able to do those things. Many of their parents began giving them beer and cigarettes before they were 10 years old!

The problem is deeper than I can fully outline here. Some outsiders have believed that I'm having the problems I am having with Joel because, as one who teaches goal setting, I've put too much pressure on him to succeed. I truly believe that is not the case. I've never (really never) challenged him to be the best at anything — only to attempt to do his best. I've not forced him to become involved in any activity (other than attend school and church), nor have I interfered when he did. I've attempted to show admiration and acceptance for his accomplishments, while (in some cases) pointing out ways he could have improved his performance. I'm not one who has demanded A's and B's, nor one who has found F's acceptable either.

As I mentioned earlier in the book, both Joel and my daughter, Kimberly, are adopted. We've explained to them, even before they could understand words, that they were special. Every person in the Bible who was adopted was so because God had a special purpose for him. We've explained that children who are adopted are not adopted because they were not wanted, but the opposite. Their natural mothers gave them up because each wanted a better life for her child than she felt she could give, and we adopted them because we wanted the same. We wanted to love them and help them to become stable adults who love life and have purpose.

I believe that Joel has had difficulty accepting his adoption. Teenage boys, especially adopted ones, have great difficulty in finding their identity. I think he has always felt that the grass is greener on the other side of the fence and that his life would have been much easier and more enjoyable if his natural mother hadn't given him up. I believe he has, at times, blamed her and us for his dissatisfaction with his life.

At present, he is once again living with me and working two part-time jobs. I believe he will come to grips with his life and get his act together. If not, I fear for his future and his very life! He, like many teenagers, doesn't seem to realize just how much today's actions determine tomorrow's opportunities.

As a note, Kimberly, now 18 seems to be maturing quite well. Some say, she's her father's daughter. That scares both of us some. She has just returned from Brazil where she spent six weeks on a missionary trip (she went to Indonesia two years ago on a similar trip). She has begun college (which I've neither encouraged, nor discouraged) and her plans include at least one of many professional careers thereafter. At present she wants to be either a marine biologist, child psychologist, policewoman, archaeologist, or sociology teacher. Who knows, she may become a race car driver.

These are the main challenges I face at the present. Oh, I have many others but these are the ones that are most important. Because of these, I've debated with myself as to whether or not I should even publish this book. I've decided that I must proceed. If I wait until the final chapters on these issues are written, I may have to wait several years. You, who have experienced similar situations as those I have described, know what I'm going through.

I can say, without hesitation, that the principles contained in this book have wonderfully sustained me. I've read my own book several times this year. I'm not suicidal, nor suffering from depression. Oh, I've been plenty discouraged over these events and have wished I could just "quit" and go hide in a hole somewhere. But, as I mentioned in Chapter 11, there is no such thing as quitting. I would still have to face myself. I love my wife (now ex-wife) and I love both my son and daughter. They are all precious to me. They are a part of me, and while they have individually separated themselves from me, I cannot. The pain is tremendous (for each of us) but God can and will sustain us all — if we will allow Him to do so. Reconciliation is possible and that is my goal!

We all have our trials and we cannot ignore them. While we are not always responsible for them, we are always responsible for how we react to them. I'll encourage you to meet your trials the way I do mine — one day at a time.

I'll close this epilog, and this book, by saying God bless you. Have a great life!